WHITMAN COLLEGE LIBRARY

D0173754

Candidates, Parties, and Campaigns

Withdrawn by
Whitman College Library

Candidates, Parties, and Campaigns

Electoral Politics in America

Stephen A. Salmore

Eagleton Institute of Politics,
Rutgers University

Barbara G. Salmore

Drew University

A division of Congressional Quarterly Inc.
1414 22nd Street N.W., Washington, D.C. 20037

JK
1976
.S25
1985

PENROSE MEMORIAL LIBRARY
WHITMAN COLLEGE
WALLA WALLA, WASHINGTON 99362

Copyright © 1985, Congressional Quarterly Inc.

All rights reserved. No part of this publication may be reproduced or transmitted in any form or by any means, electronic or mechanical, including photocopy, recording, or any information storage and retrieval system, without permission in writing from the publisher.

Printed in the United States of America

Library of Congress Cataloging in Publication Data

Salmore, Stephen A.
    Candidates, parties, and campaigns.

    Bibliography: p. 253
    Includes index.
    1. Electioneering—United States. 2. Campaign management—United States. I. Salmore, Barbara G., 1942-   . II.Title.
JK1976.S25   1985   324.7'0973   85-9721
ISBN 0-87187-348-6

PENROSE MEMORIAL LIBRARY
RECEIVED

JUL 12 1985

S.O.

ACQUISITIONS DEP'T

In memory of
Walter Salmore, M.D.
February 20, 1903—November 21, 1983
and for
Elizabeth Hiatt Salmore
Born February 20, 1976
who represent the past and future of American politics

PENROSE MEMORIAL LIBRARY

RECEIVED

ACQUISITIONS DEPT.

Contents

Preface

American political campaigns have often been the subject of anecdotal gossip and entertainment, but rarely of serious analysis. Those who have studied politics almost always have attributed electoral outcomes to anything but the actual campaigns. Some combination of factors—party loyalty, presidential popularity, incumbency, the state of the economy, and, occasionally, foreign affairs—was widely accepted as the explanation for the results. The majority party usually won, and so did incumbents, except when faced with damaging domestic events or personal scandal. This was particularly true of nonpresidential candidates, whose fortunes were closely tied to their political parties and the popularity, or lack thereof, of their parties' presidential candidates.

Starting in the late 1960s, electoral outcomes began to challenge these comfortable truisms with uncomfortable frequency. The "minority party" captured the White House in five of the six elections beginning with 1968. While the House of Representatives and the majority of governorships and state legislatures remained Democratic, the party's base in the "Solid South" was severely eroded in the Senate, and to a lesser extent in the House. It became quite commonplace everywhere for an incumbent to have an early lead of thirty points in the polls and to end up losing or winning very narrowly. The party organizations that ran most campaigns were replaced by professional consultants. The newest phenomena, political action committees, offered candidates not only money but also strategic and organizational services. The combined effect of these events has compelled analysts to focus a great deal more attention on individual candidates and their campaign organizations and to consider the diminished role of American political parties.

In this book we try to give the reader a framework for understanding how and why these changes occurred. We identify the central characteristics of successful and unsuccessful campaigns and discuss the challenges to the role of the political parties and how the parties have responded.

Chapter 1 elaborates on why and how candidates and their campaigns came to play an increasingly important role in determining electoral outcomes and sets out the major factors that influence contemporary campaigns. Chapters 2 and 3 provide historical background. We begin with a description of the era of party-centered campaigns and end with an examination of the socioeconomic and technological changes after World War II and through the 1960s, which brought an end to party-centered campaigns as Americans had known them.

The next four chapters are an intensive look at the current candidate-centered and technology-driven campaigns. We see campaigns as proceeding through three broad stages. In the first stage, candidates seek to become known, and known favorably, to voters; to assemble the information and personnel they need to make this happen; and to plan their strategy. Incumbents and challengers face such different tasks that we treat them separately, in chapters 4 and 5, respectively.

In the second stage, candidates attempt to set their campaigns' agendas, which requires them to develop specific themes and persuasive arguments. Themes may turn on issues, candidate images and records, national trends, or some combination of these. They are also affected by factors such as incumbency and the office being sought. In chapter 6, we elaborate on these points. In chapter 7, we discuss the factors affecting which paid or advertising media are used to disseminate themes as well as the relationship between campaigns and the press—the "free" media.

In the final stage, campaign organizations must attempt to counter charges by their opponents and to get enough voters to the polls on election day to ensure victory. These activities, and the factors affecting them, are the subject of chapter 8.

In the last two chapters, we return to the broader questions with which we began our study of campaigns. In chapter 9, we look at newly emerging strategies in candidate-centered campaigning and at the current and future role of the major players in them—professional consultants, political action committees, and the political parties. We devote considerable attention to examining new roles that the parties may play. In this and the concluding chapter, we discuss in some detail whether the parties will be able to reassert themselves as the central focus of campaigns, and of American politics generally, or whether they will only be one of the more important of a number of groups providing resources to campaigns.

Any work that depends as heavily as this one does on observation and interview material truly could not have been written without the help of many people. Our first and greatest debt, therefore, is to those we spoke with formally and informally about the political campaigns described in this book. Many are named in the text; those who requested anonymity know who they are and how grateful we are. Some of these people also read part or all of the manuscript and gave us numerous helpful suggestions.

Academic colleagues also assisted us. C. Anthony Broh, Richard Fenno, Julius Mastro, Larry Sabato, and Susan Tolchin made their way through various versions of the entire manuscript and offered insightful comments. Ross Baker, Jennifer Hochschild, Perry Leavell, Gerald Pomper, Neal Riemer, Alan Rosenthal, and Stephen Wayne read sections of it. John Bibby read the entire manuscript for CQ and was extraordinarily helpful, despite his friendly intellectual disagreements with some of our conclusions. Another CQ reviewer, John Petrocik, read parts of an early draft and provided many suggestions that have strengthened the final version. Any errors that remain are ours. We also benefited from other, anonymous, reviews of the plan of the book and its early chapters. All of them helped us to clarify our thoughts in important ways.

The staff at CQ Press convinced us early that we had made the right choice of publishers. We cannot sufficiently praise the encouragement, cooperation, and close attention they gave us and our work. We especially thank CQ Press director Joanne Daniels and editors Susan Joseph, Nola Lynch, and Carolyn Goldinger.

Our respective employers, Rutgers University and Drew University, made our work possible. The Drew faculty development program and the Rutgers Faculty Academic Study Program gave us each a year free of teaching and administrative responsibilities, as well as funds to defray travel and clerical expenses. We offer our thanks to both institutions. The Eagleton Institute of Politics, at Rutgers University, provides a climate that encourages the study of both academic and "practical" politics, and this book reflects in many ways the unique blend that makes Eagleton distinctive.

Finally, we take note of the two people to whom this book is dedicated. Walter Salmore was born during Theodore Roosevelt's presidency, grew up in a highly partisan family, was intensely interested in politics throughout his long life, and served as a precinct captain in Edward J. Flynn's powerful Bronx party organization. Elizabeth Salmore was born on her grandfather's birthday, near the time of the 1976 New Hampshire primary. She started watching politics on television at an early age, listened to impassioned political debates between her parents, and by the age of four was a self-proclaimed independent. Together they are the story of this book.

Studying American Political Campaigns

1

> *Political campaigns are a lot like bridge; they depend on the cards you were dealt and the way you play the hand.*
>
> —Jeff Greenfield[1]

A generation ago, the main ingredients of a successful campaign for any political office in the United States were support by leaders of the candidate's political party, effective command of the party's workers, and heavy use of shoe leather. Today, candidates more eagerly seek the support of pollsters and media advisers than of party bosses. Computer-generated letters and television advertisements replace the party canvassers. Candidates still take to the stump, but where they go is determined by what appearance will make the best "visual" for television news. This book is about the role of campaigns in American politics, the effect of the new campaign styles on American voters and their government, and the critical change from party-centered to candidate-centered campaigns.

This change is illustrated by the stories of two candidates. Each wanted to be elected governor of the largest state in the nation during a period of social and economic upheaval. Each made government's role in management of the economy the centerpiece of his campaign. Each advanced somewhat radical ideas in the context of contemporary politics, but ideas that provoked much popular attention and discussion. Each was a charismatic figure who attracted many people by the force of his personality. Each was in fact successfully elected and then reelected governor, and later president of the United States.

One of these candidates was Franklin Delano Roosevelt, elected governor of New York in 1928. The other was Ronald Reagan, elected governor of California in 1966. Almost forty years separate their gubernatorial campaigns, and thereby hangs the tale of this book. A brief look at their very different political careers tells why.[2]

Franklin Roosevelt made his career by climbing through the ranks of the Democratic party. In 1910 the local party organization in Dutchess County, New York, where he was born, urged him to run for the New York State Senate. They saw to it that he was nominated at the county convention. For his work at the 1912 Democratic national convention on behalf of Woodrow Wilson he was rewarded with an appointment as assistant secretary of the Navy. During his eight years in that position, he carefully cultivated Democratic politicians nationally, and was eventually chosen as the party's vice presidential nominee in 1920. Retired by defeat that year, and shortly thereafter stricken with polio, Roosevelt used his long period of recuperation to correspond with local and national Democrats. Party leaders asked him to make what became his famous "Happy Warrior" nomination speech for Alfred E. Smith at the 1928 national party convention. A few weeks later, the New York State party urged him to be its 1928 gubernatorial nominee. Roosevelt, unsure of his feelings, would not campaign for the post, but the party drafted and nominated him by acclamation at its state convention. His campaign manager in the race was the Democratic leader in the State Assembly. Two of his chief lieutenants were James A. Farley, secretary of the Democratic State Committee, and Edward J. Flynn, Democratic boss of the Bronx. With the support of the party, he eked out a narrow victory in a big Republican year.

As a member of the party's progressive wing, Roosevelt was embroiled in many disputes with the famous New York City Democratic machine, Tammany Hall. However, he characteristically sought compromise and, when necessary, alliance with Tammany. His position as governor of the country's largest state immediately made him a contender for the presidency in 1932. His vigorous efforts to revitalize the moribund national party machinery, which had atrophied during long years of Republican dominance, further enhanced his prospects.

Roosevelt had entered party politics shortly after completing law school. In contrast, after graduating from college in Illinois, Ronald Reagan became a radio announcer for an Iowa station, specializing in re-creating baseball games as they came over a telegraph wire. His skill won him a Hollywood screen test in 1937. A career in mostly "B" movies followed. During these years, he became president of the Screen Actors Guild and, as a New Deal Democrat, actively supported Harry Truman in 1948, as well as local Democratic candidates in California. In the mid-1950s, Reagan's movie career faltered, and he spent the next decade in corporate public relations for General Electric and the U.S. Borax

Company. He hosted programs they sponsored (first *G.E. Theater* and then *Death Valley Days*) in television's early days as a national medium and represented the corporations in public and at their workplaces. Family influences and close association with corporate executives helped shift his political thinking in a more conservative direction.

Although still registered as a Democrat, Reagan began to involve himself in conservative Republican campaigns in California in 1962 and served as co-chairman of the California Committee for Goldwater-Miller in 1964. A group of wealthy business executives who had supported Goldwater urged Reagan to run for governor in 1966. Throughout 1965, Reagan, his financial backers, and his brother (vice-president of a large advertising agency) held talks with the Spencer-Roberts political public relations firm, which had worked for Nelson Rockefeller, and against Goldwater, in 1964. As soon as Spencer-Roberts was hired in late 1965, the firm began a direct mail campaign to garner money and supporters for Reagan's candidacy, which was announced in a televised speech in January 1966. Spencer-Roberts directed and organized his successful primary and general election campaigns. Both campaigns relied heavily on the kind of informal, friendly television presentations that Reagan had perfected in his years as a performer. After two terms as governor, Reagan would become, in 1981, the president the media called the "Great Communicator."

Franklin Roosevelt was elected governor with the personnel and machinery of a great political party, after years of service in that party. Ronald Reagan was elected governor with the personnel and techniques of contemporary public relations—and only the label of a party he had joined four years previously. The changes their careers typify have come about because of technology. Television and the computer, in particular, have made it possible for voters to get political information from nonparty sources, and for candidates to reach voters and learn their concerns without the party apparatus. Successful candidates who have campaigned as individuals rather than as representatives of a party tailor their appeals to a carefully targeted constituency. Often they have few ties to other elected officials, even of the same party, and little incentive to consider broad-based national interests rather than those of the constituency that elected them—and that they hope will elect them again. Thus the impact of media-based and candidate-centered campaigns does not end when an election season is over.

The new style of campaigning has had its greatest impact on nonpresidential elections because the material the campaign disseminates is often almost the only information voters will have. Long before major presidential contenders run for office, the public has at least vague images of them because of intensive media coverage of the candidates' activities. Almost all other candidates—senators, representatives, gover-nors, mayors, and members of the state legislatures—are not covered by the media in any way that would penetrate popular consciousness. Most voters learn about these candidates as their campaigns progress. The result is that within constraints imposed by their environment and by the resources available to them, nonpresidential candidates have a great deal of freedom to shape the information voters receive about them. In short, the quality of the nonpresidential campaign has the potential to determine its outcome—victory or defeat.

Campaigns and Their Role in Elections_____

For a long time, students of politics, in contrast to candidates and campaigners, believed that campaigns had only a minimal impact on the outcome of elections. The view of campaign participants is easy to understand. They would be disheartened, if not paralyzed, if they felt that their efforts made no difference. Vigorous campaign activity and the rise of the political consulting industry—devoted exclusively to the theory and practice of the way campaign activities can affect electoral outcomes—are testimony to what participants think campaigns can do. But why did academics fail to share this view, and why is it now slowly beginning to change?

The first major academic studies of voting behavior were done in the late 1940s and 1950s when, for reasons we discuss below, campaigns were in fact not very important. Consequently, the theories put forward to explain voting choices and the outcome of elections did not include campaigns, and the accompanying research designs made it difficult to detect their effects. Thus there was a closed circle. Campaigns were left out of academic investigation, and academic research was structured so that any effects they had were unlikely to be discovered.[3] In the remainder of this chapter, we will explain why campaigns are now beginning to attract scholarly attention, what we have learned about their conduct and effects, and what the arguments and findings of this book—drawn both from academic research and from campaigners themselves—can contribute to our knowledge about them.

Until recently, political scientists contended that the outcome of most elections was explained primarily by the distribution of loyalties to the two major political parties. The vast majority of voters identified with one or the other of the parties, viewed politics through a partisan lens, and cast their votes accordingly. Moreover, for many people party identification developed early in life (it was generally passed along from parents to children), became more intense through time, and was extremely resistant to change. Voters' reactions to events were shaped by their sense of party affiliation. The seminal work on American voting behavior concluded, "The influence of party identification on attitudes toward the perceived elements of politics has been far more important than the influence of these attitudes on party identification itself." [4] If this was true, then "the behavior of the candidates during the campaign is one of the least influential factors in determining electoral outcomes." [5] It could not be otherwise, when even in our most visible elections—for president—two-thirds of the voters had made up their minds before the parties held their nominating conventions and the campaign had even begun.

Party identification thus became the major factor in voting choice, and party strength and competition the major determinant of electoral outcomes and their meaning. Only massive social upheaval, on the order of the industrial revolution of the late nineteenth century or the Great Depression of the early twentieth, could move sizable numbers of voters to consider abandoning their parties. The elections of 1896 and 1932, for instance, were "critical," or "realigning," elections, followed by a long period of party stability. [6] The effects of these two elections are examined in chapter 2; for the moment we will explore the traditional and the revised view of the role of campaigns in determining election day results.

The Traditional View:
Campaigns as a Minor Factor

The scholarly consensus on the overwhelming importance of party identification, and the lack of importance of campaign activities, derived from both empirical observation and the conceptual framework and resulting theories of the first studies of voting choice. As noted earlier, the methodology adopted to test these theories of electoral behavior only served to reinforce scholarly belief in the marginal importance of campaigns.

Before the 1950s, there was no survey research available to tell us why individuals made voting choices, but analysis of the aggregate election returns indicated that electoral competition declined sharply after 1896, and for nonpresidential office, an increasing number of constituencies were safely one-party. [7] In the 1940s, researchers began limited studies of individual voting behavior and, beginning with the 1952 election, had reliable pre- and post-election data from national samples. These early studies, conducted by the Survey Research Center at the University of Michigan and known throughout the political science community as the Michigan surveys, shaped the perception of a generation of political scientists. They revealed the significance of party identification in voting choice and generated the theories about its role.[8]

Unlike some who studied their work, the Michigan researchers recognized the time-bound nature of their data, cautioning that party identification was crucial "in the period of our studies." [9] This era, the late 1940s and the 1950s, followed closely upon the Roosevelt realignment, when party identification could be expected to be most deeply entrenched. Because of the political realities of the time, however, the studies dismissed the impact of campaigns, and their methodology made it difficult or impossible to find evidence to the contrary. With only one survey before the election and one after, it was not easy to determine the consequences of specific campaign strategies or events. Additionally, the surveys asked respondents very little about the campaign, because the theoretical constructs being tested gave them no weight. Finally, national samples of less than 2,000 respondents, and based on counties, did not permit analysis of nonpresidential campaigns.

Starting in the 1960s, it became clear that the public consensus on which the New Deal realignment rested was beginning to decay. The Michigan studies showed that the number of self-identified partisans was declining, that partisans held their allegiance more weakly, and that voting decisions were made later and later in the election season. The amount of split-ticket voting rose dramatically. It was also apparent that candidates for every office, who had previously depended on party organizations to conduct their campaigns, were responding to the electorate's volatility with major changes in campaign techniques, including heavy use of the new medium of television, a new reliance on polling and voting data analysis, and increasing participation by non-party personnel—especially public relations and advertising agencies—in campaign planning and direction.[10]

Earlier periods of voter volatility had produced the same effect. The changed or weakened party attachments in the 1890s and the 1930s had led campaigns to use the mass media of the time—printed materials in the earlier period and radio in the later one—to issue persuasive appeals. What made the 1960s different, however, was that, previously, the party organizations had devised these appeals and arranged for their dissemination. Now, it was individual candidates' organizations that performed these functions.

A Revised View:
Campaigns as a Major Factor

The importance of this electoral volatility and candidates' response to it was at first dismissed. The Michigan researchers acknowledged that "short-term forces" (that is, stimuli other than party identification) played a significant role in individual elections, but contended that they were unlikely to disturb party stability for long: "In the lengthening period of our observation, vote shifts have not been accompanied by conversion but rather have been followed routinely by actual return to the party of original choice." The chances of a "deviating election"—one in which the minority party won the presidency—were estimated as "very much less than even." [11]

This prediction was made in 1966. Since then, the minority Republicans have won four of the five presidential elections without reaching majority party status. Their presidential victories did not bring any consistent improvement in Republicans' fortunes in other electoral contests. At first, it was suggested that the United States had become a two-tiered party system in which Republican presidential candidates profited from rejection of a leftward drift among Democratic party activists, although most Democratic identifiers returned to their majority party home in voting for other races. Some researchers pointed out, however, that while national party swings in congressional elections were modest, the range in individual constituencies was five to six times as large.[12]

Initially, these puzzling data still did not lead many political scientists to study individual candidates and their campaigns. Instead, incumbency, perception of presidential performance, the state of the economy, the role of the media, and the effect of issues all became objects of attention. Studies in the 1970s documented an increasing incumbency effect, in which sizable numbers of party identifiers opted for congressional and senatorial incumbents of the other party because they were better known to an electorate increasingly detatched from party loyalties. National congressional vote swings in midterm elections were explained as strongly related to the popularity of the incumbent president and shifts in personal disposable income. The role of the media was explored, with much attention given to their greater impact on the more visible presidential contests than on other races, and the greater coverage received by incumbents. Finally, attitudes about the most salient political issues were seen as strongly affecting both vote choice and party identification.[13]

As work in these new areas of inquiry proceeded, however, the relevance of candidate and campaign effects became apparent. Incumbency was not uniformly helpful; some congressional incumbents of both parties benefited from it more than others. Incumbency was generally more valuable to representatives than to senators, and to some senators more than others. Attention was given to variations among challengers and to the factors that were more likely to produce successful challenges—chiefly, prior political experience and the ability to raise money. Any media advantage enjoyed by congressional incumbents disappeared when challengers had these resources. The apparent impact of issues on voting behavior was seen to be either time-bound or a methodological artifact.[14]

The connection between economic conditions, presidential evaluations, and the competitive stance of midterm congressional challengers also fell under new scrutiny. While analysis of election returns showed a relationship among these variables, survey data did not confirm that individual voting choices depended on attitudes toward the president or on perceived changes in personal financial status. By 1982, the models based on presidential popularity and the state of the economy also grossly overestimated the out-party swing. They predicted that the Democrats would win about twice as many congressional seats as they in fact did. Studies attempting to link voting choices to attitudes about the economic condition of the country or of groups the voter felt psychologically close to—known as "sociotropic voting"—showed only weak relationships.[15]

The combined impact of these findings directed political scientists to a more serious consideration of the effect of candidates and campaigns. In analyzing the major components of voting decisions in the presidential elections between 1952 and 1980, only twice was party identification found to be among the three most central factors, while attitudes toward the candidates were among the three most important components in seven of the eight elections. The Michigan researchers now concluded:

> Candidate evaluations have been shown to be a primary determinant of the vote, with policy considerations and even partisan orientation affecting the vote exclusively or largely through the way they help to shape feelings toward the presidential rivals. In the American system of elections, the choice is ultimately between competing candidates.[16]

Similarly, a review of the literature on determinants of the congressional vote summarized it by asserting: "It makes a difference who the candidates are and what they do. If our interest is in particular congressional races, we would do well to focus on factors related to the candidates themselves."[17] In 1984, researchers published the first major study specifically devoted to the impact of campaigns on congressional races. It stressed the critical importance of the voters' knowledge of the candidates. It is this fact that must lead us to the study of campaigns, because it is campaigns that provide voters with the information they have, primarily through their own messages, and secondarily through their influence on the media. The authors end by observing, "Understanding the campaign process requires attention to the considerable diversity among races. . . . Researchers need to think about campaigns as part of a dynamic process—a series of events with both short- and long-term consequences for the character of governance in our system." [18]

We believe that more attention to candidates and campaigns is particularly important, because, unlike the periods following the 1896 and 1932 realignments, parties probably will not reassume their central role either in determining the vote or in spearheading campaigns. Party continues to be an important factor in both, but is no longer the central factor. If voters learn about candidates through their campaigns, then what candidates do in their campaigns, we will argue, affects not only electoral outcomes, but public policy as well.

A Framework for Studying Campaigns

The greater role candidate-centered campaigns now play in American politics and governance makes it necessary to explore how such organizations are structured, what influences their outcomes, and how they differ from traditional party-based campaigns. That is the major focus of this book. In it, we discuss the function of campaigns, basic campaign resources and strategies, important contextual factors that shape campaigns, and the way these factors operate during the stages through which campaigns pass. Below, the basic arguments are summarized.

The Function of the Campaign

A political campaign is an attempt to get information to voters that will persuade them to elect a candidate or not to elect an opponent. The first problem a campaign faces is to learn what information will best serve this purpose and to acquire it. The next major step is to decide how and when its own messages should be communicated. Obtaining useful and reliable data about the voters—and getting appropriate and persuasive information to them—is what a campaign is all about.

The key methods for *acquiring* crucial information are polls and targeting data. Polls are now the major source of information about voters' preferences, attitudes, behavior, and beliefs. Polling has grown ever more sophisticated since it was introduced into politics in the 1930s, but its basic function—ascertaining what voters know, think, and do—has remained the same. Modern-day targeting techniques are merely a more sophisticated version of Abraham Lincoln's call to "find 'em and vote 'em." Past voting patterns, registration data, and turnout statistics are now grist for a computerized mill, as campaigns attempt to identify a winning coalition.

The major vehicles for *disseminating* information to voters are advertising and news coverage. Media messages under the control of the campaign embrace the various forms of paid advertising, including television, radio, billboards, and direct mail. News coverage is the journalistic reporting of campaigns in newspapers, magazines, and on television and radio. A campaign can and will attempt to influence its coverage by the press, but clearly is less able to control those messages than its own.

Information can also be obtained and disseminated through field organizations. Campaign workers who engage in door-to-door or telephone canvassing serve as conduits to and from the campaign. As is the case with the media, field organizations operate under more or less control by the campaign. In addition to workers recruited and deployed through the campaign structure, favorably disposed outsiders such as interest groups, party organizations, and independent political action committees may disseminate information of their choice about the candidate or the opponent.

Campaign Resources

The ability of a campaign to conduct its two-way exchange of information depends heavily on the resources it commands.

The three critical resources for any political campaign are money, organization, and the candidate. Money buys polls, targeting data, and advertising, while organization permits direct contact with voters. To some extent, the two are interchangeable resources. A campaign with limited money to purchase media can get its message across with an army of canvassers and supervise the way they bring the message to the voters. A campaign with enough money to buy a great deal of paid advertising can make up for organizational deficiencies, or even buy the elements of a field operation, such as paid telephone banks. The candidates themselves bring a variety of resources to the campaign, including experience, knowledge, contacts, and organizations built in past campaigns. An increasing number also bring a substantial amount of their own money to finance their campaigns.

Campaign Strategies

Campaign strategies fall into three basic types, although any campaign will be a mix of the three. First, a party-centered strategy relies heavily on voters' partisan identification, as well as on the party's organization, to provide the resources necessary to wage the campaign. Second, candidates may follow an issue-oriented strategy and seek support from groups that feel strongly about various policies. Finally, a campaign may be shaped significantly by the candidate's image. The candidates hope to gain support because of their perceived personal qualities such as experience, leadership ability, integrity, independence, trustworthiness, and the like.

There is no such thing as *the* winning mix of strategies, for each campaign takes place within a different context. The context does much to define the appropriate strategy and helps determine whether it will be successful. It is possible, however, to identify the important factors that help determine strategy.

The Context of Campaigns

Any campaign organization operates within a series of givens, which it must consider as it plans its strategy. These are aspects of the campaign environment that cannot be altered. They significantly affect not only strategy, but the amount and kind of resources the campaign requires. The two most critical contextual factors are which office the candidate is seeking and whether he or she is an incumbent. Less central but still important are partisan balance and strength in the candidate's constituency, its demographic and geographic nature, and national trends.

The office the candidate seeks affects voters' interest, evaluation of the nominee, and turnout. More people vote for candidates for an executive office like governor than for a legislative office like senator, even though both are statewide positions. Voters also measure the qualifications for executive and legislative office differently. Interest in statewide races is higher than in local races. In addition, other races on the ballot in any given year have an impact. Turnout for congressional elections, for example, is higher in presidential election years than in off-years.

The candidates' positions have a great impact on campaign strategy. In the majority of campaigns, one candidate is the incumbent, and other candidates are challengers who may or may not hold political office. Sometimes the contested office is open—that is, no incumbent is running. The strategies adopted by incumbents, challengers, and contestants for open seats are very different. Strategies will also be affected by the candidate's history of officeholding.

Although both the organizational strength of American political parties and their capacity to inspire psychological attachments have declined, party identification and activity are by no means unimportant to campaign strategists. In many areas, party activists constitute the majority of those voting in low turnout elections. In many areas, a majority of voters still identify with one party, and the strength of that identification remains the best predictor of both turnout and vote choice. This is not to say that the candidate of the minority party invariably loses, but that party balance and strength, like the other factors listed, will affect strategy and the use and amount of resources needed.

The key characteristics of a constituency are its compactness and its homogeneity. Some congressional districts in large, sparsely populated states cover areas bigger than entire small, densely populated states. Some electoral constituencies have economically, ethnically, and racially homogeneous populations, while others are highly fragmented. A constituency may be entirely urban, suburban, or rural, or it may be some mixture.

Although the most important contextual factors pertain to the candidates themselves and to their constituencies, significant national trends may often have a substantial effect. Issues of compelling interest, such as Watergate in the 1970s and the state of the economy in the early 1980s, can influence electoral contests. Other candidates for office on the same ticket, even in these days of weaker party identification, can affect the fortunes of those running with them. Campaign strategy must take the possible consequences of these trends into account.

The Stages of a Campaign

The impact of campaigns can be studied from two interrelated but different perspectives. We can look either at how campaigns attempt to influence voters or at what those influences are. The first approach focuses on campaigns as organizations and on *their* behavior, while the second examines the way their activities shape the *voters'* behavior. We concentrate on the first perspective but recognize that campaign activities are determined in large measure by the anticipated and actual response of the electorate to the organizations' messages.

During an election contest, voters' attitudes about candidates are formed in a three-phase process, which corresponds to the three components of attitudes that social scientists call *cognition, affect,* and *evaluation.* These phases are sequential and hierarchical. In the cognition phase, voters become aware that the candidate is running for office— they associate the name with the race. Political consultants call this *raw recognition,* and, in the absence of media coverage and vigorous party activity, it is surprisingly difficult to achieve. Once the candidates are recognized, the second, or affect, phase involves the development of opinions about the candidate. Based on the candidates' attributes, voters decide whether they are positively or negatively disposed toward them.

Finally, in the evaluation phase the voter decides whether to vote or not, and for whom.

A campaign can influence each phase a voter goes through in deciding who to vote for, or whether to vote at all. Candidates must become known if they are to have any opportunity to influence voters' choices. Candidates who do not achieve recognition and favorable evaluations have effectively lost the race long before election day.

A successful campaign organization also passes through a three-step process similar, but not identical, to those of the voters. In the first stage of a campaign, it must create the conditions that will make it possible for its candidate to become known to the public—by building an organization to publicize the candidate, by acquiring the necessary information about the electorate, and by generating the resources to carry out these tasks. In the second stage, it must determine the criteria by which both its candidate and the candidate's opponent are to be judged by the public. It attempts to get voters to use the campaign's criteria in evaluating the contenders, by disseminating the messages that set the campaign's agenda. In the third stage, it tries to reinforce or alter the images of the contenders the public develops, to mobilize a winning coalition, and to ensure that its supporters actually vote. Each stage demands different uses of what resources provide—polling results, targeting data, media messages, and voter contact. In addition, strategies in each stage will vary depending on the contextual factors of the campaign. These stages of a campaign are also sequential and hierarchical. A candidate who never becomes known cannot set the agenda of the campaign, acquire a winning coalition of supporters, or get them to the polls.

The discussion in this book is organized according to the stages campaigns pass through, but also necessarily attends, as campaigners do, to their effects on voters. In the chapters that follow, we elaborate on the major points in this chapter—the evolution of party-centered campaigns into candidate-centered ones, the conduct of modern campaigns, the path that campaigns are likely to take in the future, and their effects on other important aspects of American politics and governance. We begin that process in the next chapter by looking at the way American campaigns were conducted before a great watershed—the rise and spread of television.

Notes

1. Jeff Greenfield, *Running to Win* (New York: Simon and Schuster, 1980), 28.

2. See James MacGregor Burns, *Roosevelt: The Lion and the Fox* (New York: Harcourt Brace, 1956) and Lou Cannon, *Reagan* (New York: Putnam, 1982) for excellent descriptions of their early careers.

3. See the similar analysis in Edie N. Goldenberg and Michael W. Traugott, *Campaigning for Congress* (Washington, D.C.: CQ Press, 1984), chapter 1.

4. Angus Campbell, Philip E. Converse, Warren E. Miller, and Donald E. Stokes, *The American Voter* (New York: Wiley, 1960), 135.

5. Charles O. Jones, "The Role of the Campaign," in *The Electoral Process*, ed. Kent Jennings and Harmon O. Ziegler (Englewood Cliffs, N.J.: Prentice-Hall, 1968), 4.

6. See James L. Sundquist, *Dynamics of the Party System*, rev. ed., (Washington, D.C.: Brookings Institution, 1983); Walter Dean Burnham, *Critical Elections and the Mainsprings of American Politics* (New York: Norton, 1970).

7. See Burnham, *Critical Elections;* Joel H. Silbey, Allan G. Bogue, and William H. Flanigan, eds., *The History of American Electoral Behavior* (Princeton: Princeton University Press, 1978).

8. Campbell et al. The earlier important studies are Paul Lazarsfeld, Bernard R. Berelson, and Hazel Gaudet, *The People's Choice* (New York: Duell, Sloan, and Pierce, 1944); Bernard R. Berelson, Paul Lazarsfeld, and William N. McPhee, *Voting* (Chicago: University of Chicago Press, 1954); and Angus Campbell, Gerald Gurin, and Warren E. Miller, *The Voter Decides* (Evanston, Ill.: Row, Peterson, 1954).

9. Campbell et al. *The American Voter*, 135.

10. Important early studies of the new campaign techniques include Stanley Kelley, Jr., *Professional Public Relations and Political Power* (Baltimore: Johns Hopkins, 1956); Dan Nimmo, *The Political Persuaders* (Englewood Cliffs, N.J.: Prentice-Hall, 1970); and James M. Perry, *The New Politics* (New York: Clarkson N. Potter, 1968).

11. Philip E. Converse, "The Concept of a Normal Vote," in *Elections and the Political Order*, ed. Angus Campbell et al. (New York: Wiley, 1966), 15; Donald E. Stokes, "Party Loyalty and the Likelihood of Deviating Elections," in Campbell, *Elections*, 133.

12. See Everett C. Ladd with Charles D. Hadley, *Transformations of the American Party System*, 2d ed. (New York: Norton, 1978), 262-72; Thomas E. Mann, *Unsafe at Any Margin* (Washington, D.C.: American Enterprise Institute, 1978), 14-16.

13. On the incumbency effect, see David Mayhew, *Congress: The Electoral Connection* (New Haven: Yale University Press, 1974). The role of presidential performance and the state of the economy is documented in Edward Tufte, "Determinants of the Outcome of Midterm Congressional Elections," *American Political Science Review* (September 1975): 812-26. Important studies of the role of the media are Thomas E. Patterson, *The Mass Media Election: How Americans Choose Their President* (New York: Praeger, 1980); Thomas E. Patterson and Robert D. McClure, *The Unseeing Eye: The Myth of Television Power in National Politics* (New York: Putnam, 1976); and Michael J. Robinson, "Three Faces of Congressional Media," in *The New Congress*, ed. Thomas E. Mann and Norman Ornstein (Washington, D.C.: American Enterprise Institute, 1981). The role of issues is treated in Warren E. Miller and Teresa Levitan, *Leadership and Change* (Cambridge, Mass.: Winthrop, 1976); Norman H. Nie, Sidney Verba, and John R. Petrocik, *The Changing American Voter* (Cambridge, Mass.: Harvard University Press, 1976); and Gerald M. Pomper,

"From Confusion to Clarity: Issues and American Voters 1952-1968," *American Political Science Review* 66 (June 1972): 1256-68.

14. Reconsiderations of the role of incumbency and the effect of the particular office appear in Mann, *Unsafe at Any Margin;* Alan I. Abramowitz, "Name Familiarity, Reputation and the Incumbency Effect in a Congressional Election," *Western Political Quarterly* 27 (December 1975): 668-84; Alan I. Abramowitz, "A Comparison of Voting for U.S. Senate and Representative in 1978," *American Political Science Review* 74 (September 1980): 633-40; Alan I. Abramowitz, "Choices and Echoes in the 1978 U.S. Senate Elections: A Research Note," *American Journal of Political Science* 25 (February 1981): 112-18; Barbara Hinckley, "House Reelections and Senate Defeats," *British Journal of Political Science* 10 (October 1980): 441-60. The role of challengers is explored in Gary C. Jacobson and Samuel Kernell, *Strategy and Choice in Congressional Elections* (New Haven: Yale University Press, 1981) and Mark C. Westlye, "Competitiveness of Senate Seats and Voting Behavior in Senate Elections," *American Journal of Political Science* 27 (May 1983): 253-83. The role of the media in congressional elections is investigated in Peter Clarke and Susan H. Evans, *Covering Campaigns: Journalism in Congressional Elections* (Stanford, Calif.: Stanford University Press, 1983). The role of issues is reexplored in Michael Margolis, "From Confusion to Confusion: Issues and Voters 1952-1972," *American Political Science Review* 71 (March 1977): 31-43; and Arthur H. Miller, "The Majority Party Reunited? A Comparison of the 1972 and 1976 Elections," in *Parties and Elections in an Anti-Party Age,* ed. Jeff Fishel (Bloomington: Indiana University Press, 1978).

15. See Donald Kinder and D. Roderick Kiewiet, "Economic Discontent and Political Behavior: The Role of Personal Grievances and Collective Economic Judgments in Congressional Voting," *American Journal of Political Science* 23 (1979): 495-527; D. Roderick Kiewiet, "Policy-Oriented Voting in Response to Economic Issues," *American Political Science Review* 75 (1981): 448-59; Gerald H. Kramer, "The Ecological Fallacy Revisited: Aggregate- Versus Individual-Level Findings on Economics and Elections and Sociotropic Voting," *American Political Science Review* 77 (March 1983): 92-111.

16. Gregory B. Markus and Philip E. Converse, "A Dynamic Simultaneous Model of Electoral Choice," *American Political Science Review* 70 (December 1979): 1068.

17. Richard G. Niemi and Herbert F. Weisberg, *Controversies in Voting Behavior,* 2d ed. (Washington, D.C.: CQ Press, 1984), 206.

18. Goldenberg and Traugott, *Campaigning for Congress,* 187-88.

19. See Gabriel Almond and Sidney Verba, *The Civic Culture* (Princeton: Princeton University Press, 1963).

American Political Campaigns Before Television

2

No American dreams of offering himself for a post unless he has been chosen by the party.

—James Bryce, 1888[1]

The media have done to the campaign system what the invention of accurate artillery did to the feudal kingdom—destroyed the barons and shifted their power to the masses and the prince. A candidate now pays less attention to district leaders than to opinion polls.

—Stimson Bullitt, 1961[2]

A summary of recent trends in American political campaigning would begin like this: Since about 1950, American political campaigns have become increasingly candidate-centered. All aspects of the campaign—its organization, fundraising techniques, polling, and media messages—exist for the sole purpose of electing a particular candidate to a particular office. Appeals to voters communicate an "image"—a combination of the candidate's personal characteristics and his or her issue positions. Campaigns are organized and directed by "hired guns"—people who have performed the same specialized tasks in other campaigns in the past. They know what information should be gathered in polls at various stages, what kinds of media messages are required at various points in the campaign, which sorts of direct mail lists will produce the most contributions, and so on. Organizational efforts are directed at identifying, and bringing to the polls, those voters who might favor the candidate.

This description will sound banal to anyone who has come to political maturity in the television age. Yet for a century or more, as observed in chapter 1, American political campaigns were in fact party-centered, not candidate-centered. The appeals of the campaign were to party identification and loyalty; the campaign organizations were party organizations. Party domination extended beyond campaigns; for a long period, parties had substantial control of the nomination and election processes as well. Throughout the nineteenth century, candidates were chosen in party caucuses and conventions rather than in primary elections, and voters cast their ballots on forms provided by the parties, not by nonpartisan election boards. Clearly, this was a very different kind of politics.

Reasons for the Decline In Party-centered Campaigns

Some of the most important reasons why party-centered campaigns declined and came to be replaced by candidate-centered ones can be sketched here. First was the enormous growth in the voting population because of natural increase and the gradual extension of the franchise to nonproperty owners, women, southern blacks, and, most recently, eighteen- to twenty-year olds. Second was the rising tide of industrialization, the attendant movement of the population into heterogeneous urban centers, and the breakup of longstanding homogeneous rural communities. Third was the rise of the mass media and its role in personalizing and nationalizing issues, individuals, and culture. Finally, there was the altered role of government itself. As government, particularly the federal government, grew larger and assumed regulatory and social welfare functions, its relation to the public changed profoundly. American political parties, designed for face-to-face local campaigns to a limited electorate living in stable communities, were hard-pressed to cope with these disruptions in the social order.

American campaigns, of course, did not evolve from the party-centered to the candidate-centered mode overnight. Rather, the premodern campaign era can be divided into three stages: the period until about 1830-1840, from that time until about 1890, and the years between 1890 and 1950. Before the third decade of the nineteenth century, limits on the franchise and the indirect election of the president made it necessary to aim campaign messages at only a small portion of the population. As the franchise expanded and members of the electoral college were selected by voters rather than by the state legislatures, mobilization by political parties of a mass voting population became critically important. Thus until about 1890 all campaigns were in fact party-centered—it was the party, not the candidates, that was in charge.

The years from 1890 to 1950 were a transition period. Superficially, parties still dominated the nomination and campaign processes, but beneath the surface, antiparty and nonparty elements were emerging and gaining strength. The Populist and Progressive movements of the late nineteenth and early twentieth centuries engendered a number of changes that weakened the parties—the introduction of the direct primary, the direct election of senators, and the secret ballot. The development of mass media—national wire services in the late nineteenth century, radio in the first decades of the twentieth century, and television a few decades later—made it possible for voters to receive political information from sources other than the parties. The spread of the railroads and the mass production of the automobile permitted the mobility that is now characteristic of Americans and that weakened their ties to local party organizations. These innovations made possible the first insurgent candidacies—candidacies not championed or sanctioned by party organizations.

Traditional campaigning, centered on party identification and organization, was first modified in presidential campaigns; the new style of electioneering worked its way down to lower offices only gradually. Presidential candidates always had to face the most heterogeneous constituency. Because the White House was the biggest prize, especially as issues became nationalized and opportunities for federal patronage grew, presidential campaigns commanded the greatest resources, in terms of both money and organization. These resources, and the national constituency of presidential candidates, made it both possible and desirable to adopt nonparty modes of campaigning.

We have described campaigns as a process of communicating information to persuade voters to elect a candidate. As technology advanced, parties and candidates adopted the newly available means of communication, but often long after they had been used for other purposes. As we shall see, three kinds of situations may prompt campaigns to look for new ways of reaching the voters—periods of social and political upheaval, attempts by insurgents to challenge a party-backed nominee, and vigorous efforts by minority party candidates to challenge an entrenched majority party candidate. Because resources were more available to presidential candidates, and mass communication peculiarly well suited to their far-flung constituencies, it was in the race for the White House that the new techniques were first used; they were then copied by lower-level campaigns.

In this chapter we will describe the pure party-centered campaigns that characterized most of the nineteenth century, and the transition period in the first half of the twentieth century, which saw the beginning of the movement away from the party-centered campaign.

The Era of Party-centered Campaigns: 1830-1890 _____

The Importance of
Politics in Everyday Life

Comprehending the role of political campaigns in nineteenth-century America requires an understanding of the role of politics during that era. It is hard for us to imagine a world without television, without radio, without films, without organized spectator sports. For the nineteenth-century American, the two chief forms of diversion were religious observance and politics; often they reinforced each other. For one thing, the mass followings of the major parties were rooted in ethnic and religious divisions, particularly between Protestants and Catholics and between evangelical and nonevangelical Protestants. There was also a similarity between the way religious and political groups were structured. Discussing his plans for local party organizations, a Whig politician in 1840 wrote:

> The model of my primary local association is the Christian Church. The officers, the exercises, the exhortations, the singing, the weekly meetings, the enrollment of members, the contributions, and all are to be on the primitive apostolic model as presented in the Congregational churches of New England. Then I want itinerant lecturers, political preachers going about in regular circuits, next spring and summer, on the Methodist plan.... Each of all the hundreds of thousands of members of these associations will also make a weekly contribution of one cent to the great cause of our "church militant." [3]

The popular zeal for politics was readily apparent to European visitors. Alexis de Tocqueville, in a famous passage in *Democracy in America*, described the unique role politics played in American social life in the 1830s:

> The political activity that pervades the United States must be seen in order to be understood. No sooner do you set foot upon American ground than you are stunned by a kind of tumult; a confused clamor is heard on every side, and a thousand simultaneous voices demand the satisfaction of their social wants.... To take a hand in the regulation of society, and to discuss it, is his biggest concern and, so to speak, the only pleasure an American knows. [4]

Endless rounds of gatherings were a feature of both city and country life. In the cities, they resembled street carnivals. In his diary, a nineteenth-century New Yorker described a Democratic rally in New York City in 1864: "Tricolored lanterns were strung over the streets, and boys carrying more lanterns circulated among the mob of people who strolled past the dozen speakers' platforms eating peaches and oranges." [5] In rural areas, farmers came from miles around to listen to political oratory at a local picnic or fairground. Crowds reached as high as 25,000. When Stephen Douglas and Abraham Lincoln held their famous series of debates in the 1858 Illinois Senate race, throngs of people attended, even though Senate elections then took place in the state legislature, and ordinary citizens could thus not vote directly for either Douglas or Lincoln. A Chicago journalist wrote of one of their rural encounters:

> It was a glorious sight to see the long line of teams filled with men, women and children, extending down the prairie as far as the eye could reach, the flags gaily flying in the morning breeze, and the brass instruments of the numerous bands gleaming in the sun. At every house and every crossroad, the procession received accessions, until when entering Charleston, it was nearly two miles long.[6]

A Reliance on Partisanship

What enabled the political parties to organize these massive rallies was the fervent partisanship of their supporters, rooted in social and religious issues such as prohibition, antislavery, nativism, and Sunday observance. Particularly in the last third of the nineteenth century, after the cultural and sectional disputes of the 1830s and 1840s and the Civil War, the evidence is that "party loyalty was extraordinary and almost unshakable, and voting turnout amazingly high."[7] Careful studies of nineteenth-century partisanship in various regions of the country repeatedly confirm this.[8]

Historians note that although partisanship was virtually unshakable during most of the nineteenth century, the two major parties (first the Whigs and the Democrats; later the Republicans and the Democrats) were nationally very close in strength through much of the period. It was thus extremely important to the parties that their easily identified supporters come out to vote on the numerous state and federal election days. The major campaign technique in this era has been aptly described as "military." Parties commonly organized paramilitary units of supporters whose job it was to get out their vote. In the 1860 four-candidate presidential election, for instance, these quasi-military uniformed units were Stephen Douglas's Little Giants, John Breckinridge's National Democratic Volunteers, Abraham Lincoln's Wide-Awakes, and John Bell's Bell Ringers.

Urban party machines also had their generals, troop commanders, and foot soldiers. The typical city machine was organized by wards. The head of each ward was represented on a citywide council, presided over by a "boss." The ward leaders controlled the activities of the machine's foot soldiers, the precinct captains. It was the job of the leaders and the captains to turn out the mass vote. Much of this activity went on in the neighborhood bars. James Bryce described the typical ward politician of the 1880s: "A statesman of this type usually begins as a saloon or bar-keeper, an occupation which enables him to form a large circle of acquaintances, especially among the 'loafer' class who have votes but no reason for using them one way more than another, and whose interest in political issues is as limited as their stock of political knowledge." He further reported, "of the 1,007 primaries and conventions of all parties held in New York preparatory to the elections of 1884, 633 took place in liquor saloons." [9]

Party Control of the Ballot

The task of turning out a reliable vote was made easier by party control of the ballot. In the nation's earliest days, the casting of ballots had been informal and unsystematic. Some states let voters create their own ballots, or used an item like corn or beans to designate a vote. The new political parties saw the opportunity to take over the preparation of ballots. In 1829, the Massachusetts Supreme Court upheld the legality of party-prepared ballots, which became the norm until almost the end of the nineteenth century.

Each party had ballots, called party strips, of a different color, size, and shape. In most states, the names of the party's candidates for all offices appeared on the same ballot, although a few states at different times had party strips for each office. The parties had hawkers to peddle ballots "to the voters in what resembled an auctioneering atmosphere in and around the polling station." [10] This system was obviously a powerful incentive for already partisan voters to cast a straight party ticket. Splitting one's ticket required either scratching out the names listed on the ballot or fastening several ballots together. Few voters bothered to do so. Ticket splitting in states with single party strips averaged only slightly over 1 percent in the years from 1876 to 1908.

Party control of the ballot, combined with lax election laws and even laxer enforcement, almost invited vote fraud, particularly in an era when the parties were highly competitive and many elections were very close. Daniel Boorstin cites an eyewitness description of the 1827 election for the New York State legislature, the body that would cast the state's votes for president in the following year. Two hundred voters "were marched to the polls by one of the Jackson candidates who walked at the head with a cocked pistol in each hand and then without leaving the polls they voted three times apiece for the Jackson ticket." [11] Party workers frequently resorted to such "repeaters" and to "float-ers"—men brought in from other states. A Republican organizer intent on carrying a hotly contested 1888 race in Indiana instructed his local man on the scene: "Divide the floaters into blocks of five and put a trusted man with necessary funds in charge of these five and make him responsible that none get away and all vote our ticket." [12]

The Australian Ballot—
A Reaction Against Corruption

As the nineteenth century wore on, citizens became increasingly exasperated with the corruption surrounding elections. Exposure of the unsavory activities of the party machines outraged the public. For example, the inner financial workings of New York City's Tammany Hall and its notorious Tweed Ring were revealed by the *New York Times* in 1871. Reform leaders placed a spy in the city controller's office, who passed on what he found to the newspaper. Those doing business with the city were told to add increasingly larger percentages to their bills for kickbacks to the machine.[13]

The aura of corruption led reformers in many states to press for the secret, or Australian, ballot, which had been introduced in that country in midcentury. A ballot prepared by nonpartisan election authorities and cast in secret was first adopted by Massachusetts in 1888; within eight years, 90 percent of the states—almost all of those outside the South—adopted the system. The secret ballot was, as we shall see shortly, one of the changes that contributed to the gradual weakening of party organizations in the first half of the twentieth century.

Reaching the Voter

Through most of the nineteenth century, candidates communicated with voters principally through oratory. Candidates for nonpresidential office relied on shoe leather, doggedly traveling their constituencies. Direct contact with voters first became necessary with the expansion of the franchise to almost all adult white males in the Jackson era. Lincoln and Douglas traveled more than 5,000 miles when they debated in 1858, by a combination of train, carriage, and river boat. A congressional candidate in the same state in 1852 began his campaign at the end of August on horseback and did not return to his home for two months. These speaking trips were organized by the state and local party organizations.

The only candidates who did not travel were presidential aspirants. In a country without a transcontinental railroad, visiting the far corners of their national constituency was unthinkable. The presidential candidate's time was "spent chopping wood, planting crops, and dispensing folk wisdom."[14] He waited at home to be notified by a delegation from the party convention of his nomination, and then later issued a detailed letter of acceptance setting forth his views. The campaign itself was fought not by the candidates but by surrogate party speakers. The national party committees were formed in the middle of the nineteenth century, principally to coordinate the surrogates' trips and to raise funds to support speakers on the road during presidential campaigns.

Highly partisan newspapers carried the words of the orators, along with other political communication, to the public. The struggling and impoverished press was tied very early to the parties when the government authorized the establishment of up to three "By Authority" newspapers in each state to publish the content of federal legislation. The papers were selected at the discretion of the secretary of state; this was among the first instances of political patronage. Andrew Jackson cemented the alliance by awarding friendly publishers postmasterships, positions in the Customs Service, and other appointments. At least fifty-nine journalists received such patronage jobs from the Jackson administration.[15]

The printed word, which was the only form of mass communication available to campaign strategists in the nineteenth century, was almost totally controlled by the parties. It became the standard practice of nineteenth-century politicians to buy—or buy off—the small weekly newspapers, and later the dailies, that served most of the population. Henry Clay and Daniel Webster raised money to pay off newspapers sympathetic to the Whigs, and Abraham Lincoln bought a German-language newspaper to advance Republican doctrine and his own congressional and senatorial campaigns. Well-heeled party activists also bought newspapers. August Belmont, chairman of the Democratic National Committee from 1860 to 1872, purchased the *New York Morning Star* in 1851 to promote the candidacy of James Buchanan and tried to buy the *New York Times* in 1860 so that he could turn it into an organ for Stephen Douglas. Newspapers thus served as "important parts of the party organization themselves." [16] As printing presses and paper gradually became less expensive, other forms of campaign literature—broadsides, handbills, candidate biographies, and the like— supplemented the newspaper.

The Role of the Party Organization

Campaigns depending primarily on oratory and organization were not expensive affairs. Money was needed principally for speakers' travels and to meet get-out-the-vote expenses on election day. Whatever could not be raised from fat cats like the Democrats' Belmont was collected by assessing those in patronage jobs:

During the 60's, 70's and 80's the money collected by Republican congressional committees came largely from employees of the federal government. In 1878 this committee collected $106,000, of which $80,000 came from persons holding appointive positions in the public service. The contributions required ranged from 1 to 3 percent of salary, and an intensive follow-up campaign made it extremely difficult for the victim to escape.[17]

In the late nineteenth century, large amounts of political money were intended not for campaign coffers, but as payoffs to officeholders for favors or protection. The Tweed Ring, which bought votes to gain control of city or state governments, was archetypical. Once in control, politicians could sell the goods at their disposal—government contracts or favorable regulation, licences, jobs, or protection—to the highest bidders.

The political machine has been aptly described as a "business organization in a particular field of business—getting votes and winning elections. The machine, therefore, is apolitical; it is interested in making and distributing income—mainly money—to those who run it and work for it." [18] Other businesses bought the services of the machine's bosses and their candidates in the same "apolitical" way. As Jay Gould of the Erie Railroad testified to a committee of the New York State Assembly in 1873: "In a Republican district I was a Republican; in a Democratic district a Democrat; in a doubtful district I was doubtful, but I was always for Erie." [19]

An Appraisal of the Period

The picture of American campaigns in the nineteenth century that emerges is of political parties preeminently in control. In their caucuses and conventions, they nominated candidates for every office. Their workers and sympathizers militaristically drilled strong partisans to the polls, where they voted with ballots provided by the party. Their local, state, and weak national committees raised the necessary campaign funds, coordinated the travels of stump speakers to party rallies, subsidized a strongly partisan press, and printed and distributed campaign literature.

Some have seen this as a golden age of American politics, in which the vast majority of the population was highly aware of political issues, and in which almost everyone voted, often several times a year in different elections.[20] Others perceive the era, particularly its latter part, as a sinkhole of political corruption, in which votes were manufactured and bought, elections stolen, and political machines and their elected representatives did the bidding of the new big business class for mutual financial gain.[21] But everyone agrees that however elected officials

behaved, it was the organized political parties that were solely responsible for their being in office.

Yet as the nineteenth century came to an end, there were already
signs that the sway of the parties over campaigns was beginning to
weaken. The social and economic upheaval that swept the United States
in the latter part of the century was to have profound effects on its
politics, effects that would broaden and deepen through the first half of
the twentieth century.

The Era of Transition: 1890-1950

The nineteenth century was an era of strong and enduring partisanship,
but industrialization and the appearance of the powerful corporations,
or trusts, disrupted this stability. These economic changes had consequences for both voters and parties that eroded party control of
campaigns.

The Populists and the Progressives

The first threat to party stability and hegemony came from the
Populist movement, centered in the South and the West, two areas that
were described as "colonies" of the Midwest and Northeast in the latter
part of the nineteenth century. In the South, small farmers saw
themselves as captives of the northern manufacturers to whom they sold
their raw goods, of a local merchant class that charged them increasingly
exorbitant interest on loans, and of the railroads, which were the only
way of conveying goods to market. Small farmers in the western states
newly admitted to the Union shared these complaints. Additionally,
demands by powerful silver interests in the West for large government
purchases of the metal for currency exacerbated the plight of southern
and western farmers, who desired "cheap money," embodied by a silver-
backed currency.

Through the 1880s, rural America sank deeper into agricultural
depression. Farmers began to organize politically through regional
Farmers' Alliances, which had originally been fraternal organizations,
and in 1892 held a national convention to found the People's, or
Populist, party. It called for unlimited coinage of silver, a graduated
income tax, government ownership of the railroads, direct election of
senators, the secret ballot, and limits on immigration. Its presidential
nominee went on to receive more than a million votes in that year's
election. Populist politicians in the South succeeded in taking over the
Democratic party in several states and electing their leaders to governor-

ships and the Senate. State legislatures in the South and West fell under their control.

While the Democratic party split on the issues of the tariff, bimetalism, and immigration, the Republican party was being torn apart by the Progressive movement, which followed Populism a few years later. Although the Progressives did not share the Populists' positions on nationalization of industry and easy money, they joined them in their antipathy to the trusts and their support of political reform measures.

Progressives could be found in both parties, as exemplified by Republican Theodore Roosevelt and Democrat Woodrow Wilson, but they were predominantly Republican. Progressive Republicans were able to win the vice presidency in 1900 for their hero of the Spanish-American War, Teddy Roosevelt, who became an accidental president with the assassination of President William McKinley less than a year later. Roosevelt later abandoned the conservative-dominated Republican party to run a presidential race as a Progressive candidate in 1912, when he received four million votes, came in second, and split the Republican vote to give the election to Woodrow Wilson, the Progressive-leaning Democratic governor of New Jersey. In the Midwest, Republican progressives, disenchanted with the conservative economic policies of their state parties, sporadically mounted state Progressive campaigns. Among their notable leaders was Robert La Follette, who received almost five million votes in the 1924 presidential election.

The Populist and Progressive movements had a major impact on party organizations and their campaign strategies. Populists and Progressives succeeded at the polls because the social and economic unrest that brought them into being tore large numbers of voters loose from their accustomed party moorings. A new note of uncertainty was introduced into campaigns beginning in the early 1890s. Helped by the advent of the Australian, or secret, ballot and an increasingly less partisan press, Populists began to win elections, and dealt the Republicans a severe defeat in the congressional elections of 1890.[22]

The Panic of 1893, the worst depression in the nation's history, struck shortly after the inauguration of the conservative "gold Democrat" Grover Cleveland, leading many to believe the Populists had a real chance of becoming one of the two major parties. In the 1894 midterm elections, Democrats lost control of the House and Senate, and their 1896 presidential convention nominated William Jennings Bryan, after being overwhelmed by the famous speech in which he declared, "You shall not crucify mankind upon a cross of gold." The country was in turmoil, and both parties saw that agitated voters, moving in all directions, could not be summoned to their party homes in the old ways: "Instead of a campaign carried on in a few dubious states, the field of action was enlarged to include half the country."[23] Uncertainty and political instability produced significant changes in political campaign styles, which were seen for the first time in the 1896 presidential campaign.

The Watershed Campaign of 1896

In the Democratic campaign, Bryan broke precedent by conducting what amounted to the first candidate-centered campaign. Blessed with extraordinary oratorical gifts, and embodying a highly emotional cause—the silver issue—Bryan was the first presidential candidate to take his case directly to the people. Between July and November of 1896, he made five hundred speeches, personally addressing thirty to forty million people as far west as Nebraska, as far south as Tennessee, and as far north as Boston, traveling 18,000 miles in four swings around the country.[24] To a nation accustomed to presidential candidates who were neither seen nor heard, it was an astounding performance—one that convinced many in the opposition camp that he was leading in the race.

The Republican campaign, under the direction of candidate McKinley's patron, Mark Hanna, realized it would also have to take dramatic action to counter the appeal of the "Boy Orator from the Platte." The departure from electioneering as usual saw the advent of another innovation. As Hanna's biographer tells it, the Republicans "decided to oppose Mr. Bryan's personal appeal with an exhaustive and systematic educational canvass of the country."[25] A later, more dispassionate historian describes it this way: "Hanna conducted the first modern advertising campaign, selling his candidate like soap to the American people. Cartoons, posters, inscriptions, were turned out by the carloads. Hanna set up twin headquarters in Chicago and New York, dispatched an army of 1,400 trained speakers, sent out over 120 million campaign documents."[26]

Unlike the Bryan campaign, the Republicans' effort did not feature new campaign tactics. The party organized the traditional surrogate orators and production of campaign literature. What made McKinley's campaign different was its deliberate orchestration: the careful attention, first to finding and targeting likely Republican voters, and then to winning them to the Republican side through a series of persuasive negative messages about the Democratic candidate and program as well as positive messages about the Republicans' own. One of the tactics party workers relied on was painstaking canvasses of doubtful areas. When a house-to-house canvass of Iowa in September showed Bryan leading, in "the next six weeks, speakers and campaign documents were poured into every town and village."[27] A second canvass in late October showed the state safe for McKinley. The flood of almost three hundred different campaign documents was carefully tailored for target groups and for different stages in the campaign. To reach the immigrant workers, who had been strongly Democratic, literature was printed in German, French, Spanish, Italian, Yiddish, and other languages. The early phases of the campaign dealt mostly with the silver issue, detailing the Republican view that it was a quick fix that would benefit only a minority sectional and class interest. Later, as the silver issue seemed to lose appeal, campaign literature switched to other issues such as protectionism.

Running such a campaign cost a great deal of money. The uncertainty that had already crept into politics had started to drive campaign costs up, a fact that generally benefited the Republicans. The new captains of industry had unbelievable amounts of capital at their disposal and a willingness to spend it to protect themselves from the Populist threat. The outlays in 1896, however, were unprecedented. Bryan's war chest of $675,000, provided primarily by silver interests, was very large for the period but paled into insignificance compared with the $3.5 million the Republicans reported they had spent. The money was raised by a canvass of business as thorough as the canvass of voters: "Inasmuch as the security of business and the credit system of the country were involved by the issues of the campaign, appeals were made to banks and businessmen, irrespective of party affiliations. . . . Responsible men were appointed to act as local agents in all fruitful neighborhoods for the purpose of both soliciting and receiving contributions." [28]

Thus the campaign of 1896 made significant departures from campaigns as usual—particularly in Bryan's personalization of his candidacy, in the Republicans' targeting of voters and marketing of their message, and in their liberal use of money not for bribery of officials or voters but for legitimate and ordinary campaign purposes. Additionally, Bryan's campaign was the first successful insurgent campaign, in which a candidate could take over a party convention through the force of his personality, ideas, and personal following. These phenomena were to have an important impact in the next fifty years, a period that marked the transition from party- to candidate-centered campaigns.

The Return to Politics as Usual

What we see clearly now was not as evident at the time. Although in 1896 the Republican party employed a new strategy, the fundamental tactics remained the same, and the effort was a *party* effort. As the electorate settled into a pattern of Republican voting after 1896, the

Republicans actually spent less in every presidential election from 1900 to 1916, when they saw a chance to recapture the prize Roosevelt had "stolen" from them as a third-party spoiler in 1912. The volatility of the congressional vote, which reached its apogee in the 1890s, ended. (The Democrats, who had held 61 percent of the seats in the House of Representatives after their great victory in 1892, saw themselves reduced to just over 29 percent in 1894.) Voters who had switched parties in 1896 stayed with them, voting the party and not the candidate. Even in 1896, split-ticket voting remained under 5 percent in the Australian ballot states and was generally lower thereafter.

In nonpresidential races, the route of electoral success in most of the country continued to be service in the locally dominant party organization, traditional campaigns mounted by the parties, and relatively low campaign expenditures. Warren G. Harding, running for senator from Ohio in 1914, relied on the Republican organization and spent $6,000. Even as late as 1940, Harry Truman had to raise less than $9,000 for his Senate reelection campaign, despite the fact that he had two serious opponents: he put his faith in the St. Louis Democratic organization. Examining data from several states in the late 1920s and early 1930s, an exhaustive study of campaign finance reported, "One is forced to conclude that in the great majority of cases campaigning for a seat in the House of Representatives is not an expensive business." [29] Academic analysts and practicing politicians agreed that in the early 1940s, $5,000 was more than enough to run a very well financed congressional campaign. Lyndon B. Johnson, who in 1940 was able to draw on a campaign fund provided by Texas oilmen and contractors, saved close to a hundred Democratic members of Congress that year with strategically placed contributions of $100 to $1,000. [30]

Moreover, the party machines, which were expected to wilt under the onslaught of the secret ballot, the institution of the federal civil service, the direct primary, and the personal registration systems that took hold in most states between 1910 and 1920, remained as strong as ever for most of the first half of the twentieth century. In 1910, a leading Progressive journalist wrote gleefully:

> And to have told the campaign managers of '84 or '88 that within a quarter of a century the whole nation would be voting a secret ballot, for candidates nominated in two-thirds of the American states by a direct vote of the people, without the intervention of conventions or caucuses, and that further than that every dollar spent by a candidate or by a party committee would have to be publicly accounted for, both coming and going—such a tale would have set ... the managers of those days to cackling and derision. ... Now the political machine is in a fair way to be reduced to mere political scrap iron by the rise of the people. [31]

However, it was noted, "With a few exceptions, the bosses found ways to either deflect or to use the new reforms that were meant to unseat them." [32] The way the machines operated under the new system is captured in this account of an election in Hudson County, New Jersey, where the Hague machine reigned for most of the first half of the twentieth century. Speaking of the Hudson County results in the 1925 New Jersey gubernatorial election, a latter-day Hudson County politician comments:

> This was the time of paper ballots. It was relatively easy for [Frank] Hague's people manning the polls to erase ballots, change ballots, destroy ballots, miscount ballots—while Hague-controlled policemen looked the other way or pressured inspection officials to stand aside. . . . Election superintendent John Ferguson [said] "we know it is futile to arrest anyone belonging to the Democrat organization in Hudson County on Election Day. The accuser usually finds himself in jail as the arrested party by the time he gets to the station house . . . the only way to have an honest election in Hudson County is with a militia, and if the present conditions are to continue, it is futile and ridiculous for us to attempt to hold further elections." [33]

The First Nonpresidential Insurgent Campaigns

The major effects of the weakened party loyalty brought on by the Populist and Progressive movements and the personalized and marketing candidacies of 1896 were seen in the two regions where they had had the greatest impact—the West and the South. The direct primary, perhaps the most significant of Progressive reforms from the perspective of campaigns, gave insurgents in these areas a chance to appeal directly to voters rather than only to the participants at party conventions or caucuses. Once nominated, however, insurgents took over party organizations as campaign vehicles for the general election. Of the leading Progressive and crusader for the direct primary, Robert La Follette, V. O. Key observes, "La Follette and the voters who followed him perhaps wanted to go to heaven but they insisted on traveling under Republican auspices." [34] Still, Populism and Progressivism introduced a fluidity into politics that made it possible to mount campaigns outside the party apparatus, in a way that was still not possible elsewhere.

In the South, politicians like Louisiana's legendary Huey Long were able to use Populist appeals to defeat the conservative courthouse gangs that dominated state politics in much of the old Confederacy. Using his own newspaper and the technological innovations of radio and sound truck, which were developed in the early decades of the twentieth century, Long was elected governor and then senator. He was preparing to mount a challenge to President Roosevelt when he was assassinated in 1935. [35]

The most important progenitor of the candidate-centered campaign, however, may have been the California gubernatorial contest of 1934, a race notable for two developments. It was the first time a neophyte attempted to launch a political career at the statewide level with the help of a personal organization and the first time that business interests, usually dependent on party machines, struck back with their own nonparty-based effort. The real contest was between the EPIC movement of Democratic candidate and political amateur Upton Sinclair and Whitaker and Baxter, a public relations firm that later would become the first independent political consultants for hire.

EPIC (End Poverty in California) was the organizational creation of Sinclair, a muckraking Socialist reporter, novelist, and scriptwriter, who decided to run in the 1934 Democratic gubernatorial primary. California, like the rest of the nation, was still in the grip of the Great Depression, with more than a million citizens receiving public relief. The EPIC platform called for steeply graduated inheritance and income taxes and for pensions for dependent widows and children. It also proposed a rather vague plan for state purchase of fallow farmland and idle factories to make work for the unemployed—a plan Sinclair's alarmed opponents described as socialism. Sinclair was entering the primary of the distinctly minority party. As he wrote, "The Republican Party has named the governors of California for more than forty years, and during that period the Democratic Party has been a small and feeble minority . . . split among themselves, living in the memory of old-time factional fights." [36]

Stepping into this Democratic vacuum, Sinclair formed about 2,000 neighborhood EPIC clubs and launched the *EPIC News*, which achieved a circulation of almost two million by the end of the campaign. The candidate also bought what radio time he could afford for speeches and wrote his best-selling book, *I, Governor of California*. EPIC precinct captains were present in virtually every district of the state; "tireless and dedicated, they were Sinclair's greatest source of political strength, and far more productive of results than the official party machinery." [37] Sinclair won the Democratic primary by better than two to one.

The California Republican party also had a history of factionalism, based on the old conservative-Progressive split in the party. Hiram Johnson, elected governor in 1910, and later senator until his death, was a leading Progressive. Johnson, who made a career of fighting the Southern Pacific Railroad, pushed through all of the Progressive political agenda—direct primaries, and initiative, referendum, and recall elections. At the time Sinclair ran for governor, however, the conservatives had the upper hand in the Republican party. Its state committee chairman was Louis B. Mayer, president of Metro-Goldwyn-Mayer studios. The major industries of California were among the first to hire public relations and advertising firms and, by the time of Sinclair's race, had employed them to wage publicity campaigns against referenda questions considered detrimental to business. However, they had never been used for or against a candidate in an election. Sinclair's economic program was seen as so threatening that the film industry and other corporations decided that such a campaign was necessary and provided the Republican party with the financial backing to carry it out.

Whitaker and Baxter, the public relations firm hired by the Republicans, produced enormous numbers of pamphlets, circulars, and newspaper advertisements with alarming themes. One handout resembled a piece of American currency, emblazoned ONE SINCLIAR DOLLAR at the top, and ENDURE POVERTY IN CALIFORNIA at the bottom. "Good only in California or Russia," it proclaimed. Other literature accused Sinclair of being opposed to organized religion and in favor of "free love." With little money and no organization capable of penetrating the frightened Republican middle class, Sinclair lost the general election by more than 200,000 votes.

The Sinclair campaign, as well as Huey Long's, demonstrated how insurgent candidates with charismatic personalities and strong issues could run independently of weakened party organizations and wage campaigns through the mass media of the time. Reliance on newspapers was traditional, but a new medium was entering the political arena.

Radio was first widely used in the presidential campaign of 1928. By the early 1930s, it had spread to state-level campaigns. Gubernatorial and senatorial candidates in New Jersey and Massachusetts in 1930 reported that a fifth to a third of their total campaign expenditures went for radio broadcasts. Radio came to be regarded as another way to make stump speeches to a large audience. A 1940 Democratic handbook for precinct leaders advised them to encourage supporters to tune in when important party leaders made broadcast addresses. "Radio is the streamlined way of reaching voters in a streamlined age," it concluded.

Air time was typically bought in chunks of fifteen minutes to an hour, for the communication of traditional political oratory by the candidates or surrogate speakers. Some of radio's most accomplished users employed it less for campaigning than for maintaining a political base once they had been elected. Franklin Roosevelt delivered his famous fireside chats. During a protracted newspaper strike, New York's Mayor LaGuardia read the funnies over the air on Sunday mornings. Governor Lee ("Pappy") O'Daniel of Texas, a political neophyte who had the state's most widely listened-to radio program before his election, continued it from the governor's mansion. O'Daniel may thus have been the first politician whose career was entirely the creation of the media.[38]

An Overview of the Era of Transition

As the twentieth century reached its midpoint, campaigns in most of the country continued to be party-centered affairs. In response to the loosening of party identification that had occurred at the turn of the century, organizational efforts to get sure party voters to the polls were supplemented but not supplanted by merchandising techniques. Insurgent candidacies became commonplace in those regions most affected by the Populist and Progressive movements, as candidates espousing their ideas moved into the Democratic and Republican parties, respectively, and challenged the traditional organizations through the direct primary. Candidates of the local minority party could sometimes win in times of strong national tides, but, for the most part, traditional majority party candidates reigned supreme.

The California public relations campaign against Upton Sinclair however, was a straw in the wind. As the second half of the century began, these techniques were adopted first at the presidential level; in the next twenty years, they filtered down to statewide campaigns, and then even lower. By the 1980s, California, once again leading the way, would see a million-dollar media race for a seat in the State Assembly. The beginnings of that process are described in the next chapter.

Notes

1. James Bryce, *The American Commonwealth*, ed. Louis Hacker (1888; reprint, New York: Putnam, 1959), vol. 1, 180.
2. Stimson Bullitt, *To Be a Politician* (Garden City, N.Y.: Doubleday, 1961), 65.
3. Jasper P. Shannon, *Money and Politics* (New York: Random House, 1959), 19-20.
4. Alexis de Tocqueville, *Democracy in America* (New York: Knopf, 1945), vol. 1, 259-60.
5. David Black, *The King of Fifth Avenue: The Fortunes of August Belmont* (New York: Dial Press, 1981), 254.
6. *Chicago Times*, September 21, 1858, quoted in Paul M. Angle, *Created Equal? The Complete Lincoln-Douglas Debates* (Chicago: University of Chicago Press, 1958) 232-233.
7. Joel H. Silbey and Samuel T. McSeveney, eds., *Voters, Parties and Elections: Quantitative Essays in the History of American Popular Voting Behavior* (Lexington, Mass.: Xerox College Publishers, 1972), 2.
8. See V. O. Key, Jr., and Frank Munger, "Social Determinism and Electoral Decision: The Case of Indiana," in Silbey and McSeveney, *Voters, Parties and Elections*, 31; Samuel T. McSeveney, "Voting in the Northeastern States

During the Late Nineteenth Century," in Silbey and McSeveney, *Voters, Parties and Elections*, 196; Paul Kleppner, "The Political Revolution of the 1890s: A Behavioral Interpretation," in Silbey and McSeveney, *Voters, Parties and Elections*, 186.

9. Bryce, *The American Commonwealth*, vol. 1, 166, 205.
10. Jerrold G. Rusk, "The Effect of the Australian Ballot on Split-Ticket Voting, 1876-1908," *American Political Science Review* 64 (December 1970): 1221. The description here draws heavily from Rusk.
11. Daniel Boorstin, *The Americans: The Democratic Experience* (New York: Random House, 1973), 257.
12. George H. Mayer, *The Republican Party: 1854-1964* (New York: Oxford University Press, 1964), 219.
13. See Samuel P. Orth, *The Boss and the Machine* (New Haven: Yale University Press, 1919), 71-80.
14. Mayer, *The Republican Party*, 12.
15. See Richard Rubin, *Press, Party and Presidency* (New York: Norton, 1981), 20-38 and *passim*, for an extensive discussion of the relationship between the press and the political parties.
16. Rubin, *Press, Party, and Presidency*, 52.
17. Louise Overacker, *Money in Elections* (New York: Macmillan, 1932), 103.
18. Edward C. Banfield and James Q. Wilson, *City Politics* (Cambridge, Mass.: Harvard University Press, 1963), 115-16.
19. Overacker, *Money in Elections*, 177.
20. See Mayer, *The Republican Party*; Walter Dean Burnham, "The Changing Shape of the American Political Universe," *American Political Science Review* 59 (March 1965): 7-28; Burnham, "Theory and Voting Research: Some Reflections on Converse's 'Change in the American Electorate,' " *American Political Science Review* 68 (September 1974): 1002-23.
21. See Philip Converse, "Change in the American Electorate," in Angus Campbell and P. E. Converse, *The Human Meaning of Social Change* (New York: Russell Sage, 1972); Jerrold Rusk, "The American Electoral Universe: Speculation and Evidence," *American Political Science Review* 68 (September 1974): 1028-49; and the interesting fictional treatment by Gore Vidal, *1876* (New York: Random House, 1976).
22. Among the most important reasons why the press became less partisan toward the end of the nineteenth century were the rise of the wire services, with clients in both parties; the growth in advertising revenue that accompanied increasing population and readership, making newspapers financially independent of the parties; and the rise of mass-circulation muckraking magazines with Progressive attitudes.
23. Herbert J. Croly, *Marcus Alonzo Hanna: His Life and Work* (New York: Macmillan, 1912), 212-13.
24. Wayne C. Williams, *William Jennings Bryan* (New York: Putnam, 1936), 162.
25. Croly, *Marcus Alonzo Hanna*, 212.
26. Francis T. Russell, *The Shadow of Blooming Grove* (New York: McGraw-Hill, 1968), 125.
27. Croly, *Marcus Alonzo Hanna*, 217.
28. Ibid., 220.
29. Overacker, *Money in Elections*, 60.
30. See Robert A. Caro, *The Years of Lyndon Johnson: The Path to Power* (New York: Knopf, 1982), chapters 31-32.

31. William Alan White, *The Old Order Changeth* (New York: Macmillan, 1910), 49-50, 53.
32. Richard Hofstadter, *The Age of Reform* (New York: Vintage Books, 1960), 258. See also Richard L. McCormick, "The Party Period and Public Policy: An Exploratory Hypothesis," *Journal of American History* 66 (September 1979): 279-98.
33. Thomas F. X. Smith, *The Poweriticians* (Secaucus, N.J.: Lyle Stuart, 1982), 75-76.
34. V. O. Key, *American State Politics* (New York: Knopf, 1956), 93.
35. See V. O. Key, *Southern Politics* (New York: Knopf, 1949) and T. Harry Williams, *Huey Long* (New York: Bantam, 1970).
36. Upton Sinclair, *I, Governor of California* (Los Angeles, published by the author, 1935), 41-42.
37. Walt Anderson, *Campaigns: Cases in Political Conflict* (Pacific Palisades, Calif.: Goodyear, 1970), 117.
38. Caro, *The Years of Lyndon Johnson*, 698-702.

The Rise of the Candidate-centered Campaign

3

> *We organize a campaign as an independent business. And we start a new business every two years, with a new organization, new people, a new board of directors. We have experts. Our writers are good writers; our TV script people are good; we decide on strategy and tactics ourselves.*
>
> —Clem Whitaker, political consultant, 1955[1]

We have seen that, in the nineteenth century, parties regulated the flow of political information through their domination of the press. They controlled the nomination of candidates through their caucuses and conventions. Their organizations financed campaigns and distributed ballots. But by the early part of the twentieth century, the daily press was becoming independent—and often critical of candidates. The direct primary began to threaten party control of nominations; the parties had already lost control of the ballot. The combined onslaught of the Populists and the Progressives made some insurgent candidacies possible.

In the middle decades of the century, however, a series of events occurred that would affect politics, and thus campaigns, even more profoundly. Among these were the aftermath of the Great Depression of 1929, suburbanization, rapid developments in technology (particularly of television and the computer), the civil rights movement, the Vietnam War, and Watergate. The political fluidity induced by these events made the 1890s pale in comparison, and the effect on campaign techniques was massive and unprecedented. With the advantage of hindsight, one can see that most campaigns of even the 1950s were more similar to those of the 1880s than of the 1980s. The decades after the 1950s would see the eclipse of local party organizations as a factor in most campaigns and the rise of the candidate-centered campaign run by professional consultants—a style of campaigning that demanded greatly increased amounts of money to purchase expensive technology. These developments were first evident in presidential campaigns; only gradually did they move to lower-level races. The detailing of this chapter of the story will bring us to the present.

The Changing Historical Background _____

Although the political outcome was different, the election of 1932 was as much of a watershed as the race in 1896 had been. As we have seen, the 1896 campaign was fought and won by the Republicans with the argument that their platform held the key to economic prosperity, and indeed it seemed to be so. The United States prospered for decades thereafter, and Republicans enjoyed great political favor. With the exception of Wilson's two terms, Republicans occupied the White House continually from 1896 to 1932, and for almost three-quarters of that period, had a majority in both houses of the Congress and of the governorships and state legislative seats. Their long tenure ended with the Great Depression, the election of Franklin Roosevelt to four consecutive terms, and the implementation of the New Deal. Now the Democrats would hold both houses of Congress for forty of the forty-eight years between 1932 and 1980 and the presidency for two-thirds of that period. Thus the 1932 election brought on a realignment similar to that of 1896; campaigns were conducted in the same party-based way.

Again, however, events were gradually eroding the organizational strength of both parties and the psychological ties that bound the electorate to them. The party machines were buffeted by the changing role of government, by the increased size and mobility of the population, and by the presence of television in most living rooms. Beginning with Roosevelt's New Deal, and extended by Lyndon Johnson's Great Society, the federal government's greater role in social welfare programs and the regulation of business prompted those in need of assistance to look to Washington rather than to local government, to the bureaucrat rather than to the precinct worker: "To the voter who in case of need could now turn to a professional social worker and receive as a matter of course unemployment compensation, aid to dependent children, old-age assistance and all the rest, the precinct worker's hod of coal was a joke." [2]

Population growth in the first half of the century had been limited by stiffer immigration laws, the Depression, and the two world wars. After World War II, the population exploded. In addition, the franchise was gradually extended to southern blacks and those between eighteen and twenty; women, granted the vote in 1920, participated in increasing numbers. Almost 50 million people voted in the 1952 presidential election; sixteen years later, 73.2 million. Stimson Bullitt described the changes graphically: "In 1956, Eisenhower was given more votes in New York and Ohio alone than Wilson received from the entire nation in 1912. . . . In losing a race for Congress I received 10,000 more votes than John Quincy Adams did when he was elected President." [3]

Party organizations, designed for campaigning to a limited electorate on a personal basis, were not an efficient means for reaching this vastly growing pool of voters. Moreover, the strength of the organization had depended on tightly knit and stable neighborhoods. With postwar prosperity, the spread of the automobile, and increased highway construction, the mobility of the population expanded enormously. Approximately a fifth of the population changed addresses every year. Many went to new and sparsely populated communities, leaving behind family and friends—and the neighborhood political organizations.

Television, too, had an impact on voters' behavior. Among the other dramatic roles the medium played, it claimed an increasing amount of the leisure time Americans had devoted to other forms of recreation, including political activity: "The precinct captain who visits in the evening interrupts a television program and must either stay and watch in silence or else excuse himself quickly and move on." [4] Having lost the patronage jobs they depended upon to the civil service, and much of their rank and file to the suburbs, most party machines gradually subsided into impotence.

Still, the party could count for a while upon the psychological pull that kept voters in the fold. Although this factor is important even today, its strength has diminished. Just as the Panic of 1893, industrialization, and urbanization had produced social turmoil, the events of the 1960s and 1970s also caused great upheaval. The breakdown of racial and sexual codes, the apparent change in America's place in the world, and the political cynicism engendered by Vietnam and Watergate made core groups in both parties reconsider their affiliations.

George Wallace's third-party candidacy in 1968 and John Anderson's race in 1980 were echoes of the minority party candidacies of the earlier period of dislocation. From the 1950s to the 1980s, the number of people calling themselves strong partisans declined by 10 percent, while the number styling themselves political independents rose by about 15 percent. More worrisome to campaign strategists was the number of split-ticket voters. By the 1970s, between two-thirds and three-quarters of the independents and the Democrats and one-half of the Republicans divided their ballots between the parties at one point or another.[5] Split-ticket voting, in other words, became the norm. Party was thus fading as both an organizational device and a psychological voting cue.

At roughly the same time, however, technology was providing campaign strategists with new ways to determine what voters were thinking and with new methods to send out the desired messages. For the first task, the chief tool was data-processing equipment; for the second, the medium was television. When campaign strategies were devised, the most important applications of these technological developments were polling, targeting, and political advertising.

Scientific polls became possible in the 1930s, with the perfection of probability sampling techniques. The first known scientific poll was taken for a Democratic candidate for secretary of state in Iowa in 1932. The lucky beneficiary, who won her race, happened to be George Gallup's mother-in-law. Gallup began his series of public polls on presidential races in 1936, and Republican candidates Thomas E. Dewey and Wendell Willkie hired private campaign pollsters during the 1940s. However, polling did not become a major element in presidential campaigns until the 1960 Kennedy-Nixon election, when analyst Lou Harris became a senior adviser to the Kennedy campaign. Theodore White's classic account of this race gives what now seems an amusingly quaint picture of Lou Harris bent over a slide rule.[6] The party also commissioned a computer simulation of demographic groups in the electorate and their likely responses to various aspects of the Kennedy campaign—a project fictionalized in a best-selling novel named for the number of demographic groups in the model— *The 480.*[7]

Polls had become necessary to presidential campaigns for two reasons. First, the decline of party organizations removed the chief source of information about political opinions and voting inclinations at the grass roots. Second, the Eisenhower landslides of the 1950s demonstrated that an appealing presidential candidate could attract large numbers of voters from the opposition party. Campaign organizations needed to know from which groups wavering voters might come, what concerned them, and how they would respond to various candidates and issues. As computers became more widespread, moreover, it was increasingly possible to target communications by phone and mail to potential supporters, requesting both money and votes.

Polling and targeting came later to races for lower offices, because in state and local contests voters were less ready to desert their parties. An important reason for this was that television paid a great deal more attention to presidential campaigns than to other races— giving the otherwise partisan voter information on which to base a defecting vote.

Campaigns in the Television Age _____

In 1946 there were only 7,000 television sets in American households. By 1952 there were 19 million, and by 1960 the number of homes with sets reached 45 million. During much of the 1950s, 10,000 people were buying TV sets every day.[8] Seldom had an innovation with such potential spread as rapidly. In November 1951, the coaxial cable linking all the nation's television sets was completed, thus making possible the first nationwide broadcasts. In 1963 the national networks expanded their evening news broadcasts from fifteen minutes to half an hour, and in the same year, for the first time, pollsters reported that more people had come to rely on television than on newspapers for their information about public affairs. Television would make "image" campaigns possible in a way that was never possible before. Viewers could see candidates in the flesh with no mediating influences—not through the lenses of party workers or those of a partisan press.

Presidential Candidates

The age of television campaigns began with the presidential election of 1952, in which Republican Dwight Eisenhower ran against Democrat Adlai Stevenson. By 1952 the Democrats had been in power for twenty years. They still depended on their declining but not yet dead party organizations and on interest groups, particularly the blue-collar unions, who had profited so enormously from New Deal legislation. The party had paid scant attention to communications technology, thinking little about the power of television, which had been virtually nonexistent only four years earlier.

For the rival party, the prospect was different. The Republicans, in the minority and closer to business, which had already discovered the impact of television advertising, thought about it a great deal. Republican voters might be in relatively short supply, but money and public relations skills were not. Soon after their 1952 convention, the Republicans set up a strategy board for the presidential campaign. To this group, Robert Humphreys, public relations director of the Republican National Committee, presented a formal "Campaign Plan," which one writer has described: "Prepared in standard advertising agency format, the plan outlined basic strategy, organization, appeals, types of speeches, literature, advertising, television and radio programs, the relative weight to be given to the various media, the kinds, places and times of campaign trips and rallies, and the areas in which efforts were to be concentrated."[9] It was the first time such a detailed marketing strategy had ever been drawn up for a presidential campaign.

The Democratic campaign for Stevenson was considerably less centralized and much less professional in a public relations sense. The director of the campaign worked out of Springfield, Illinois, the state capital and Stevenson's base of operations as governor. His handpicked choice for national committee chairman had headquarters in Washington, while the head of the volunteer organization was based in Chicago. Rather than coming from the world of advertising and public relations, as did Humphreys and his subordinates, the propagandists of the Democratic campaign came directly from journalism or from jobs as government information officers. There was "little evidence that the Democratic publicity professionals exercised important influence on the strategy decisions made by Stevenson and his principal advisors. They served more as tacticians than as strategists . . . and were therefore not well integrated into any over-all campaign plan." [10]

The differing backgrounds and philosophies of the campaign organizations became evident in the way they approached advertising on the new medium of television. The Democrats regarded television as both parties had previously regarded radio—as an extension of the stump speech. Fully 96 percent of the Democrats' television time was devoted to traditional speeches. For instance, they bought eighteen half-hour blocks of time on a national hookup for Stevenson. The Republicans bought similar time blocks for speeches, but the heart of their television campaign was the massive purchase of spot announcements to present the first political commercials. These spots was carefully targeted to forty-nine counties in twelve critical states, and to the Deep South, where the Republicans correctly sensed a chance for breakthroughs. The party spent about $1.5 million on the spot ads over the last three weeks of the campaign, which was characterized by the advertising executive who devised the plan as "an unheard of saturation campaign in the TV-radio field" for a "national advertiser." [11] The spots were the staged interviews with which we are now so familiar:

> ANNOUNCER: Eisenhower answers the nation!
> VOICE: Mr. Eisenhower, what about the high cost of living?
> EISENHOWER: My wife, Mamie, worries about the same thing. I tell her it's our job to change that on November 4.

There were forty-nine different spots for television and twenty-nine for radio. The Democrats attempted to retaliate, but had only $77,000 to spend. The high echelons of the Stevenson campaign did not yet understand the new medium as a vehicle for marketing messages, rather than as another forum for making speeches. The Republicans did. As early as May 1952, they had televised a program devised by Humphreys called "The Case for a Republican Congress," which put the Democratic party on trial by Republican congressional leaders and professional actors. The Republican efforts were aimed at getting away from formal speeches; they presented the Republican political message as a show.

Although the Republican media campaign concentrated on the GOP's very attractive "nonpartisan" war hero candidate—a most appropriate strategy for the minority party—it was still the party machinery that ran the campaign, an employee of the party who devised it, and the party national committee that hired Ted Bates and B.B.D. and O., the advertising agencies that created and placed the spot ads. This approach changed in succeeding years, however. Insurgent Barry Goldwater captured the Republican nomination in 1964 with a campaign team from outside the party. Richard Nixon, although a more mainstream party candidate, in 1968 also established a candidate-centered organization; rather than hiring an outside advertising agency, he created a short-lived one, the November Group, whose only client was his campaign.

Television gradually became the central focus of presidential campaign advertising. In 1952 advertising expenditures were split almost evenly between television and radio, and both media could make a major impact. The two most important paid media events were Richard Nixon's famous "Checkers" speech, in which he defended himself against charges of having profited from a political slush fund, and Eisenhower's speech announcing, "I will go to Korea." The first was televised, but the second was carried only on radio. In 1956 and 1960, however, spending for television in presidential campaigns outpaced radio by better than two to one, and by 1980 the ratio was approximately eight to one.[12]

At the same time that presidential campaigns were devising ways to send their commercial messages to the public, the contests were coming under increasing scrutiny by print and television journalists. In 1960 Theodore White began his series of books about presidential campaigns, with an unprecedented reliance on insider accounts of the politics of nominations and elections. In the same year, the first televised presidential debates were widely credited with giving Kennedy his narrow margin of victory. In 1968 a journalist insinuated himself into the Nixon entourage and published an account of the way Nixon stage-managed his appearances and shaped his media coverage.[13]

With the development of smaller and more mobile equipment, television journalists were able to cover national conventions from the floor, seeking out interesting stories rather than being forced to follow the proceedings from the rostrum. The most striking images of the 1968 Democratic Convention were not of the speechmaking at the podium, but of the delegates themselves watching the clashes between antiwar demonstrators and the Chicago police outside the convention hall on portable televisions. Thus "investigative" and "advocacy" journalism became the hallmark of both print and television coverage. American presidential elections were now a spectator sport. The players in the game were the candidates, with their teams of pollsters and media consultants, and a vigilant press corps, which not only described but explained and judged what the candidates were doing. The role of the national news programs was now to *"act as the shadow cabinet."* [14]

The new style of presidential campaigning, which relied not on party workers and political machines but on highly paid professional consultants and expensive broadcast media, drove up costs enormously. Through the 1950s, costs had been increasing, but this was due almost entirely to the expansion of the electorate. Between 1912 and 1956, presidential campaigns fairly consistently cost 19 to 20 cents per vote cast. This figure rose to 29 cents in 1960, 35 cents in 1964, 60 cents in 1968, and $1.31 in 1972, the last presidential election before the advent of public financing and controls on spending. Inflation accounted for only a small part of the increase. In the period 1960-72, the cost of living increased by 41 percent, but the cost per vote in presidential elections more than quadrupled. [15]

Another factor in driving up the costs of presidential campaigns was the rapid increase in the number of contested primaries. In the 1960 election, sixteen states held presidential primaries, of which only about half were seriously contested. The number shot way up in the 1970s, and the 1980 presidential campaign saw thirty-seven primaries. As late as 1968, only 40 percent of the delegates to presidential conventions were selected in primaries, with the rest chosen in state party caucuses and conventions. By 1980, 75 percent of the delegates were selected in primaries, most of them bound to support particular candidates.

Although the number of delegates chosen in caucuses increased somewhat in 1984, these meetings did not resemble the party gatherings of old. Spurred by candidates' television and radio advertising in caucus states, reached by direct mail, and encouraged to attend by occupational or cause groups to which they belonged, political activists of all stripes outnumbered party organization regulars. Aside from procedure, in fact, there was little to distinguish the Iowa caucuses, for instance, from the New Hampshire primary; they had both become media- and candidate-centered events. Before the late 1960s, candidates had little need to engage in advertising during the preconvention phase; they could utilize the much less expensive strategy of courting potential caucus and convention delegates from the party. After that period, effective campaigns in all states required an expensive advertising campaign to reach potential caucus participants and primary voters, along with the attendant research and "get-out-the-vote" expenses.

Thus, in the last third of the twentieth century, American presidential elections have become almost entirely candidate- and media-centered events. Candidates make their way through an increasingly complex maze of state primaries. The television networks present special programs each Tuesday night during the primary season, but the party nominating conventions have become so insignificant that the networks have abandoned the traditional gavel-to-gavel coverage. Weekly public polls chart the candidates' progress, beginning as early as two years before the election, before any of them have even formally announced they are running. The multiballot party convention has become a thing of the past; a candidate arrives at the convention with the nomination all but locked up in the primaries and caucuses. Throughout, the candidates are followed by a huge entourage from the press, which reports on their every move. What has happened to nonpresidential candidates as these events have unfolded?

Nonpresidential Candidates

As noted already, most candidates for nonpresidential office were affected later by the new developments in electronic campaigning than their presidential counterparts. One of the first systematic studies of the activities of professional political consultants concluded that the "California syndrome," which saw Whitaker and Baxter (directors of the anti-EPIC campaign—see chapter 2) and then other firms enter state politics in the 1930s, was slow in spreading. Despite a slow but steady expansion of activities in the 1950s, "in 1960, professional campaign managers were working in fewer than ten states on a regular basis." [16] Television provided little information about nonpresidential candidates, and the electorate was more prone to rely on party identification and incumbency as voting cues.

Although state and local governments still had enough patronage to keep machines viable for gubernatorial and mayoral campaigns, congressional candidates, with little patronage at their disposal, could depend less on party organizations and had to construct more personal followings. A report in 1959 concluded, "The feeling is strong that local, state and national party organizations are indifferent and/or ineffective in lending support" to congressional campaigns. One House member observed:

> I don't think there is any element of the party that is particularly interested in or concerned with the election of members of Congress. The National Committee is preoccupied with the White House. The state committee has its eyes on the state house and the county committee is interested only in the court house. The congressman is just sort of a fifth wheel on the whole wagon.[17]

Instead, representatives turned to organized groups in their constituencies—unions, small businesses, civic associations—in which many of
them had been active before they were elected to the House. Those who
later entered the Senate tried to expand these networks. Almost 80
percent of the senators serving between 1947 and 1957 had been in
public office at least five years before election to the upper house.
Almost two-thirds had served as representatives, governors, or state
legislators immediately before their election.[18]

However, as party organizations continued to weaken through the
1960s and split-ticket voting increased, candidates for nonpresidential
office found it necessary to employ the research and media professionals
who had already ensconced themselves at the presidential level. The
number of campaigns using such services advanced in a direct relationship with the increase in split-ticket voting. In 1962, 168 campaigns
involved professional consultants; two years later the number had
increased to 280. Four years after that, in 1968, the number jumped to
658.[19]

At first, most of the candidates purchasing the services of consultants were nonincumbents and Republicans.[20] As with all campaign
innovations, this one was heavily employed early by the out-party. More
Democrats benefited from the advantages of incumbency and from
outside help from favorably inclined constituency groups, particularly
labor unions. The Republicans, with fewer shock troops but more
money, struck back by buying assistance.

The candidate-centered campaign took root first and most widely in
Senate contests. Unlike governors and mayors, senators did not have the
services of state and local party organizations, nor was it as easy for them
to practice, at the statewide level, the "friends and neighbors" politics of
the representative. Senators were most liable to the charge that they had
lost touch with the state. The return rate of Senate incumbents in the
1960s and 1970s averaged only about two-thirds, as opposed to the 90
percent or so for House incumbents. Consequently, a survey of the sixty-
seven Senate candidates in contested races in 1970 found that sixty-two
employed advertising firms, twenty-four engaged national polling
firms, and twenty had entrusted total management of the campaign to
consultants. A similar picture emerged in 1972. An earlier study,
comparing the periods 1952-57 and 1964-69, found that the number of
Senate campaigns employing consultants increased by about 400 percent
in primary elections and 500 percent in general elections.[21]

Additionally, the Senate, more than the House, attracted wealthy
political amateurs willing to spend their own funds to finance a
professional campaign. Among the 100 senators elected or reelected
between 1966 and 1970, only twelve, evenly divided between Democrats

and Republicans, had held no previous public office, and about half of these had been practicing attorneys, the traditional route to political office; only two were businessmen. However, the group elected between 1976 and 1982 was significantly different. The number holding no previous elective or appointive office more than doubled. Only about a fifth of these were attorneys; twice as many were businessmen; and about two-thirds were Republicans. While the House of Representatives remained the leading incubator for prospective senators, the number who came to the Senate from the state legislatures was halved. This latter group, which came up through the party ranks, was replaced not only by business executives but by former astronauts, a Vietnam POW, a professional athlete, and a television news director.

Although, as statewide officials, senators are more visible than representatives (but much less so than presidential candidates), it is more difficult for them to develop personal organizations in their larger constituencies. Television could provide an answer to this problem, because senatorial constituencies tend to coincide somewhat with television's media markets. (In most instances, a representative who bought TV time would be wasting resources, because advertisements would reach a large audience outside the representative's district.) Other statewide officials gradually succumbed to the lures of the media-based and professionally run campaign as party organizations and loyalties continued to weaken. From the 1950s to the 1960s, the proportionate use of consultants by candidates for these offices rose only about 150 percent in primaries and a little over 200 percent in general elections, less than half the rate for Senate candidates.[22] The real breakthrough came in the early 1970s. In the 1972-73 election cycle, candidates employing at least one professional consultant numbered thirty-eight of forty-two gubernatorial candidates, thirty of thirty-seven aspirants for state attorney general, twenty of the thirty-two candidates for state treasurer, and nineteen of the thirty-one running for secretary of state.[23]

A typical early practitioner of the new candidate-centered campaign for an obscure statewide office was John Danforth, who was elected state attorney general in Missouri in 1968 (and later U.S. senator). Danforth was the first Missouri Republican to win a statewide election in twenty-two years, and the first to go to the state capitol in twenty-eight years. At the age of thirty-two, he had spent his entire adult life outside Missouri until two years before his election. At least half of his campaign budget was spent on media, primarily television. His menu of television ads consisted of eighteen different spots, which were played 376 times in the last two weeks of the campaign. Extrapolating this rate of saturation on a national and yearly basis, his chief consultant compared it to the advertising expenditures of General Motors or Procter and Gamble, the country's two largest advertisers.[24]

Representatives, as noted, tended to bypass the new style of campaigning. The various reasons for this reinforced each other. First, because their constituencies were small and hard to reach by television on a cost-effective basis, they were somewhat insulated from well-financed challengers seeking instant recognition through television. Second, they were relatively free from scrutiny by the independent media. The information constituents received about them was almost entirely self-generated—either through newsletters, questionnaires, and the like, or in the form of press releases about pork barrel projects for the district. Through the 1960s and 1970s, representatives also increased the size of their local district offices and staff, which helped constituents cut through the red tape of the federal bureaucracy. Third, having to run for reelection every two years, rather than every four or six years like statewide and other federal officials, turned the nursing of their constituencies into what amounted to a permanent campaign. A constant presence in the district maintained the strength of the representative's electoral coalition and tended to discourage challengers. Fourth, the less glamorous life of the representative did not especially appeal to the kind of wealthy business executive who, tiring of life as the chief executive officer of a large corporation, found the possibility of being chief executive of a state or a member of the world's most exclusive club, the Senate, attractive.

Most of all, the weakening of the parties worked to the benefit of incumbent representatives. In the polling booth, voters more or less divorced from party might be swayed to go with a gubernatorial or senatorial candidate who had said something they agreed with or had looked attractive on a television commercial. When the same voters came to the congressional column, though, they would be likely to press the lever for the only candidate they had ever heard of—the incumbent.

Thus a survey of 1980 voters found that while 92 percent recognized the name of their congressional incumbents, only 54 percent could identify the challengers. More than 90 percent said they had had some contact with the incumbent, either in person or through the media, as compared to 44 percent who remembered some contact with the challenger. On the other hand, the figures were more nearly equal for Senate incumbents and challengers.

While representatives could generally ward off a challenger, senators faced with strong campaigns by well-known opponents had good reason to feel threatened. The propensity of voters to split tickets in Senate and House races was about the same. In 1956, only 9 percent of voters defected from the party in their congressional vote, but this figure had risen to 23 percent in 1980. The figure for Senate votes was similar—12 percent in 1956, and 21 percent in 1980. As time went on, party defectors in House races increasingly opted for the incumbent. In the off-year elections of 1958, for instance, defectors chose the incumbent by about a two-to-one ratio; twenty years later, this preference escalated to ten to one. In the Senate, the story was different. Although no figures are available for the earlier year, defectors in 1978 favored Senate incumbents by a margin of only three to one. Their more visible, better-financed, and professionally managed challengers had an easier time surmounting the advantages of incumbency.[25]

The Restructuring of Campaign Finance

Officeholders and their challengers both found that running campaigns in the increasingly partyless atmosphere of the 1970s was becoming more and more expensive. Statewide candidates had to lay out huge sums on polling, over-the-air media, and voter targeting and contact. Members of Congress and state legislators who did not use television still had to pay for radio time, direct mail lists, production and postage costs, and telephone banks. The ability of challengers to mount expensive candidate-centered campaigns made even the most secure incumbents begin to feel shaky.

Adjusting for inflation, the average campaign war chests of House candidates increased from about $87,000 in 1976 to almost $193,000 in 1984, while the comparable Senate figures went from about $350,000 to well over $1 million. In the six years between 1976 and 1982, House campaign expenditures rose by 97 percent, while the general cost of living went up by only 54 percent. Senate campaign spending doubled between 1982 and 1984.[26] These figures, of course, masked broad variations. Half-million dollar congressional campaigns and Senate races costing over $5 million were not uncommon.

The pressure to reach an expanding, immensely volatile electorate through expensive technological means was the chief reason for the escalation in campaign costs. The Watergate scandal of 1972-74 symbolized the dangers of the new campaign style. The unfolding saga, with its revelations of massive illegal contributions to Richard Nixon's 1972 presidential campaign, demonstrated the need for more fundamental campaign finance reforms than the modest congressional legislation of 1971, which had dealt primarily with public disclosure of contributions. Amendments to the 1971 legislation, and court cases dealing with various aspects of the finance laws, reshaped the financing of federal campaigns.

These campaign finance reforms reflected several themes: the need to limit the contributions of wealthy individuals and business interests, the corresponding need to increase small individual contributions, and the increasing nationalization of American politics. Although complex in detail, the major provisions of the new regulations, as they affected senators and representatives, may be summarized in four major points:

1. Individuals may not contribute more than $1,000 to any single candidate in each election, primary or general.
2. Groups, such as business, labor, or cause organizations, may not contribute more than $5,000 to any single candidate in each election, primary or general. The vehicle for such contributions is the political action committee.
3. The direct monetary contributions of political parties to campaigns are severely limited, but their ability to contribute indirectly, through provision of "in-kind" services, can be substantial.
4. Neither individuals, political action committees, nor parties are limited in the amount they can spend on "uncoordinated" expenditures—outlays for any form of political communication that are separate from a particular candidate's campaign. Nor are candidates limited in what they can spend on their own campaigns.

These provisions led to important changes in the environment of federal campaigns.[27] The next two sections examine the impact of the new regulations.

The Effects on Individual and Group Contributions

The need to raise small amounts of money from large numbers of individuals put a premium on direct mail solicitation—and on efforts to obtain contributions from people who lived outside the candidates' constituencies but shared their policy views. Past campaign contributors grew accustomed to a deluge of mail from out-of-state candidates urging them to "elect a progressive Democrat to the Senate," or "help the Republicans retain our Senate majority." Like-minded candidates shared the names of contributors who had, in the Washington lingo, "maxed out"—contributed the maximum amount permissible to one candidate— but might be willing to contribute to other candidates with similar policy stands. The proportionate contribution of out-of-district individual givers and political action committees rose steadily between 1978 and 1982. Nonconstituent donors accounted for more than half of all contributions over $100.[28]

The second provision, which systematized the giving of group contributions through the medium of political action committees, had a major impact on campaign financing. Political action committees, or PACs, were first able to contribute significantly in 1974, and their increase in both numbers and absolute levels of giving has been enormous. The number of PACs registered with the Federal Election Commission grew from 608 in 1974 to 4,243 in 1984, and their contributions to House and Senate candidates jumped from $55 million in 1980 to $103 million in 1984. PAC outlays now approach one-third of all funds contributed to congressional candidates and more than half the war chests of over 100 incumbents, especially committee chairmen.

Political action committees fall into four basic categories: corporate, labor, trade, and "nonconnected." The first three types donate more than four out of five PAC dollars. Their motive for contributing, as might be expected, is the impact that congressional legislation and the federal regulatory activity that Congress oversees has on their endeavors. Oil companies, for instance, are interested in deregulation and tax policy affecting their companies. Trade associations, like milk producers, automobile dealers, and real estate agents, have a stake in issues such as dairy price supports, quotas on foreign car imports, and mortgage rates. Labor unions have a wider agenda but are specifically concerned about wage legislation, the establishment of closed shops, and similar matters. Nonconnected PACs, which include environmental, right-to-life, feminist, and various other ideological groups on both the left and the right, also realized that legislation affects their interests. In addition, an increasing number of leading political figures, especially presidential aspirants and those in congressional leadership positions, are forming their own PACs.

In general, business and labor PACs are much more likely to contribute to incumbent officeholders, while nonconnected PACs tend to give to challengers. On average, business PACs give about two-thirds of their money to incumbents, while nonconnected PACs donate more than half to challengers. Additionally, business PACs are more likely to contribute money (up to $10,000 to a candidate for his or her primary and general elections) directly to campaigns, while nonconnected PACs usually participate in independent campaign activities or "uncoordinated" spending. Labor PACs do both.

Independent campaigns may be waged either for or against a candidate, but, to date, most have been negative campaigns, to defeat a candidate, and have been conducted chiefly by conservative groups against liberal candidates. In fact, more than half of the almost $6 million of independent spending in 1982 came from the National Conservative Political Action Committee (NCPAC), which waged extensive negative campaigns against eight targeted liberal senators and the top Democratic leadership in the House. NCPAC, together with four other conservative PACs, accounted for two out of every three dollars of uncoordinated spending.[29]

Business PACs are also more likely to donate to Republicans; their contributions to Democrats are almost exclusively confined to incumbent officeholders serving on congressional committees that regulate their industries. Although labor PACs give a small amount to incumbent Republicans, more than 90 percent of their donations go to Democrats. The Democrats' narrow advantage in PAC money to date is attributable to their monopoly on donations from labor groups and their larger number of incumbent officeholders.

The Effects on Party Contributions

Republicans. Another major infusion of funds into campaigns, beginning in the 1970s, came from the Republican party's national committees based in Washington. State and local Republican parties were more active than their Democratic counterparts, but few of the organizations below the national level in either party played a substantial role in congressional or senatorial races. Although between the 1960s and the 1980s there was some strengthening of the state parties, particularly as permanent headquarters were set up and activities such as campaign schools and registration drives were undertaken, nevertheless the parties recruited candidates for fewer offices, contributed less money directly to campaigns, and raised funds at a rate that barely outstripped inflation.[30] The most important party activity, in other words, was at the national level and affected federal candidates.

Behind the Republicans' national fundraising drive was a well-orchestrated campaign to engineer a comeback. Until 1980, the Republicans, except for a brief period during the Eisenhower presidency, had been in a decided minority in both houses of Congress for fifty years. They had barely recovered from their severe defeat in the 1964 Goldwater debacle when they suffered an equally devastating loss in the 1974 elections as a result of Watergate. The Republicans therefore determined that only a massive and well-financed effort by the national party to build up its grass roots could make their candidates competitive.

Aware of the premium the new campaign finance laws placed on the garnering of small contributions, the Republicans used the technological developments of the 1970s to embark on a spectacularly successful direct mail campaign, which, by the 1980s, had raised enormous sums from a donor base of more than two million names. Between 1976 and 1982, all Republican committees together increased their receipts almost five times, from about $46 million to $215 million. While they had outraised the Democrats roughly two and a half to one in 1976, this figure escalated to better than five to one in 1982, and remained at almost that level in 1984. The National Republican Congressional Committee (NRCC), which supported House candidates, outpaced its Democratic counterpart on the order of ten to one. Its receipts increased 50 percent or more in every election cycle between 1975-76 and 1981-82.

Further revisions in the campaign finance laws made the overflowing coffers of the national Republican party increasingly valuable to its congressional and senatorial candidates. New legislation permitted parties to go beyond the $5,000 limit by making further expenditures as "agents" for state and local parties, which could pay for "in-kind" services, such as polling and media production costs. The upshot was that, by 1984, national party committees could give a maximum of almost $72,000 to each House campaign. Much more was available to Senate candidates, whose permissible party contributions were governed by the size of the state's population. Senate candidates could receive as much as $1.5 million.

By the elections of the 1980s, the Republicans could afford, if they chose, to contribute to the legal maximum in every federal campaign. In fact, they targeted their expenditures to marginal House contests, giving very little either to safe incumbents or to seemingly hopeless challengers. With many fewer Senate seats being contested in any given election, almost all Republican Senate candidates received the maximum permissible amount.

In 1984, the Republicans devised another method to expand the limits on party-generated contributions to Senate campaigns. The National Republican Senatorial Committee (NRSC) solicited contributions to several closely contested races from individuals and forwarded them to candidate campaign committees as individual contributions made through the "conduit" of the NRSC. For example, the two Republican Senate incumbents who lost in 1984, Charles Percy of Illinois and Roger Jepsen of Iowa, reported NRSC conduit contributions of $76,000 and $57,000, respectively, in addition to the party's own maximum legal contribution.[31]

In addition, the Republican party used its money for institutional activities that benefited all its candidates and that were a form of independent expenditure not connected to particular campaigns. It spent millions on polls to identify vulnerable Democrats and their weaknesses, devised elaborate targeting programs for selected districts, offered training schools to congressional candidates it recruited, and deployed field representatives to advise campaigns. The party's media center produced generic national television advertising, telling voters in

1980 to "vote Republican for a change," to "stay the course" in 1982, and that "America is back" in 1984. The party media center also became increasingly involved in the production of advertising for individual House candidates. In 1984, twenty-five of them got "full-service" National Republican Congressional Committee assistance, which included writing advertising copy, sending NRCC film crews to the candidate's district, and editing the film. The NRCC also announced a new strategy for the 1986 House elections. Borrowing a technique from NCPAC, the committee planned to begin a $4 million negative advertising campaign against about fifty selected Democratic incumbents as early as April of the election year.[32]

Beginning in the late 1970s, the Republicans turned their attention to the state legislatures, hoping to get control of more of them by 1980, and give Republicans a greater say in shaping the congressional redistricting following the 1980 census. GOPAC, a unit of the Republican National Committee, contributed a half million dollars, ran 120 campaign seminars, and deployed fourteen field personnel in this effort in 1978 and 1980. This effort did not meet with much success, and by 1984 the number of state legislative houses controlled by the Republicans had dropped to thirty-one, down from the thirty-five of 1980, or less than one-third of the total. Consequently, the RNC made plans to spend $15 million on state legislative races by 1990, with the hope of being more effective in the next reapportionment period.[33]

Finally, the Republican party cooperated closely with a number of friendly PACs, meeting weekly with interested Washington-based PACs to inform them about targeted races. The coordinator of this activity in 1982 boasted, "We're making sure that everyone gets from 150 to 400 grand extra, and that's a big wallop out there in a congressional district." [34]

Democrats. The opportunities to contribute to federal campaigns were of course theoretically open to the Democratic party as well, but it had substantially less money to offer its candidates. Their average donation was only a fourth of the Republicans' in Senate races, and only a tenth in House races. There were three factors behind the paucity of Democratic money. First, the Democrats were in a sense the victims of their own success. With large majorities for so many years in both houses of Congress, they did not have the same need to raise money in pursuit of electoral success, nor as compelling a message to send to would-be givers. Second, because of the party's heterogeneity, whatever message the Democrats transmitted would be rejected by either its conservative or liberal wing. As a consultant close to the national committees observed, "It's so broad, as soon as they ran an institutional ad for half the party, the other half would scream and holler and you can't do it. The only thing they can be is against something." Third, much of their support was among the economically disadvantaged. As a staffer at a Democratic national committee said:

> Our inability to raise the money probably has something to do with not knowing which buttons to push, but it has something to do with our constituency. If the Democratic party is the party that represents minorities and poor people, those are the very people who cannot contribute to us. How many middle class people do you know that became wealthy as a result of Democratic policies and then became Republicans? Republicans are wealthy people. Are we Democrats not motivating them, or are they not out there?

Nevertheless, the loss of control of the presidency and the Senate in 1980 mobilized the Democrats to emulate the direct mail fundraising efforts of their Republican counterparts, and they have met with modest success. By 1984, the Democratic Senatorial and Congressional Campaign Committees (DSCC and DCCC) could make the maximum party contribution in most of the closest races. It is still too early to tell how far the Democratic efforts can go.

The Democrats were not without their own resources, however. One party staffer observed, "Republicans pay for things Democrats don't pay for. People volunteer to work on Democratic campaigns." The "volunteers" are frequently labor union activists or members of other groups associated with the Democratic party. A Republican consultant who earlier worked with Democrats remembered the constituency groups and union activists who flocked to Democratic campaigns: "They had the capability; it was expected that they would do it. The only thing you had to do, when they had their local dinner, the congressman had to show up, stroke the leaders, and buy a table. Republicans don't have it." Additionally, the Democrats' recent domination of entry-level positions in the state legislatures gave them a larger pool of candidates who had developed their own resources: "Without a strong contingent of state legislators, a party's talent pool is severely restricted." [35] One of the reasons the Republicans had to raise money and recruit candidates was that there were fewer potential candidates engaged in self-recruitment.

An Appraisal of the Role of Parties. The dramatic success of the Republicans at raising money and strengthening their national organizations would seem to argue against a thesis of party decline, at least in their case. However, if one reviews the ostensible major functions of parties—to structure the nomination process and provide alternative policy agendas—it is questionable whether the Republicans have in fact arrested the move to candidate-centered politics. Although we will discuss this issue in detail in Chapter 10, it can be persuasively argued that current party activity merely subsidizes candidate-centered campaigns. By concentrating on aiding candidates who are "electable," staying out of primary races, and not demanding programmatic commitments from the candidates it supports, the party may be simply a giant, well-financed PAC that can make larger contributions than most other PACs.[36]

The Nationalization of Politics

The provisions of the new campaign finance laws contributed to the nationalization and homogenization of politics. Candidates who in the past had run modestly financed campaigns, depending upon party workers and local party financial support, found themselves seeking funds from individuals nationwide who shared their positions and from the national party apparatus (until recently a shell) rather than from the enfeebled state and local organizations. PACs, too, took an essentially national rather than local view. Although some PACs based their giving on local considerations (such as whether they had plants or offices located in a particular constituency), the major rationale for supporting candidates was their positions on issues and their ability to influence legislation of interest to the PAC. The consultants candidates hired often did not have local roots either, but roamed the country; they were recommended by candidates who had used them in earlier races. Their specialization might be moderate Republicans or populist Democrats, but it made no difference to them whether the candidate was in New Jersey or in Arizona; the techniques, and often the message, were the same.

Thus, by the 1980s, the candidate- and media-centered campaign had penetrated to every level of American politics. The local party bosses were all but gone, and media consultants, pollsters, direct mail specialists, and professional organizers had come to the fore. How did these new specialists approach particular campaigns? What factors made for the success or failure of given campaigns? These are the questions we address in the next five chapters. We begin at the beginning—the first stage of candidate-centered campaigns.

Notes

1. Quoted in Theodore H. White, *America in Search of Itself: The Making of the President, 1956-1980* (New York: Harper & Row, 1982), 68-69.

2. Edward C. Banfield and James Q. Wilson, *City Politics* (Cambridge, Mass.: Harvard University Press, 1963), 121.
3. Stimson Bullitt, *To Be a Politician* (Garden City, N.Y.: Doubleday, 1961), 68.
4. Banfield and Wilson, *City Politics*, 122.
5. See William J. Crotty, *American Parties in Decline*, 2d ed. (Boston: Little, Brown, 1984), 34-36, for a discussion of the growth in split-ticket voting.
6. Theodore White, *The Making of the President, 1960* (New York: Harper & Row, 1961), 23.
7. Eugene Burdick, *The 480* (New York: McGraw-Hill, 1964). The actual project is described in Ithiel de Sola Poole, Robert B. Abelson, and Samuel Popkin, *Candidates, Issues and Strategies: A Computer Simulation of the 1960 and 1964 Elections*, rev. ed. (Cambridge, Mass.: MIT Press, 1965).
8. White, *America in Search of Itself*, 165.
9. Stanley Kelley, Jr., *Professional Public Relations and Political Power* (Baltimore: Johns Hopkins, 1956), 1. For details of the plan, see Harold L. Lavine, ed., *Smoke-Filled Rooms: The Confidential Papers of Robert Humphreys* (Englewood Cliffs, N.J.: Prentice-Hall, 1970).
10. Kelley, *Professional Public Relations*, 160.
11. Ibid., 188. The Eisenhower-Stevenson television campaigns are also discussed in detail in Edwin Diamond and Stephen Bates, *The Spot: The Rise of Political Advertising* (Cambridge, Mass.: MIT Press, 1984), chapter 3.
12. Herbert E. Alexander, "Broadcasting and Politics," in *Elections and the Political Order*, ed. Kent Jennings and Harmon Ziegler (Englewood Cliffs, N.J.: Prentice-Hall, 1966), 86; Herbert E. Alexander, *Financing Politics: Money, Elections and Political Reform*, 3d ed. (Washington, D.C.: CQ Press, 1984), 127.
13. Joe McGinniss, *The Selling of the President, 1968* (New York: Trident Press, 1969).
14. Michael J. Robinson, "Television and American Politics," *The Public Interest* 48 (Summer 1977): 21.
15. See the data in David Adamany, "Financing National Politics," in *The New Style in Election Campaigns*, ed. Robert Agranoff, 2d ed. (Boston: Holbrook Press, 1976), 381-84.
16. David Rosenbloom, *The Election Men* (New York: Quadrangle Press, 1973), 50-51.
17. Charles L. Clapp, *The Congressman: His Work as He Sees It* (New York: Anchor Books, 1964), 397, 398.
18. Donald R. Matthews, *U.S. Senators and Their World* (Chapel Hill: University of North Carolina Press, 1960), 53, 55.
19. Rosenbloom, *The Election Men*, 53.
20. See *Congressional Quarterly Weekly Report*, April 5, 1968.
21. Data from *National Journal*, September 26, 1970; Agranoff, *The New Style in Election Campaigns*, 8; Rosenbloom, *The Election Men*, 51.
22. Rosenbloom, *The Election Men*, 51.
23. Agranoff, *The New Style in Election Campaigns*, 8. The absolute numbers for the three latter offices are smaller because not all states elect these officials.
24. Harry N. D. Fisher, "How the 'I Dare You!' Candidate Won," in Agranoff, *The New Style in Election Campaigns*, 79-86.
25. The data in this paragraph appear in Thomas E. Mann and Raymond Wolfinger, "Candidates and Parties in Congressional Elections," *American Political Science Review* 74 (September 1980): 617-32. Some methodological questions about the validity of the recognition data are raised by David John

Gow and Robert B. Eubank, "The Pro-Incumbent Bias in the 1982 National Election Study," *American Journal of Political Science* 28 (February 1984): 224-29 and Robert Eubank and David John Gow, "The Pro-Incumbent Bias in the 1978 and 1980 National Election Studies," *American Journal of Political Science* 27 (February 1983): 122-39.

26. Data constructed from *New York Times,* December 4, 1984, A29; *New York Times,* October 26, 1984; *National Journal,* April 16, 1983, 780.

27. The campaign reform ethos also had some effect on the states. Approximately half the states have enacted contribution limits for state elections, and about a fifth have also passed spending limits. Generally, however, the restrictions are much less stringent than federal legislation. See Alexander, *Financing Politics,* chapter 7.

28. Janet Grenzke, "Campaign Financing Practices and the Nature of Representation," paper delivered at the Annual Meeting of the American Political Science Association, Washington, D.C., August 30-September 2, 1984, 6.

29. Michael Barone and Grant Ujifusa, *Almanac of American Politics 1984* (Washington, D.C.: National Journal, 1983), 1336.

30. See David A. Leuthold, *Electioneering in a Democracy* (New York: Wiley, 1968), chapter 3; Cornelius P. Cotter, James L. Gibson, John F. Bibby, and Robert J. Huckshorn, *Party Organizations in American Politics,* (New York: Praeger, 1984). An assessment of the Cotter et al. findings appears in David E. Price, *Bringing Back the Parties* (Washington, D.C.: CQ Press, 1984), 34-36.

31. See the *Des Moines Register,* October 16, 1984, 2, and the *Chicago Tribune,* October 17, 1984, 6.

32. For a summary of Republican activity through 1982, see Larry Sabato, "Parties, PACs and Independent Groups," in *The American Elections of 1982,* ed. Thomas E. Mann and Norman J. Ornstein (Washington, D.C.: American Enterprise Institute, 1983). The NRCC 1984 media activity is described in *Congressional Quarterly Weekly Report,* December 22, 1984, 3152, and March 9, 1985, 459.

33. See *Congressional Quarterly Weekly Report,* October 25, 1980, 3188-92, and March 9, 1985, 459; *Public Opinion* 7 (December-January 1985): 27.

34. Elizabeth Drew, "Politics and Money: I," *The New Yorker,* December 6, 1982, 54ff.

35. John Bibby, "State House Elections at Midterm," in Mann and Ornstein, *American Elections of 1982,* 127.

36. An argument suggested in F. Christopher Arterton, "Political Money and Party Strength," in *The Future of American Political Parties,* ed. Joel L. Fleishman (Englewood Cliffs, N.J.: Prentice-Hall, 1982), 101-39.

Creating a Credible
Campaign: Incumbents

4

When there's an incumbent governor running for reelection, it's so difficult to separate what's political from what's not. The governor was pretty shrewd about it. It used to be that the labor commissioner put out the unemployment rate every month. Once it became clear that the labor commissioner was going to be a primary challenger, they had him announce every time the unemployment rate went up, and had the governor's office announce it every time it went down.

—Statehouse political reporter

There is an old saying that American political campaigns do not begin until after the World Series, when Americans shift their attention from one great spectator sport to another. With the lengthening of both the baseball and the campaign seasons, this axiom may no longer hold true. Nevertheless, the end of summer is the time when campaigns begin to become visible to the public. Of course, the seeds of most campaigns take root many months—sometimes several years—before the autumn of election year. By late September, they have developed in significant ways that determine whether the candidate has any real chance of winning. Some may already have made decisions that will almost certainly lead to failure. Others have made important strides toward success.

In understanding why this is so, it is helpful to distinguish between the *internal campaign* and the *external campaign*. The external campaign is the visible one directed to voters; the internal campaign is the activity going on within the apparatus set up to conduct the race. By early fall, serious candidates for any public office, from a seat in the state legislature to a race for the governorship or the U.S. Senate, must have formulated a grand strategy and be in a position to implement that strategy.

Formulating a strategy requires information about the electorate, gathered from polling and analysis of other data, primarily past voting patterns. A campaign organization must be in place to determine what information is needed, to commission its collection, to analyze it, to devise the strategy, and direct its implementation. Collecting the information and sustaining the organization requires money. This process must start long before the contest enters the consciousness of the public, and it is the job of the internal campaign.

By September the internal campaign must have completed these tasks, although the external campaign—to the general public—may have barely begun. Even if candidates have not yet publicly laid out their major appeals, they must have achieved sufficient recognition and acceptance from prospective voters. With the decline of party as a voting cue, the candidate becomes the major cue. A candidate who is unknown, or known and disliked, does not have much time to rectify a blank or negative image. Therefore, the first stage of a successful external campaign involves *becoming known and becoming liked.*

Although all credible campaigns must meet these requirements, many factors, all noted in chapter 1, affect the way this stage of the campaign is played out. Foremost is whether there is an incumbent is in the race. Incumbents start with tremendous advantages; no matter what the office, they begin their campaigns with a much better than even chance of winning reelection. Other factors shape a campaign's early activities, including the office for which the candidate is running, the relative strength of the political parties in the constituency, the geographic and demographic nature of the district, and prevailing national trends. In this chapter we shall discuss how incumbents plan their campaigns and how strategy decisions are affected by the context in which the campaign operates. The following chapter does the same for challengers.

Assets of Incumbency

As we have noted, the incumbent in any race usually begins with formidable advantages, the most important of which are recognition, money, and time. Widespread positive recognition goes a long way in satisfying the requirements of the early external campaign. Money and time are necessary ingredients for the internal campaign. Incumbency also has possible disadvantages, though, and two in particular can sometimes defeat an incumbent: having negative recognition—the perception that the incumbent has not done a good job—and complacency. In this section, we look at the way successful candidates seek to use the advantages of incumbency and cope with some of the disadvantages during the internal campaign. The liabilities of running as an officeholder are discussed in greater detail in a later section.

Recognition

Because of their previous campaigns and their activities in office, incumbents usually are much better known than their opponents. How well informed voters are likely to be about an incumbent depends in part on the office the candidate is seeking. Knowledge is greater when (1) the constituency is broader (representatives are better known than state legislators; senators are better known than representatives); (2) the office is executive rather than legislative (governors have greater recognition than senators); (3) the office is more widely covered by the media (both print and over-the-air media report on the activities of governors more than of senators). The more exposure voters have to a candidate, the easier it is for them to make a positive or negative judgment. It is within this framework that incumbents must plan how to exploit the recognition that incumbency gives them.

The Case of House Members. It is always to candidates' advantage to be able to shape the information voters have about them. The office of U.S. representative is a good example. Members of Congress receive very little coverage, and even less critical scrutiny, from the media, but they have substantial resources for direct communication with their constituents.

Except for the handful in the House leadership or the unhappy few involved in scandal, media coverage of representatives consists primarily of their own press releases: "Most newspapers in the country simply have no congressional coverage they can call their own. This is fine with most congressmen. Among the various high crimes and misdemeanors with which they charge the press, noncoverage is not one of them." [1] A thoughtful reporter describes the relationship between representatives and the press:

> Between the big story and the local sewer grant lies a vast unreported landscape . . . which is almost never seen in the daily paper, let alone on local television. In this wasteland, a symbiotic relationship flourishes between congressman and correspondent, a relationship based on mutual need and sometimes mutual laziness. This relationship permits the typical invisible congressman to become visible in a highly selective way in his home district. [2]

Even if the will were there, it would be difficult for the media to cover representatives. Large urban areas elect too many for metropolitan newspapers or television stations to report on them in any reasonable fashion. Within the New York City television market, for example, there are fourteen congressional districts wholly within the city and eight suburban districts north and east of the city but in New York State. Additionally, ten districts in northern and central New Jersey and one in Connecticut are totally dominated by New York television. Television stations, faced with the prospect of covering thirty-three representatives, thirty-two of whom will be of little or no interest to 95 percent of their viewers, generally opt to cover none. In less densely populated areas, a representative's district many stretch across a number of media markets, none of which consider the official to be "their" representative.

Evidence exists that the nature of the office itself affects the coverage it receives. In Wyoming in 1982, for example, there were races for governor, for senator, and for the one at-large (statewide) congressional seat. Both the senate and gubernatorial races received extensive front-page coverage in the three newspapers in Casper and Cheyenne. But the House race got exactly one front-page story late in the campaign, with a telling headline: "Who vs. What's His Name: Wyoming's Other Campaign." Asserting that the senatorial and gubernatorial races "are both household conversation topics and certainly issues for debate in social circles," the reporter went on to observe of the House race, "But what about Ted Hommel vs. Dick Cheney? Discussion about that contest is almost as hush-hush as hemorrhoids." [3]

Representatives, as noted earlier, generally are ready to fill the void created by the lack of media attention. Their major resources for communication, in addition to news releases, are the congressional frank (free mailing privileges to all "postal patrons"—all households in their districts) and district offices and staff. Since representatives face another contest less than twenty-one months after each Congress convenes in January of odd-numbered years, it is not surprising that these resources almost immediately become tools for reelection. Nearly anything short of a campaign brochure appears to fall within the rubric of "official business," the legal limitation on the use of the frank. Questionnaires, newsletters, and invitations to town meetings pour out of congressional offices, increasing dramatically as election time draws closer. The volume of postal patron mailings in September of election years, as compared with the same month in nonelection years, is more than double. [4]

Nominally, of course, newsletters are intended to inform citizens about legislative or other government matters, and questionnaires and town meetings help representatives elicit the views of constituents and carry out the functions of the office. There is no doubt they do this. But another clear effect is to bring the member recognition—and positive recognition. As one top aide in a congressional office commented: "The thing that makes you the concerned congressman is the town meeting. It's immaterial how many people show up; it's the fact that I mailed 200,000 postcards that we're having it. We don't care if six people show up, as long as we got the extra mail out."

Similarly, district offices, which aid individual constituents in cutting red tape at the Social Security Administration, the Immigration and Naturalization Service, or the Veterans Administration, or help local governments deal with federal agencies, garner much favorable feeling for incumbent members of Congress. Such activities to assist constituents are known as casework. A manual for congressional caseworkers distributed by the National Republican Congressional Committee (NRCC) advises its readers:

> A CONSTITUENT is the LIFEBLOOD of this and every other congressional office. Let your constituents know that you are willing to serve. This can be accomplished by co-ordinating with your press aide by inserting articles in the Member's newsletters advising of the Congressman's willingness to help or by sending out postcard mailings with the same message. Make it impossible for the constituents not to know that the Congressman is accessible and anxious to help.

Among the many who could be cited, two representatives who excel at the creative, effective, and entirely legal use of congressional resources for campaign purposes are liberal Democrat Bob Edgar of Pennsylvania and conservative Republican Jim Courter of New Jersey. Both faced the prospect of running in massively redistricted constituencies in 1982. Edgar represents a suburban Philadelphia district that "continues to vote Republican in just about every election but its House contest." [5] As soon as redistricting was completed, new residents of Edgar's constituency received a franked letter beginning, "Dear New Constituent, WELCOME TO MY CONGRESSIONAL DISTRICT!!!" The letter, which went on to detail Edgar's view of a representative's role, managed to note that he had served 4,000 constituents annually in his two district offices; that he was chairman of the Northeast-Midwest Congressional Coalition, which was "actively involved in bringing the [aircraft carrier] Saratoga to Philadelphia"; and that in the previous year he had responded to more than 21,000 letters, held a public forum every month at different locations in the district and a series of specialized meetings with business groups, veterans' groups, and workers. Within a month of this mailing, and at the height of discussion of the gender gap favoring Democrats, Edgar's office was out with another specialized mailing under the frank, entitled "From Washington to Women." The enclosed "Report to Women" invited recipients to "attend an informal discussion on women, the economy and the family with Congressman Bob Edgar."

In the 1982 election, Edgar ran more than twenty points ahead of Jimmy Carter's 1980 showing and placed even with Ronald Reagan, in his Republican-leaning district. A study of several 1982 congressional campaigns observed of Edgar's race, "the greatest hurdle which faced the Republican had nothing to do with his campaign. Rather it had to do with his opponent. Bob Edgar was one of the strongest Democratic candidates in the eight election races examined here." [6] In 1984 Edgar survived a race that many analysts predicted would be his toughest yet and made plans to run for the Senate in 1986.

Residents of the new areas of Jim Courter's district became regular recipients of "Congressman Courter's Courier," his handsomely produced bimonthly newsletter. Immediately before the September deadline on franked mail, they received a postcard invitation to a town meeting and the final preelection issue of the "Courier." Courter represents a safely Republican district, but often takes positions on issues substantially to the right of opinion in the district. His newsletter, therefore, concentrated on highlighting Courter's more "moderate" votes, citing his support for a nuclear arms reduction resolution (but not his opposition to a nuclear freeze) and his support for increased veterans' benefits (but not his vote to fund the MX missile project). In 1982 Courter ran five points ahead of President Reagan's 1980 performance in his Republican stronghold. Redistricted once more in 1984, Courter again ran five points ahead of President Reagan's statewide showing in New Jersey.

In addition to the advantages stemming from the resources of the office, incumbent House members usually benefit from running in districts where their partisans are dominant. Congressional districts are shaped by the state legislature, and their propensity to draw districts that are as safe as possible for one party is notorious. The partisan redistricting that occurred in 1980 gave rise to oddly shaped districts that journalists and pols dubbed with names like the "fish hook" and the "swan." Outraged Republicans in one state with a Democratic dominated legislature complained that one coastal district was "only contiguous at low tide." It is therefore not surprising that, on average, more than 90 percent of incumbent members of Congress who choose to run for reelection are successful.

Senators and Governors. Incumbent statewide officials—senators and governors—face a different situation. Voters know their senators in a different, and more impersonal, way than they know their members of Congress. Representing entire states, up for election only once every six years, and denied the "postal patron" frank, senators cannot maintain the same kind of close ties with their constituents. (While senators by law can send mail to each person in their state, the mail must have the householder's name on it.) A national study found that the amount of contact senators had with their constituents was about equal to that of representatives, but that the nature of the contact differed. Constituents were much more likely to say they had met their representatives personally, seen them at meetings, or talked to their staffs. Conversely, they were more likely to say they had seen their senators on television or heard them on the radio.[7] A study of reporting by Washington-based journalists found that television coverage of activities in the Senate was twice as frequent as of events in the House of Representatives, and mention of the names of particular senators occurred three times more frequently than of individual representatives.[8]

Thus, senators look primarily to the media to maintain favorable recognition. Any important domestic or foreign policy event finds them heading for the Senate television studios, local news programs, and the Sunday morning talk shows. Newspapers routinely call them for reaction to such events. But this coverage is uncritical and unanalytic, permitting senators to frame a response in whatever they regard as the best possible light. Their task is made easier by the nature of the statewide press corps, which is usually based in the state capital and engaged most of the time in covering state politics, particularly the activities of the governor. A political reporter observed, "It's less important to find out what a senator thinks of an issue than a governor. The senator is not going to be guiding the policy of the country the way a governor guides the state." A good Senate campaign staff can take advantage of this relative lack of close scrutiny by shaping the early media coverage of the candidate in a favorable way. A Senate press secretary describes the process:

> We have an operation that runs on a campaign footing. We have a very active press and mail outreach, even though our next election is four years off. For example, we recently did something manufactured for TV. We went to a house mentioned in a HUD scandal and we packaged the whole event. When we went to the site, we had every TV station in the city. We had a live shot from the house at noon go back to the number-one-rated station. Everything was made simple. They got us making the charges. They got the HUD people on the right answering them, the aggrieved residents on the left. They got the lock being broken, the visuals. Even though we're not campaigning, that's the quintessential campaign "hit."

Another staffer in the same office gave the rationale for planning such events: "His name ID hasn't gone up since he was elected. It's like nothing has happened in a year. It isn't good enough. It's only two or three years until the Republicans decide if they're going to target that seat."

Other than the president, governors are the officials of whom the public has the clearest view gained from mass media sources. Like senators, but even more strongly, governors become known to voters because they see them on television.[9] In one of the nation's largest states, a former governor, out of office for four years, was debating whether to run against an incumbent senator who was serving his fourth term and was chairman of a major Senate committee. A poll the former governor commissioned to explore his chances a year before the election found that the senator's recognition level among voters was 67 percent, while the ex-governor's rating was 72 percent. The pollster commented, "What a graphic illustration of news coverage that four years after a governor has left office he is better known than a senator who has been in office for better than two decades!"

Covered on an almost daily basis by the print media, whose bureaus are based in the statehouses, governors, as initiators of controversial policy proposals, are constantly in the limelight—and any slip they make, no matter how minor, can result in negative appraisals of their official behavior. Consultant Vince Breglio described the particular susceptibility of a governor to a bad press:

> A governor's record is far more crucial than a senator's record. Governors have their hands on the throttle of all the things that directly influence people in a state. A race for governor is a microcosm of the presidential race. They see in that chair all the power to make good things happen or bad things happen. That's not true with senators or representatives. For a governor, it's meat and potatoes—what's his or her record? If the farmers haven't had rain, the governor's going to get blamed.

One factor in determining how clear an evaluation of the governor the public develops is the location of the state capital. A consultant who works on many governors' races explained:

> It's very critical what proportion of the state is served by the media market the state capital is in. In Mississippi, say, 50 percent of the people are in the Jackson media market, and they all know about state government. It's the same with Denver and Colorado. New York State is very well covered by TV, but state politics isn't because Albany is a jerkwater town. In a state like West Virginia, only about a quarter of the population lives in that media market. An incumbent has the opportunity to tell people what his record is during a campaign, whereas in other states they already know.

Traditionally, the high visibility of governors, and their association with often unpopular legislation like tax increases, made them more vulnerable to defeat than senators or representatives—but in recent years a governor's prospects for reelection have improved. Between 1956 and 1976, the average incumbent governor received 55 percent of the vote, compared to the average incumbent senator's 61 percent. Gubernatorial candidates were also more likely to face serious challenges. If a "serious challenge" is said to occur when an incumbent receives less than 60 percent of the vote, or loses, then 57 percent of incumbent senators had serious challenges, as compared with 77 percent of governors. Excluding the southern states, where the Democratic party continues to monopolize governorships despite many Republican successes in Senate races, 67 percent of senators had serious challenges, while for governors the figure was 84 percent. However, in 1964 the difference in electoral outcomes for senators and governors began to shrink, and in recent years 70 to 75 percent of incumbent governors have been successful in races for reelection.[10] Increasingly stronger institutional resources, and thus greater ability to dominate state government and state media coverage, have made it more likely that a gubernatorial incumbent will win another term.

Recent changes in state constitutional provisions for gubernatorial elections have significantly strengthened the office. Until not long ago, many governors were up for election in presidential years, when they ran the risk of being buried in landslides by the opposition party's candidate; many were limited to two-year terms or were not permitted to run for reelection. The trend is now strongly against all these provisions. Between 1948 and 1980, the number of governors elected in off-years has risen from sixteen to thirty-seven. Those serving two-year terms have decreased from twenty-one to four, and those denied the chance to run for reelection have decreased from eleven to four.[11] Most of the changes occurred after the mid-1960s, when extensive ticket-splitting began.

For most governors, then, the advantages of constant attention from the media outweigh the risks. A reporter explained the process from the media's point of view:

> Symbolically, it's appropriate that in the statehouse, reporters are summoned by a bell. There's a bell in all their offices and whenever there's an event, it's a Pavlovian response, the bell rings, and everybody just gets up and takes their pencils and goes into the governor's office. That bell was rung on a lot of bullshit. It was not a case where you declined to answer the bell. If you spend thirty minutes in the governor's office, minutes with other competing reporters there, you're bound to write something, and they know that.

Even though reporters are aware of this manipulation, they are still likely, when campaign time rolls around, to give a reasonably competent governor the benefit of the doubt. As this same journalist added,

"The press that covers the candidates is basically the statehouse press. Despite the political guys they throw in, the statehouse regulars are still the cutting edge of the press. They've had four years of working with this guy. There's a built-in institutional bias." So while governors can suffer from mistakes made under close media scrutiny, a state chief executive who uses the media well can also create an image that will be relatively impervious to charges made in the campaign season—unlike senators, who have not established the kind of working relationship that governors have with the media. A consultant who works in both senatorial and gubernatorial campaigns said:

> No advertising is likely to significantly alter a governor's image. So much has been said about him over so many years that voters are relatively immunized to negative information about him. When senators' images are similar to governors', it must be regarded as their peak, whereas for a governor, it is probably a floor below which he cannot sink, and above which he will probably be able to rise.

Thus we see that incumbents, from representatives on up the scale, enjoy substantial advantages in recognition, not merely because they have previously campaigned and thus garnered some notice but because they use the resources associated with incumbency to build positive recognition during their terms of office. For the most part, they can shape the kind of publicity they receive to ensure that, as they enter the campaign season, the voters' views of them will be favorable.

Money

Incumbents also enjoy a significant advantage when it comes to raising money, particularly early money. A healthy bank balance at the start of a campaign permits a candidate to do the polling and other research necessary to develop an effective strategy. It also enables the candidate to hire other consultants, such as media and direct mail specialists. In recent years, direct mail solicitation has become an increasingly important source of campaign funds, but candidates must have a lot of ready cash to pay for the production of the appeals and the cost of mailing.

By August 1983, Senate incumbents running for reelection in November 1984 already had raised more than $10 million in campaign funds, as compared with less than $8 million raised by their counterparts in the 1982 election cycle at the same time.[12] By February 1984, Senator Alfonse D'Amato of New York, who won a three-way race in 1980 with only 45 percent of the vote, had moved to consolidate his position by raising $1.3 million for his 1986 race, still two and one-half years away.[13]

For all officials, but particularly House and Senate members, a major source of early money is the political action committee, or PAC (see chapter 3). Of the $10 million raised for 1984 races by Senate incumbents as early as August 1983, 25 percent was contributed by PACs. At least twelve senators had raised more than $100,000 from PACs by that date.[14] Even when PACs prefer a challenger, they are aware that most incumbents are reelected and that they are likely to have to continue to deal with them.

Thus, congressional incumbents are in a strong position to receive early PAC money, particularly if they serve on committees that oversee legislation related to heavily regulated sectors of the economy. In July 1982, for instance, members of the House Energy and Commerce Committee, which shapes such diverse legislation as clean air and water bills and transportation regulation, had received $2.9 million in PAC contributions. The members of the House Ways and Means Committee, which writes the tax code, had collected $2.1 million. On the other hand, members of the Judiciary and Foreign Affairs committees received only half or less than these amounts from PACs. As Elizabeth Drew stringently observed, "It is worth roughly half as much to watch over foreign policy and guard the Constitution as it is to write tax laws and preside over regulation and energy policy."[15]

Incumbents do not have to travel very far to obtain substantial PAC funds; much of the early fundraising goes on at Washington receptions. Since legislators do not have to specify how and where contributions are raised, it is difficult to quantify the impact of capital fundraisers, but a survey by Congressional Quarterly reported: "Almost every available source agrees that there are more Washington fundraisers (perhaps double the number five years ago), that ticket prices have soared, and that they are scheduled earlier in each campaign cycle." The report commented:

> The Washington fundraiser is especially important to incumbents because it is a card that can be played early in the campaign. PACs that normally make their major giving decisions later on usually have enough loose money so their Washington representatives can attend fundraisers early in the off-election year. This gives the incumbent a head start.[16]

It is obvious too that state-level incumbents have an edge. Almost all incumbents in races for the governorship and the state legislatures benefit from those who do business with the state, are regulated by the state, or are employed by the state. The Citizens' Research Foundation study of state-level elections found similar patterns of financing in states as various as Kansas and Florida, Texas and New York. Incumbents benefited heavily and early. In Maryland, Governor Marvin Mandel raised almost $1 million at a testimonial dinner in May 1973 for the gubernatorial and legislative elections to be held eighteen months later. Those who bought and sold tickets to the dinner included an engineering firm recently awarded major contracts for a new Chesapeake Bay bridge, the owners of basketball and hockey teams that had received state permits to build a new stadium, developers requiring sewer permits from the state, and so on. In Florida, of every dollar raised by winning legislative candidates (80 percent of whom were incumbents) 63 cents came from just five groups: registered lobbyists, the building industry, attorneys, insurance companies, and the medical profession.[17]

Most states revised their campaign finance laws in the wake of Watergate. Occasionally, however, the still relatively unregulated financing of state-level campaigns results in scandals reminiscent of Watergate. Pennsylvania's incumbent governor, Milton Shapp, declared in 1974 that as an antidote to Watergate, he intended to minimize his campaign spending, to raise money in small contributions at the grassroots level, and refuse contributions from state employees. He did, however, accept several hundred thousand dollars from the Pennsylvania Democratic State Committee. In 1975 the chief campaign fundraiser for the committee was convicted of criminal conspiracy and criminal solicitation. Witnesses testified that he had met with state officials prior to the election in a county highway shed and ordered them to extract specified contributions from state employees.[18] In the 1982 Wyoming gubernatorial election, an irate businessman renting office space from the state produced a transcript of a tape recording in which a state committeeman allegedly attempted to extort a month's rent—$3,400— for the incumbent governor's campaign. The transcript quoted the committeeman as saying that if the contribution was not made, the administration "might make it pretty goddamn rough on you" when it came time to renogotiate the rental agreement. The conversation continued:

> BUSINESSMAN: They want it all right now?
> COMMITTEEMAN: Oh, they want the check right now because they can't do no advertising after . . .
> BUSINESSMAN: After the election.
> COMMITTEEMAN: Even after the first of the month. They need it now.[19]

Time

The third major advantage of the incumbent is time to organize. Incumbents begin to plan for reelection at least a year in advance. Their first task is to build a campaign organization and appoint a campaign manager (or director, as these persons are increasingly called) to head it. Good campaign managers are in notoriously short supply. As one comments, "It's the biggest problem there is. Anyone who's done it once or twice is either too old or too smart to do it again." Moreover, they must either have no other job or have an occupation they can abandon for several months and then return to, such as law or a position on an incumbent's staff. Managers are traditionally drawn from among the candidate's closest friends, from a group of perennial managers in the various states, or from the incumbent's office staff. A cadre of professional managers for hire has also recently emerged.

Reporting to the manager are those in charge of field organization, campaign administration (which maintains the payroll, the Federal Election Commission reports, and so on), fundraising, press relations, issue and opponent research, and candidate scheduling. Increasingly, these last three functions—press, research, and scheduling—fall under the aegis of a "communications director" who coordinates all nonadvertising aspects of the candidate's message. Outside this formal staff, which runs the campaign from day to day, may be consultants hired to do polling, media advertising, direct mail fundraising, and voter contact. Finally, many campaigns have a "kitchen cabinet"—an informal advisory group of old friends and supporters, important party figures, and volunteer fundraisers.

The candidates themselves are both the most and least important members of a good organization: "He or she may play a large role in the selection of the campaign staff and be the final arbiter in struggles among the staff, but a candidate is not so much a member as an object of the organization." [20] The old adage about doctors who treat themselves applies to campaigns as well: "A candidate who directs his or her own campaign has a fool for a manager." As one experienced manager noted:

> Ultimately, every campaign reflects the candidate, and the campaign flows from that. But a campaign the candidate wants to manage doesn't have a manager at all. A manager's authority is constantly undermined by the candidate intervening in decisions that aren't properly his. A candidate can't be his own manager because of scheduling requirements, and because so much of a winning campaign is dependent on the candidate being out talking to voters. The three major resources of a campaign are money—which is focused on too much—the candidate's time, and staff time. All those things have to be budgeted. If you have an interventionist candidate, he's squandering a valuable resource—his time.

Most incumbents have already learned this, and are comfortable leaving the details of the campaign to the staff. Their managers have run their previous campaigns or at least worked with or known the candidate well in another capacity. They have proved their loyalty and reliability and earned the candidate's trust. A congressional staffer who alternates between running campaigns and serving as the Washington chief describes his boss's campaign activities:

> I would say he was pretty well directed. He was like an actor on a movie set. He had a couple of directors who knew him very well. It wasn't like we were telling a robot what to do; we just told him what he would do anyway. He had a lot of trust in us. In many cases I would pick him up at the airport and tell him where we were going.

The Role of Consultants

The number of consultants in a campaign is determined both by the candidate's tenure in office and by the position sought. Incumbents have experienced staffs and a record to defend. Compared with challenger campaigns, there are more ground rules for consultants, and a sense among the staff about what sort of message they want to convey in the campaign. Some of the staff members and consultants may have worked together before in the candidate's previous races. The staff and consultants, all with prior political experience, are more likely to respect each other professionally and understand their roles better.

House Members

Generally speaking, representatives have less need for consultants than do candidates running in statewide races—especially senators and governors. The congressional constituency is smaller and more homogeneous and, for incumbents particularly, is less likely to require an extensive polling program or heavy over-the-air media planning. Because elections occur every two years, much of a representative's previous campaign team remains intact, providing an experienced core strategy group for the next race. Many representatives develop in-house expertise and have staffers capable of devising mail and radio messages and analyzing polling data. Moreover, many do not face serious competition. A manager for a Republican incumbent who regularly rolls up pluralities exceeding two-thirds of the vote said a year before his boss's most recent race:

> We have it all laid out until next December what next year's mail program will be—deadlines, print. We'll probably do an issues pacification program, which is a circle around all of the pro-ERA, NOW women, and we'll mail the hell out of them the first three months of the year on favorable issues, We won't do anything very involved, no phone banks.

House incumbents who do fear a tough race have the time to mobilize for it and the money to hire outside professionals. A pollster described a long-term Democratic House incumbent who came within a point of losing in 1980:

> He was twenty years behind the times. He was still stuck in 1964. You open an office, you get yourself some combs and nail files and plastic bags with your name on it . . . you do all the events that are done in the district, election day you pay a few guys and that's it, that's the campaign. He didn't want to believe he was as deeply in trouble as I told him he was.

In 1982, facing the same opponent, the representative "believed." The pollster continued:

> He really thought he was in trouble. Jim Wright [House majority leader] was pushing consultants in his district. For $20,000, they do four polls in the year before the election, on issues, name ID, simple short questions—and they'll come out with a four-point plan of action, do sample press releases and letters, tell you what groups to target mail to. . . . He bought a computer system for the first time. . . . After the 1980 campaign, he was so nervous, he kept his campaign office open and in fact it's still open [March 1983].

The representative raised three times as much as he had in 1980, half again as much as his opponent, and won this time by almost two to one.

Senators and Governors

For those in statewide office with four- or six-year terms, although reelection thoughts are never absent, formal campaign planning—often including the appointment of consultants—begins at least a year and a half before the election. The 1984 campaign organization of Minnesota incumbent Senator Rudy Boschwitz provides a good example. Boschwitz's campaign manager, who began work in the spring of 1983, was a native of the state and had previously worked on the national Republican senatorial and congressional campaign committees (NRSC and NRCC). He oversaw the campaign's finance, communications, and organizational divisions. Four consultants—for conceptual and organizational strategy, polling, and media—worked with the manager. A kitchen cabinet, composed of trusted Minnesota advisers and headed by Boschwitz's 1978 manager and former Washington office chief (now practicing law in Minnesota), met every three weeks to review the general campaign operation. By the end of March, the campaign had raised more than $3 million, through efforts that began with the appointment of a full-time fundraiser in 1981. A major source of funds was Boschwitz's "Washington club," 850 contributors primarily from Minnesota, who pledged $250 per year to the campaign through 1984. Another source was PACs, mostly out of state, which by March had contributed almost $400,000.[21]

The heavy involvement of professional political consultants in Boschwitz's early campaign is typical of such races, not only because of the need for expertise in reaching a large and diverse constituency through the media but because of the frequent lack of in-house campaign veterans. As Mitch Daniels, executive director of the NRSC and a former Senate campaign participant, said of Senate incumbents:

> Most of them don't have any organization at all. Senators are very ill prepared for their races. As they get to the election cycle, all the combat marines on their staffs are gone. A lot of the staff has drifted in since the last election. People in House offices are far better politicians because they're at it all the time. Senators have less of a standing organization, but they're self-sufficient financially so they sort of assemble one that is partly mercenary and partly political organization.

Incumbent governors also begin to plan early, and in similar ways. Governor John Carlin of Kansas, up for reelection in 1982, retained a campaign management firm in the spring of 1981. His chief strategist, pollster Bill Hamilton, described what he proposed Carlin should do:

> He seemed to be in relatively rough shape. We found early that John had problems. We suggested two things that fit with him philosophically. First, go back to the town meetings, get out there with average people. The second was to look at the severance tax [on energy companies] as a key issue for the election. We took the fact that people knew revenues were down, and they wanted government services in the areas where government should provide them. John tried to push the severance tax through the state legislature. They wouldn't do it. That was fine—not for the state, but for the campaign. We were about eighteen months out and had the time to do these things.

Liabilities of Incumbency

Despite its many advantages, incumbency is a mixed blessing. Being in an official position may carry with it a number of potential difficulties, principally complacency and negative recognition.

Complacency

Successful candidates "run scared." In the previous section, we considered a long-time congressional incumbent whose brush with defeat spurred him two years later to massive efforts that paid off. In the same state, a member of the delegation had captured 59 percent of the vote in 1980 and apparently saw no reason to worry much about 1982, despite substantial redistricting changes. He did no polling to assess the mood of the district and raised little more money than he had in 1980. He ran a low-key campaign in which his "manager," the administrative assistant in his Washington congressional office, remained in the capital and directed two inexperienced district staffers by telephone. His percentage of the vote dropped 13 percent in two years, and he is now an ex-representative.

But few incumbents these days fall victim to complacency—if they did, they would not remain incumbents. Many more are like another representative who regularly wins overwhelming victory, yet worried some months before the election about his most recent opponent—not at that time a credible challenger:

> He's a retired war hero military guy—not too bright or good on the issues, but he looks good. If someone dumped $400,000 in his lap and put him on TV in his uniform, he could be formidable. I am convinced that there is no district that is unwinnable these days.

This representative held his Republican opponent to a quarter of the vote, but felt compelled to outspend him five to one to do it—and to ensure that no one in the future would think it worthwhile to "dump $400,000" in an opponent's lap.

Negative Recognition

Much more troublesome for incumbents is the danger of negative recognition. It can take a number of forms, producing varying degrees of difficulty for a campaign. Incumbents may acquire negative reputations if they (1) are involved in personal scandal, (2) are thought to have handled salient issues incorrectly or incompetently, (3) are on the wrong side of the trends of the times. An incumbent who does no advance planning to mitigate these dangers is an officeholder at risk.

Scandal. History is replete with examples of those whose incumbency could not survive personal scandal. The fondness of the media for drama, and the warts-and-all style of the "new journalism," make it certain that scandalous behavior while in office will receive wide publicity and destroy most incumbents' favorable press.

Not every kind of scandal is equally injurious. Over time, voters have become more tolerant of entirely personal pecadillos, if they do not affect the incumbent's conduct in office. Few of the cultural conservatives who were among Ronald Reagan's strongest supporters seemed to know or care that the guardian of family values had been divorced.

Governor Jerry Brown's vacation trips with singer Linda Ronstadt apparently drew more approval than condemnation from perhaps envious voters. In 1983 one of the most conservative electorates in the nation elevated to the Mississippi governorship a man who had been accused of (but denied) homosexual acts with black transvestites.[22]

An almost sure route out of office, however, is to be convincingly accused of financial irregularities involving public funds. Idaho Representative George Hansen had previously survived several indictments for financial wrongdoing but was finally narrowly defeated in 1984 because of them. All of the legislators indicted in the 1980 Abscam scandal, in which FBI agents posing as Arab sheiks bribed them for congressional favors, were either defeated or forced to resign. When charges of official corruption can be substantiated, politicians may as well start packing up their offices; there is rarely a way to surmount such accusations.

Dangerous Issues. Charges that an officeholder has handled issues inappropriately or incompetently are another matter. Dealt with properly by an incumbent, they may be survived, even if they are basically true. The type of charge that is effective often depends on the office being contested. Incumbents in executive office—president, governor, mayor—are most subject to charges of incompetence, since, to paraphrase the famous sign on Harry Truman's desk, the buck stops there. It is no accident that the media regularly report the results of polls rating the "job performance" of presidents and governors but that such a question is usually not asked about legislators. Legislators are less likely to be accused of incompetence because they can only participate in major policy decisions collectively; they cannot singlehandedly make policy the way executives do (or seem to).

Voters unhappy with government policy are likely to attach their hostility to the executive or the legislative *institution*, not the individual legislator. Legislators' credit-taking and advertising in constituent communications provide an answer to the question "If, as Ralph Nader says, Congress is the 'broken branch,' how come we love our congressman so much?" [23] However, legislators are subject to different criticisms about the way they handle their jobs: that their voting is "out of sync" with the district or, particularly in the case of senior legislators, that they have become more interested in big picture issues of importance in the state and national capitals than in the parochial concerns of their own constituencies—that they have lost touch with the district.

In recent elections, illustrations abound of the particular vulnerability of incumbent executives to voter disapproval. Four presidents in a row—from Lyndon Johnson to Jimmy Carter—either retired, resigned, or lost a reelection bid because of a clear public judgment that they had exercised ineffective or irresponsible leadership. In 1982, incumbent Republican governors in five states of the recession-devastated Midwest chose not to seek reelection when the states' economies failed to respond to their programs; another lost amid charges of fiscal mismanagement. Other Republican gubernatorial incumbents in economically depressed industrial states squeaked through with substantially reduced victory margins. In general, the popularity of governors wanes with each passing year as they cope with and become identified with their states' pressing problems. In the first seven decades of this century, even though the return rate of incumbent governors grew, the proportion of the vote received by those running for reelection declined with each year in office.[24]

Incumbent executives are turned out of office when voters are dissatisfied with their leadership abilities; incumbent legislators may lose if, as we have noted, a perception grows that they are out of touch. Legislators have two careers—as representatives of their districts and as members of a lawmaking body with wider policy responsibilities. Often the interests of the district will be at odds with those of the state as a whole or the nation.[25] The massacre of Democratic senators in 1980 provides an example. Although other factors played a role in this unprecedented and unexpected slaughter, the twelve who were defeated in primaries or in general elections included many—Birch Bayh, Frank Church, Herman Talmadge, George McGovern, Warren Magnusen, Gaylord Nelson—who were powerful committee chairmen with national interests. They were accused, at least in part, of forgetting the folks back home.

McGovern, Bayh, and Church also suffered because of quests for the Democratic presidential nomination at the expense of the home folks. Although all lost their Senate seats, their performances were strongly related to the way they chose to deal with their national as opposed to state roles. McGovern, who received 39 percent of the vote and ran only seven points ahead of President Carter in South Dakota, refused to trim the issue positions he had taken in 1972 and continued to cultivate his position as a national liberal spokesman. He said of his 1980 race, "When I was trying for the fourth term, that was an easy defeat to accept. The state wanted somebody more conservative, and I wasn't about to change, so they got rid of me. Okay, that's the system." [26] Bayh, who got 46 percent of the vote and ran eight points ahead of Carter in Indiana, made heroic but ultimately unsuccessful efforts to repair his Indiana base after his presidential races in 1972 and 1976. A Bayh staffer described the effect of the races on the 1980 Senate election:

> His visible stance on a large number of liberal issues has just chipped away at his broad support at home. It made people feel like he just

doesn't share their values anymore.... He cares deeply about Indiana and understands and knows the state as few do. But, it hasn't looked that way to folks at home for a long time and I can understand that.... The liberal label has stuck.... This compounded with his attendance record and public perception that he doesn't care about Indiana is a lot of baggage for a guy, who barely survived in the past, to carry into an election.... All of it together may prove too much. This is a lasting legacy of his presidential campaigns.[27]

In contrast, Frank Church, who lost by only 4,000 votes in 1980 and ran 24 points ahead of President Carter, kept Idaho in mind even in the heat of his brief presidential campaign in 1976. Church was known nationally as chairman of the Senate Foreign Relations Committee, for his opposition to the Vietnam War and support of the SALT and Panama Canal treaties. But his Idaho reputation rested on his leadership on environmental legislation important to the state, such as reclamation and water issues. His campaign press secretary commented, "He never made the mistake, even when he ran for president, of staying away from that state. He gave up his campaign five days before the Ohio primary to return to Idaho when a dam broke because he wouldn't erode that base." Moreover, Church concentrated his campaign in Idaho and neighboring western states—Nebraska, Montana, and Oregon. Shortly afterward, the *Almanac of American Politics* would observe that his "Presidential campaign seems to have hurt him less than it did some of his rivals in their home states. He campaigned, after all, as a westerner, and he tended to solidify rather than reduce his identification with Idaho." [28]

Although many Senate Democrats represented states swept by Ronald Reagan in 1980 and 1984, they survived because they did not occupy visible leadership positions and were attentive to their constituents. A similar pattern emerged in the 1980 House elections, where powerful Democratic representatives in the House leadership—men like former majority whip John Brademas of Indiana and Ways and Means Committee chairman Al Ullman of Oregon—were defeated, and Agricultural Committee and Democratic Caucus chairman Tom Foley of Washington came close. They faced the dilemma one representative expressed:

I'm beginning to be a little concerned about my political future. I can feel myself getting into what I guess is a natural and inevitable condition—the gradual erosion of my local orientation. I'm not as enthused about tending my constituency relations as I used to be and I'm not paying them the attention I should be.... I'm getting into some heady things in Washington, and I want to make an input into the government. But I'm beginning to feel that I could be defeated before long. And I'm not going to change. I don't want the status. I want to contribute to government.[29]

Trends of the Times. Such incumbent ploys are often very effective. Incumbents face the most difficulty, however, when charges against them combine with strong national or state tides that are flowing away from the stance represented by the particular officeholder. Fortunately for incumbents, particularly in the House, these tides are rarely strong enough to outweigh the many advantages incumbents possess, if only they use them properly.

Let us look more closely at the 1980 election, which would seem to belie these arguments. After all, the Democrats lost the presidency, twelve Senate seats, and thirty-four seats in the House. Certainly many losing Democratic candidates attributed their defeats to the tides running in the Republican direction. As Bayh strategist Eve Lubalin put it:

> He had huge leads from May till the poll we took a week after the Republican presidential convention, at which point it was a dead heat. The simple truth about the campaign that we knew one and a half years in advance was that the presidential race was going to be absolutely decisive. How you did something about it given that overwhelming trend in the state was maddening. The voters didn't even know his opponent. He lost his lead to a total stranger.

However, "no explanation of House elections relying on national forces is very helpful when we find that no fewer than 73 of the 185 Democratic House incumbents who faced Republican opposition in both 1978 and 1980 actually improved on their 1978 vote." [30] Despite the substantial losses in the House, in fact 89 percent of all Democratic incumbents were reelected.

Senators, more in the glare of the media and more closely tied to the issues represented by national trends, had more difficulty in 1980 than House members. But even in the Senate, where only ten of the twenty-two incumbent Democrats running managed to hold on to their jobs, four got a larger share of the vote than they had in their last election in 1974 (an excellent Democratic year), and one was not even opposed by a Republican.

Governors can also get caught in national trends, but have more resources to withstand them than do senators. Pollster Bill Hamilton commented, "There are things senators have less control over because they're part of a body that does certain things and has an image, as opposed to a governor that usually has a little more control over what he does, or at least can separate himself from a cantankerous legislature. With a governor, you feel you have more control over your own destiny."

There is no doubt that national trends have some impact, but the extent of that impact will depend on the office, the nature of a particular constituency, the characteristics of particular candidates, the quality of their campaigns, and the nature of the opposition; rarely do tides run strong enough, in themselves, to threaten a large number of incumbents.

Coping with Liabilities

What does an incumbent do in the face of the various kinds of dangers we have discussed? In the words of a consultant, "the most important thing you do as an incumbent is negative research on yourself. You anticipate negatives and preempt them." Discovering one's weaknesses is a critical early task for incumbents; it is done primarily through early polling. As one strategist for an incumbent representative facing a potentially tough primary in a newly drawn district (which he eventually won easily) described their early surveys: "Who was ahead was the last number we looked at. I don't think the candidate batted an eyelash when he saw himself 15 points down in the first poll. We checked poll results for ad content and strategy, gauging the theme. We played the devil's advocate, giving our worst case."

These excerpts from a long memo to Indiana Democratic senator Birch Bayh, written in the early spring of 1980 by Eve Lubalin, his campaign issues director, graphically illustrate how experienced campaigners use early poll information:

> I think your potential vulnerability is well illustrated in the "Jesus Christ" question that matched you against a "Republican new to politics, attractive, outspoken, and in harmony with the voter's opinions." In the first poll you edged this guy out 46-36. In the second he edged you 49-37. *You need to make sure your opponent does not become this hypothetical Republican.* The working assumption is that Senate campaigns do not "really" begin until after Labor Day. The summertime is a time to get around the state to county fairs and do radio media. The consensus is to use this early period to reinforce your strengths by:
>
> —reinforcing the warm, close feeling many voters have about you to blunt personal attacks on your integrity and character.
>
> —continuing to identify yourself with state concerns and avoiding entanglement with national issues unless they work to your advantage or are unavoidable.
>
> —working at buttressing your strong job performance rating and providing yourself with a base for your campaign themes—your experience, foresight, effectiveness, success, caring nature and delivering for the state—by discussing your past successes and solutions for the future.
>
> —using the time to fill in a surprising vacuum on where you have been on certain "positive for Indiana" issues so that voters can distinguish you and your record from the Senator your opponent will try to paint—liberal, non-responsive, co-opted by the Eastern Establishment, and part of the Congress which has created the mess we are in.

The key to incumbent "damage control" in the earliest stages of a campaign is to campaign without campaigning—to retain the aura of officeholder and use the resources of the office before openly entering the fray. Republican strategist Vince Breglio said:

> One of the problems incumbents have, if they're doing a good job, is starting political activity too soon. Some of our incumbents had commercials on the air as early as April, the standard stuff you'd put on to vote for the incumbent again. The result of that is to politicize your image, making that person a candidate, not a senator. Once you put candidate instead of senator in front of someone's name, all of a sudden the perceptual screen of the electorate seems to change. It's now okay to challenge his views, take this guy on.

But Breglio agrees with Democratic strategist Bill Hamilton "that doesn't mean it's okay to wait." Instead of a full-blown media effort that signals "campaign," the incumbent must act in an official role in a manner calculated to gain approval from supportive constituencies, and perhaps make more discreet contact with the groups that need shoring up. Breglio explained:

> How do you start without provoking that candidate image? You do it by going to direct mail and you do it with rifle-shotting particular messages to particular groups of people with as much accuracy as you can muster. Targeting in that sense has clearly exceeded the value of the broadcast media for incumbents. You can do it right up to September without showing a broad-brush flag that says, "Hey—I'm a politician." Yet you've been able to take your political message to those who need it most with a very personal appeal.

This survey of the advantages and disadvantages of incumbent officeholders in the early stages of their campaigns is not encouraging for those who challenge them. It would seem that no challenger should run and expect to win unless the country is poised on the brink of upheaval and the incumbent is about to be indicted. Often this advice is not far from the mark. However, there are frequent occasions when no incumbent is in the race, and, in every election year, some incumbents are in fact beaten. So let us next consider, in chapter 5, what a successful challenger must accomplish in this stage of the campaign to remain in contention.

Notes

1. Peter Clarke and Susan H. Evans, *Covering Campaigns: Journalism in Congressional Elections* (Stanford, Calif.: Stanford University Press, 1983), 16.

2. Lou Cannon, *Reporting: An Inside View* (California Journal Press, 1977), 181-82.
3. *Wyoming Eagle,* October 13, 1982, 1.
4. *Congressional Quarterly Weekly Report,* August 16, 1980, 2387. Legislation currently prohibits postal patron mailings within sixty days of general elections; thus early September is the last permitted mailing time in congressional election years.
5. Michael Barone and Grant Ujifusa, *Almanac of American Politics 1984* (Washington, D.C.: National Journal, 1983), 1015.
6. Stuart Rothenberg, *Winners and Losers: Campaigns, Candidates and Congressional Elections* (Washington, D.C.: Free Congress Research and Education Foundation, 1983), 119.
7. Thomas E. Mann and Raymond Wolfinger, "Candidates and Parties in Congressional Elections," *American Political Science Review* 74 (September 1980): 617-32.
8. Stephen Hess, *The Washington Reporters* (Washington, D.C.: Brookings Institution, 1981), 101-02. Senators are also increasingly trying to build up specialized mailing lists to make up for not having a statewide frank. For example, Kentucky Senator Walter Huddleston, who lost narrowly in 1984, sent out 198 targeted mass mailings in 1983 and 1984. These included a list of Tobacco Institute publications to tobacco farmers, a letter to attorneys about the effect of proposed FTC regulation of their profession, and an account of progress on construction of a tunnel to residents of the affected area. All Senate mass mailings in 1984 cost federal taxpayers $37 million. See the *Louisville Courier-Journal,* October 19, 1984, 1; *New York Times,* March 15, 1985, B7.
9. See the data reported in Malcolm E. Jewell, *Parties and Primaries: Nominating State Governors* (New York: Praeger, 1984), 262-63.
10. Jim Seroka, "Incumbents and Reelection: Governors and U.S. Senators," *State Government* 53 (Summer 1980): 161-65; also see William H. Flanigan and Nancy J. Zingale, "Ticket Splitting and the Vote for Governor," *State Government* 53 (Summer 1980): 157-60; J. Stephen Turette, "The Vulnerability of American Governors, 1900-1969," *Midwest Journal of Political Science* 15 (February 1971): 108-32.
11. Andrew McNitt, "The Impact of State Legislation on Political Campaigns," *State Government* 53 (Summer 1980): 135-39; Larry Sabato, *Goodbye to Goodtime Charlie: The American Governorship Transformed,* 2d ed. (Washington, D.C.: CQ Press, 1983).
12. *New York Times,* August 8, 1983, A11.
13. *New York Times,* February 17, 1984, B3.
14. Ibid.
15. Elizabeth Drew, "Politics and Money: I," *The New Yorker,* December 6, 1982, 122.
16. *Congressional Quarterly Weekly Report,* May 17, 1980, 1333, 1343.
17. As reported in the state studies in Herbert E. Alexander, ed., *Campaign Money: Reform and Reality in the States* (New York: The Free Press, 1976).
18. Ibid., chapter 9.
19. *Casper Star-Tribune,* October 27, 1982, A16.
20. Xandra Kayden, *Campaign Organization* (Lexington, Mass.: D. C. Heath, 1978), 3.
21. Richard E. Cohen, "Boschwitz Hopes Incumbency Can Work to Senate Republicans' Advantage," *National Journal,* June 23, 1984, 1217-22.

22. See the further discussion of this case in chapter 8.
23. Richard Fenno Jr., "If, as Ralph Nader Says, Congress Is the Broken Branch, How Come We Love Our Congressmen So Much?" in *Congress in Change*, ed. Norman J. Ornstein (New York: Praeger, 1975).
24. Turette, "The Vulnerability of American Governors," 118.
25. Richard F. Fenno Jr., *Home Style: House Members in Their Districts* (Boston: Little, Brown, 1978), chapter 7.
26. *Washington Post National Weekly Edition*, March 5, 1984, 8.
27. Eve Lubalin, "Presidential Ambition and Senatorial Behavior: The Impact of Ambition on the Behavior of Incumbent Politicians," Ph.D diss., Johns Hopkins University, 1981.
28. Michael Barone and Grant Ujifusa, *Almanac of American Politics 1980* (Washington, D.C.: National Journal, 1979), 227.
29. Fenno, *Home Style*, 216.
30. Gary C. Jacobson and Samuel Kernell, *Strategy and Choice in Congressional Elections* (New Haven: Yale University Press, 1981), 74.

The Challenger: Running While Not Campaigning

5

The governor [Hugh Carey] appears to have dyed his hair again, and that is being perceived as a sure sign he's running again. I'm sure he is ... but I don't know if it's for President, for Governor, for Evangeline Gouleitas [Carey's fiancée] or for all three! In the meantime—and in the dark, I'm going forward with fund-raising and a poll and a temporary meeting place, to be ready for whatever.

—Mario Cuomo[1]

The problems of the challenger in this stage of the campaign are simply summarized: he or she is not the incumbent. Most challengers, especially strong ones, wait for a "target of opportunity," and it rarely presents itself very far in advance. With few exceptions, challengers do not initially have the recognition or the organizational and financial resources available to almost all incumbents. Those who cannot acquire them quickly are doomed to almost certain failure.

This chapter considers challengers and their problems. First, we analyze their backgrounds—who they are and where they come from. Second, we consider how they become credible contestants—by building recognition, raising money, and organizing. Finally, we look at how they put it all together in time.

Who Are the Challengers?

Challengers' backgrounds vary most notably by office, by party, and by size of state. Some positions, like governor or senator, are more likely to be the goal of challengers who have already served in government. Party plays a role, because in many cases, Republican party organizations are more active in candidate recruitment. The size of the state helps determine the number of officeholders likely to be considered serious contestants for higher positions. This section expands on these points.

The Challenger's Prior Service in Government

Prior service in the state government is virtually a requirement for the governorship. More than forty of the fifty governors serving in 1984 came to office from other positions in state government—lieutenant governor, state attorney general, or member of the state legislature. Five of the seven who had been businessmen just before becoming governor had previously held positions in state government. U.S. senators rarely run for governor, although there is some traffic in the other direction.

Members of Congress run for governor relatively infrequently; only four of the governors elected between 1980 and 1984 were former representatives.[2] Representatives who served between 1953 and 1974 were three times more likely to run for senator than for a four-year gubernatorial term, and eleven times more likely to run for senator than for a two-year gubernatorial term. This finding is ascribed to the longer length of the Senate term, the similarity of the legislative functions, and the traditional (but disappearing) lower likelihood of an incumbent's defeat in the Senate.[3] Representatives grow tired of the incessant campaigning during their two-year terms, and may yearn for the relative peace and stability of the six year term in the Senate. As one newly elected senator said, "I set a certain standard of expectation when I was in the House, going home every weekend, but I'm not going to do that now. One of the reasons I ran for the Senate was so that I wouldn't have to go home every weekend."[4]

Looking at the lineup after the 1984 elections, former representatives were among the more than 70 percent of senators who had held prior office. Most often, representatives who succeed to the Senate are from relatively small states, in which their congressional districts comprise a significant proportion of the state. Thus they have already achieved substantial recognition over a wide area at the time they first run for election as Senate challengers. Examples included both senators from Connecticut, Hawaii, Idaho, Maryland, Montana, and North and South Dakota. The next largest contingent of senators were former governors, who also tend to come from small- to medium-sized states— for example, both of the senators from South Carolina and Arkansas. They also obviously began their races as challengers with wide recognition.

Senators from both parties in the largest states were overrepresented among the minority who had no prior electoral record when they first ran. They included a number of business executives, a scattering of academics, and a few "celebrities" (professional athletes, astronauts, and the like) and represented states such as New York, New Jersey, Texas, Ohio, and Minnesota. California, the largest state, had two senators with previous political experience in 1984, but among their recent predecessors were a professional actor and an academic. The cost of gaining recognition through advertising in these states is so high that successful contestants must either have previous wide public recognition when they first run (like former U.N. ambassador Daniel Patrick Moynihan of New York or professional athlete Bill Bradley of New Jersey), or be wealthy enough to buy saturation advertising (like businessmen Dave Durenberger and Rudy Boschwitz of Minnesota).

The Challenger's Resources

Another factor determining the credibility of challengers consists of the resources, contacts, and organization that candidates can bring to a race. Members of the state legislature who run for governor have often built up resources that can be used for a further run within the state, but are not as readily available for a Washington-based office. A consultant points to a former state senate majority leader who ran for both the governorship and the House of Representatives: "Any bill in the state Senate had to go across his desk. Everybody had to ante up when he ran for governor. Look at the contributor list—they all gave to the legal limit. As a congressional candidate, he couldn't raise it like he did for the governorship." A local reporter observes of the same candidate, "Inside the walls of that statehouse, he was given twenty points more than when he walked outside the statehouse or left the county."

The Challenger's Party Affiliation

The final factor affecting legislative recruitment is the candidate's party banner. In chapter 3 we detailed the stronger role that the Republican party plays in recruiting efforts, noting the relative paucity of Republican officeholders at lower levels available and willing to move to higher office, and the much greater financial and organizational support that the Republican party can offer its candidates. The result is that, particularly at the congressional level, successful Republican challengers are more likely to be amateurs with less of a record of service than their Democratic counterparts. As noted earlier, prior political experience exercises a powerful effect on the likelihood that a congressional challenger will be successful: between 1946 and 1980, about 20 percent of experienced challengers defeated incumbents, as opposed to 5 percent of those with no prior political experience. This relationship held for both parties.[5] Strong challengers (defined as those with prior experience) are more likely to run when they perceive the trends as propitious for victory.

In every year since 1974, fewer Republican than Democratic challengers have held previous office. The difference diminished for open seats (with no incumbent running), which have traditionally been regarded as the best bet for a challenger, but is still there, and consistent.[6] Perhaps because of the enormous infusion of funds on the Republican side, *successful* Republican challengers in the most recent elections have been notably less experienced than their Democratic counterparts. In 1980 open seats were won by twenty-six Republicans and eighteen Democrats. Of the Democrats, 72 percent were experienced challengers who had held prior elective office. Only 54 percent of the Republicans had similar experience. Similarly, in 1982, 66 percent of the thirty-five successful Democratic contestants for open seats had prior elective experience, as opposed to 55 percent of the twenty-two successful Republicans. The pattern held again in 1984, when 68 percent of the nineteen successful Republican contestants for open seats had previously held office, compared to 88 percent of the eight successful Democratic open seat winners. Although 1980 and 1984 were good years for Republican challengers, and 1982 was a bad year, the profiles of Democratic and Republican candidates who were successful in capturing open seats changed little. Republican amateurs who could mount a credible campaign in promising districts were assured of adequate funding from their party; Democrats were more likely to be on their own. This frequently meant that only Democrats with a track record could run and win.

Overcoming the Disadvantages of the Challenger _____

In our discussion of incumbents, we pointed to three of their chief advantages: recognition, money, and time. To become credible, a challenger for any office must negate these advantages. He or she must also have a substantial level of recognition or acquire it quickly; must turn the incumbent's recognition into a negative rather than a positive factor; must raise sufficient early money for information gathering, organization, and advertising; and must start early enough to be able to build an organization and formulate a strategy for the external campaign. A challenger who, by early September, has not achieved substantial recognition, has not increased the negative perceptions of the opponent, has not acquired sufficient money, and is not in a positive or at least neutral position in relation to national trends has probably already lost the election, even if the public is barely aware that a campaign is going on.

The Pressures on the Challenger

For the challenger, recognition, money, and time are closely linked. Incumbents acquire recognition through their activities in office and their ability to publicize them. Most challengers, even if they are currently serving in some other office, do not receive the same kind of publicity the incumbent gets. It is therefore usually necessary for challengers to buy coverage, in the form of paid advertising—through television, radio, and direct mail. Further, the money that challengers can raise affects, to a great extent, the amount of free media coverage they receive. Raising and spending money is what makes the challenger credible to the press. "High-resource" challengers—those with publicity expenditures above the median for all candidates—are able to match or exceed incumbents in their newspaper coverage.[7] Similarly, a few challengers determine years in advance when they are going to make a race, but most decide, start to raise funds and organize, and announce perhaps nine months before the general election, as they perceive a target of opportunity. To run effectively against an incumbent who has typically been planning the race for a year or more, a challenger must be able to compress time, creating an instant organization by hiring experienced consultants. This, of course, also costs money.

Ideally, a challenger's professional staff is similar to the incumbent's, which we described in chapter 4. The difference is that challengers do not have the perquisites of incumbents. They do not have an existing staff with appropriate campaign experience, and they are less likely to be familiar with the national consultants who specialize in statewide races. Because in most races challengers are assumed to be the underdogs, and consultants' reputations depend on their "win and loss" records, they find it more difficult to persuade the leading consultants to work for them. At the same time, they need the consultants more than the incumbents do, both for their experience and for the credibility their presence bestows. The challenger's need for hired guns, and the difficulties in retaining the well-known ones, who are most likely to be both competent and credible, becomes a vicious circle.

For example, Mario Cuomo, elected governor of New York in 1982 after a surprise victory in a primary against Mayor Edward Koch of New

York City, recorded in his campaign diaries the frustrations in finding a campaign manager and consultants to do his polling and media work. His first choice for a campaign director, the well-known consultant David Garth, opted to go with Koch. His second choice declined because he was involved with the Senate campaign for incumbent Daniel Patrick Moynihan in the same state. In a diary entry seven months before primary election day, Cuomo wrote:

> We're caught in a circular problem. . . . many of the money people are reluctant to commit to me. They are waiting for signs of organization and potential success before they "invest," but they are almost indispensable ingredients in forming up the effort in the first place. I must get a "name" campaign manager and a headquarters as soon as possible.[8]

Two days later, Cuomo commented further on the price exacted by the failure to get the staff he needed: "The value of a Garth is clear from the way our campaign is shaping up—or rather, isn't. It has no form. It is not being driven by anyone along any particular path."[9] The Cuomo campaign muddled through with a neophyte staff (who had had some statewide experience in his lieutenant-governor campaign four years earlier), the advantage of errors by Koch, and Cuomo's own savvy and experience. As late as July, Cuomo was writing most of his own television commercials; he prepared his afternoon speech for the state party nominating convention at 5:30 a.m. the same day.

When and if challengers finally hire the consultants they need, their organizations are particularly prone to conflict and struggles for turf. Such conflict is never absent in a campaign but is more likely in challengers' efforts, where the participants have not worked together before and consultants may discount the abilities of the day-to-day staff. The deputy manager of a gubernatorial campaign describes the hostility between the staff and the polling and media consultants:

> The campaign manager talked to them, but I would have to say there was nobody in the campaign that was their boss; they basically did what they wanted to. A flunky worked with us. He would issue orders. This underling would call and say, "We're coming to shoot commercials and I want this, this, and this," and I'd say, "Did you think of——" and he'd say, "I didn't ask you for your thoughts; this is what we want."

The field director in another gubernatorial campaign had similar recollections:

> I was press secretary and field director, running the daily operation, doing the press, working with all the local organizations, and moving the mail. I was working sixteen hours a day, six days a week, and here's this consultant who comes in one day a week and is getting paid five grand a month. There's natural resentment, there's suspicion, there is jealousy, and there is competitiveness.

Congressional and Legislative Campaigns

Challengers for the state legislature or the House of Representatives find recognition extremely difficult to come by. The media generally do not give much coverage to such candidates. Moreover, legislative districts at the state and federal levels are usually drawn to the substantial advantage of one party. Challengers, almost always from the other party and running in low-turnout elections in which party activists are overrepresented, begin with two strikes against them. The legislative or congressional challenger who seeks to buy media advertising finds that television, which is most effective at building quick, widespread recognition, is not only very expensive but usually not well tailored to the district.

The time-honored method of gaining recognition at the local level is shoe leather, and the attempt to reach personally as many voters as possible remains a leading stratagem for the legislative or congressional candidate. Legislative districts and many congressional districts are still small enough for door-to-door campaigning. Interviews with more than two hundred state legislators in nine states revealed that "many of them won their first election by door-to-door campaigning, and they are convinced that this is the most effective way to maintain contacts and visibility." [10] Reflecting on his first races for both the state legislature and the House of Representatives, Jim Florio of New Jersey said: "You have to go strategically around the district. Breaking in is a very physical thing. There is no substitute for physical work." [11] The theme is echoed by Larry Pressler, now senator from South Dakota, in describing his first congressional race in 1974: "I tried to shake 500 hands a day. That is where you really take their hand and look at them and talk to them a little bit. I succeeded in doing that seven days a week. I put in a lot of twelve hour days starting at a quarter to six in the morning at some plant.... You would not believe the physical and mental effort this requires." [12]

These days, however, the doors on which a challenger knocks are not selected randomly. Analysis of swing precincts directs the candidate to particular locations, and the friendly or at least neutral voter who answers the door is likely to receive a computer-generated letter in the next few days, addressing the voter by name and favorably recalling a small child, the attractive landscaping, and so on. [13] Such letters, a technique known as direct mail, are increasingly important in campaigns for the state legislatures and the House. Although most analysts who have written about direct mail concentrate on its use as a fundraising tool, [14] campaign professionals regard it as an important method of informing and persuading voters, especially in lower-level races where television is very expensive and not cost-efficient. [15]

A typical challenger using direct mail was Ralph Salerno, who ran an ultimately unsuccessful race against the Democratic president of the New Jersey State Senate in 1983. Along with a ten-day, $18,000 radio buy in July, his campaign sent a districtwide mailing including a picture postcard of the candidate and his family, a three-page letter detailing eight campaign issues and making veiled negative attacks against the incumbent, and a prepaid envelope in which recipients could enclose campaign contributions or offers to volunteer. The mailing brought in a welcome $3,700, but more important was the recognition gain for the candidate. As the architect of these efforts commented, "We thought it was important to establish early credibility for him. He had never held political office before; he was unknown. He was running against the Senate president."

In addition to opportunities to meet and greet the voters and to send out direct mail solicitations, a key asset for a local level challenger seeking recognition is early support from politically active groups willing to serve as surrogates for the candidate in canvassing or fundraising. These include the remnants of the party organizations, labor unions, civic associations, and special-interest groups like environmentalists, feminists, and others. They serve as an organizational base for the challenger and as a counterweight to the existing organizations of most incumbents. Organized support is especially important in primary elections, which many challengers have to negotiate successfully before moving on to the general election; it is vital to the challenger who has held no previous office. For example, Representative Chris Smith was part-time executive director of New Jersey Right-to-Life when he first gained the Republican nomination in his district. A salesman in a family sporting-goods business, he had no political record aside from his antiabortion activities.

Candidates without existing group ties can often create them. Consultant Hank Parkinson described a two-year program he designed to elect an unknown optometrist to the Kansas state legislature:

> We arranged for him to join a group of eye doctors in Mexico fitting indigents for eyeglasses.... Through direct mail we made sure that all Lions Club members in the southeast corner of Kansas were made aware of Dr. Whittaker's work—important because our man was active in the organization, which has sight-saving as a major service project.
>
> Included with the direct mailings were return cards with which Lions Club program directors could indicate if they wanted Dr. Whittaker as a speaker. The response was gratifyingly heavy. Each speech appearance was publicized without fail.... In about four months, Dr. Whittaker was a pretty well-known figure in that part of Kansas.[16]

Dr. Robert Whittaker served one term in the state legislature before winning the Republican congressional primary as a dark horse and an easy general election victory in Kansas's Fifth District.[17]

Candidates who have previously held local office are more apt to turn to what remains of the local party organizations, which still recruit candidates for the state legislature. Not uncommonly, such candidates have been active in local parties, or have held county office, where many party activists still subsist in what may be the last patronage-rich environments. Pete Curtin, a Democratic campaign consultant who works with legislative and congressional campaigns, described an early primary campaign for a congressional race, in which the candidate had previously held county office:

> Whatever is there of the party organization, you work it to the highest level possible. Hook the candidate up close with the county committee members. A lot of that is personal contact on the part of the candidate, but we sent out 3,500 pieces of direct mail in connection with his announcement—every county committee member, every election board member, every party official, the leaders of every constituent group identified with the Democratic party. It was a "Dear Joe," not a "Dear Democrat," letter and included in it was a copy of his announcement.

This candidate embodied both the old and new techniques of high touch and high tech. In addition to personal campaigning, he reached out, in Curtin's words, "to the traditional Democratic family," with computerized direct mail. He won his primary easily.

Although both Democratic and Republican challengers utilize all of these strategies in this stage of the campaign, Democratic candidates below the statewide level are more likely to depend on personal organizations deriving from past officeholding or interest-group contacts, while Republicans rely more on paid mail and telephone. These different strategies reflect the strengths and weaknesses of each of the parties.

Democrats. The Democrats have enjoyed a numerical advantage among psychological party identifiers for half a century. Party affiliation is still critical in most elections below the statewide level. In explaining the continuing dominance of Democrats in the state legislatures, Republican consultant Dave Murray, said: "On the grand scale of elections, the further you go down the ladder, the more people have a tendency to vote party line as opposed to issues and personality, because there's a dearth of information. People don't want the information; it's not that important." Thus, in the majority of legislative and congressional districts in which Democrats are the "natural" majority, they need only reinforce an existing base—always a simpler job than persuading independents. The Republicans' task has been to convert the opposition's partisans. Additionally, the Democrats are a party of constituencies. Democratic candidates start out with a road map; they know they can probably find support among such groups as union members, minorities, public employees, feminists, and the like—or, in the words of Democratic strategist Tim Ridley, "Democrats know where the mother lode is."

Therefore, Democratic challengers at the legislative and congressional levels are more likely to have run lower-level races, to have strong interest-group ties, and to represent districts where their partisans are in the majority. In our earlier discussion of recruitment at the congressional level, we noted these differences. These Democrats generally have a personal fundraising base. Labor PACs and a growing number of liberal-issue PACs contribute substantially and disproportionately to Democrats. However, neither the Democratic party nor the liberal PACs can come close to matching the opposition's resources. Thus, an increasing number of wealthy Democrats are opting to finance their own efforts. Of the twenty-two House members who contributed more than $75,000 to their own 1982 campaigns, sixteen were Democrats, and the top four were successful challengers.[18]

Republicans. Faced with minority party status since the Great Depression, Republicans have traditionally been bereft of any substantial interest-group support. Religious fundamentalists, through organizations like the Moral Majority, have played an important role in some Republican campaigns in recent years, but some groups' activities are limited if they wish to retain their tax-exempt status. Thus, by the mid-1960s, many observers actually believed that the Republicans would cease to be one of two major parties. As late as 1978, a distinguished political scientist could convincingly write, "The United States lacks a competitive two-party system at present because of the exceptional weakness of the Republican party." Almost as an aside, he added in a footnote, "The Republican weakness to which we refer here, is, of course, primarily that of 'the party in the electorate, rather than of party organization." [19]

As we have seen in chapter 3, however, it was in fact the national Republican party organization, beginning in the mid-1970s, that was in large measure responsible for a steady increase in the Republican share of the House vote, after the low ebb of Watergate in 1974, and for the election of many Republican challengers. Assurance that the party would back them to the hilt persuaded strong Republican candidates to run even in "bad" years.

Candidates who have accepted Republican party assistance lose some freedom in running their campaigns, but the loss is less ideological than procedural. They remain free to adjust their issue appeals to their constituencies. One congressional candidate from Texas told a reporter: "I let the NRCC [National Republican Congressional Committee] know my positions on the issues at the first. They did not encourage us to take any particular theme." Another from Illinois added: "They wanted to talk about national issues and I wanted to talk about local issues. It was a long discussion, and I disagreed with them, but they gave me money anyway." [20]

What the national committees do require of candidates is that their money be used for purposes considered worthwhile. As much as possible, contributions are made "in kind"—as payments for polls, phone banks, direct mail, media production, and the like, frequently done by committee-approved vendors. The committees can thus shape the campaigns professionally. Major effort is put into voter contact— early identification and persuasion of independents, and even Democrats, to vote Republican. Not every Republican House challenger can expect a large infusion of party funds, however. Republican strategists concede many seats with heavily Democratic populations and effective Democratic incumbents. Only challengers in potentially winnable districts are the beneficiaries of national party largesse. The more modestly financed Democratic Congressional Campaign Committee follows the same strategy. A DCCC staffer commented: "There are 435 races, but you're probably looking at under 100 that are really contests. Those don't change very much, and every year you take a look at those same races."

By 1983 this model had moved to state legislative races. In New Jersey, the state Republican party set up the Republican Legislative Campaign Committee (RLCC) and funded it with a million dollars. The hope was to take over both houses of the state legislature, which the Democrats controlled narrowly, by winning ten targeted races. Control in 1983 was especially desired because the state's final congressional redistricting plan for the 1980s was still up in the air; the U.S. Supreme Court had thrown out the plan devised by the Democrats in the legislature as a deliberate political gerrymander. The RLCC executive director described its role: "We set this thing up as a business. We saw our money as an investment in candidates to help them win and they would contribute their wins to make a majority." Just as a business franchisee might be required to market products in a particular way, RLCC candidates, like those supported by the congressional committee, had to run their campaigns in a manner approved by the funding source:

> We looked at the entire state, past voting, margins in previous races, town numbers, and found the most likely places for us to win seats. We sat down with the individual candidates and said, here's how much

money we agree you need to win, and we're going to give it to you, but we're only going to give you in-kind assistance. We spent money only on polls, mail, radio, and phone banks. We recruited, found, and placed campaign managers to give us more control in many cases, particularly with nonincumbents who weren't conversant with campaigns.

Ultimately, the effort was unsuccessful, and the legislative balance remained roughly the same, although the Republicans managed to avoid the midterm losses usually associated with having a party's governor in office, as they did in New Jersey.

Summary. This review of races below the statewide level seems to paint a picture of successful Democratic challengers who win with grassroots organizational campaigns that mobilize a natural majority, and of successful Republican challengers who conduct well-financed, high-tech efforts. Indeed, in the six congressional elections between 1974 and 1984, on average, the Democratic challengers who defeated Republican incumbents spent less than the losing incumbents, except in 1980, a very bad Democratic year in the House. On the other hand, all the Republican challengers who defeated Democrats spent more than the losing incumbents.[21] The same pattern appears in races in which challenger seriously threatened incumbents, holding them to under 60 percent. In these competitive contests, Democratic challengers almost always spent less than Republicans did.

It would be an error to think, though, that winning Democratic candidates were running cheap campaigns while the Republican candidates were spending huge sums. In fact, the *winning* challengers in *both* parties spent approximately a third more than all challengers—in other words, *all* winning challengers had well-financed campaigns; Democratic challengers who cannot raise a good deal of money do not fare well either. However, the amount that is *sufficient* to win is usually lower for Democratic challengers.

The picture sharpens as we look at the political background of successful challengers. Of the twenty-six Republican challengers who defeated Democratic incumbents in 1980, fifteen, or 58 percent, spent more than their opponents. Their expenses were closely related to their previous political experience, however. Among those who had never run for office before, 75 percent spent more; of those who had run for office before, 50 percent spent more; and of those who had won office before, 38 percent spent more. In 1982, when twenty-two Democratic challengers defeated Republican incumbents, almost all—twenty—spent less than their opponents. The two who spent more were among the six who had never previously run for office. All the previous officeholders spent less than the Republican incumbents in defeating them.

Thus, although there are always exceptions to the rule, a reasonable conclusion is that recent successful Republican congressional challengers have outspent successful Democrats, mainly because Republicans tend to be inexperienced challengers who need to buy recognition and because Democratic candidates begin with a larger partisan base that is less expensive to persuade. In addition, Democratic challengers are more likely to have gained recognition from their previous political records, but even Democratic neophytes can usually get by with less than their Republican counterparts.

Statewide Races: Senators and Governors

Challengers for the office of senator and governor face a different set of problems from those of legislative and congressional challengers; moreover, there are some differences between a race for senator and one for governor. The task of the typical Senate challenger is to show that the incumbent is out of touch with the state, while a gubernatorial challenger must demonstrate superior leadership capabilities. Senate challengers, like incumbents, raise money from Washington-based political action committees and national party sources, whereas gubernatorial contestants must seek funds from in-state sources, with the help of the state party organization. These differences will be explored further in the case studies presented in the section "Examining Some Challenger Campaigns." This section concentrates on the similarities among statewide challengers for the Senate and the governorship and on their differences from lower-level office.

Senate Races. Senate campaigns differ in two ways from contests for the House. They are more likely to be competitive, and the media play a larger role. Both of these differences can significantly affect the activities of statewide challengers.

As for competition, the figures speak for themselves. Although 1982 and 1984 were good years for Senate incumbents, producing only two and three incumbent defeats, respectively, more than a third of the incumbents who sought reelection in 1976, 1978, and 1980 were bested, compared to about a tenth of the House members. Successful Senate incumbents also had closer races. In the same period, about seven in ten House incumbents won reelection with at least 60 percent of the two-party vote; only about four in ten Senate incumbents did as well. These data paint a considerably brighter picture for Senate challengers than for House challengers.

We noted in chapter 4 that statewide candidates receive much greater media attention during their campaigns than do congressional office-seekers. Although this observation is often true, a number of

Senate campaigns resemble House campaigns in which a hopeless challenger runs. They are neither competitive nor well covered by the media. Mark Westlye points out that "a substantial proportion of Senate races are low-key affairs that attract scant notice: media coverage is limited, spending by the challenger is relatively low, and the outcome is often a foregone conclusion." [22]

The 122 Senate races between 1972 and 1980 in which incumbents figured could be divided almost evenly between hard-fought and low-key. The challengers in low-key races, as in most congressional races, were much less well known than the incumbents, with recognition rates averaging 60 percent, as opposed to 92 percent for challengers in hard-fought contests. In hard-fought races, voter defections—votes by partisans for the Senate candidate of the other party—were moderately high and in both directions, whereas in low-key races, defections were strongly in the direction of the incumbent. When a race for the Senate does not have the excitement of competitiveness, the media tend to treat the contest as they do the typical House election—and the absence of coverage reinforces the voters' lack of interest.

What makes a Senate race hard-fought or low-key is not entirely clear, although there are clues. Lightly populated states are more likely to have less competitive races when incumbents are involved. Between 1968 and 1980, two-thirds of the Senate races in the twelve most populous states were decided by fewer than ten percentage points, whereas the same proportion in the twelve least populous states were decided by more than ten percentage points. Researchers speculate that less densely populated Senate constituencies are more like congressional districts—more homogeneous and more strongly one-party: "For incumbent legislators, the more constituents there are, the more difficult they are to please." [23]

However, this is not the entire answer. Larger states like New Jersey and Ohio in 1985 had two senators of the same party elected by widely varying margins. The explanation must also lie in the quality of their campaigns, their attractiveness as candidates, and the strength of their challengers. Like representatives, senators whose vote totals approach or exceed two-thirds devise strategies to make themselves appear so invulnerable that strong challengers decline to run against them, even though Senate challengers traditionally stand a better chance of winning than do their House counterparts. The weak challengers who do run are less able to raise money, have no previous experience that would gain them widespread recognition, are thus not taken seriously by the media, and do not receive the free media coverage they need to acquire recognition.

Most media organizations make their election coverage plans in the internal campaign period during the summer. One political reporter observed the winter before a federal election, "We basically decide we're going to cover the elections that will be in doubt." Comparing the Senate race that was going to take place in his state that fall with the contest for the other Senate seat two years previously, he was already practically dismissing the fall contest: "There probably will have been a lot more stories two years ago than this year mainly because it's not perceived as a close race." In fact, no challenger to the incumbent had even emerged definitively at that point. Like the reporter, potentially strong challengers presumably read the polls that gave the incumbent the highest favorability rating of any politician in the state and knew about his $4 million war chest.

Another factor influencing the competitiveness of Senate contests is whether a challenger must face an incumbent or simply another challenger. Open seats almost always attract two strong candidates. Half the incumbent races Westlye studied were low-key, but less than a fifth of the races for open seats were. Whereas only about a third of open House seats are hard-fought, four out of five open Senate seats are. The higher media profile of the Senate contest and the greater heterogeneity of most Senate constituencies mean that party identification and recognition are less crucial than in House contests, and either candidate has a reasonable chance to win.

The greater chance of winning a Senate race makes it easier, in many cases, to raise campaign funds. Republican Senate challengers generally can expect to receive more party money and support than their Democratic counterparts can count on, although their proportionate advantage is not as great as for Republican House challengers. The major difference is that the Republican party, unlike the Democrats, can afford to give every Senate challenger the maximum permitted by law, and in most cases it does. The executive director of the National Republican Senatorial Committee said:

> I just feel very strongly that this committee is uniquely positioned to recruit candidates and therefore has a party responsibility to do so; and to be effective in the long haul, has to keep its commitments. We'll fulfill every commitment we made even though we know some of them will never come close.

Because there are only 33 or 34 Senate races in each two-year election cycle, as opposed to 435 House races, PACs are more likely to contribute to any promising Senate race. Wealthy individuals are increasingly financing their own campaigns for the Senate as well. Although political amateurs are still less common in the Senate than in the House, the decline of the parties and the growing importance of paid media advertising in Senate campaigns have attracted a growing number of affluent political novices to Senate races. In 1982, 20 percent of all money spent on senatorial contests came from the candidates themselves, up from 8 percent in 1978, and almost all of the heavy spenders were challengers.[24] This is especially true in the largest states, which require the greatest media expenditures. The Senate has always had its share of members who amassed power and wealth in nonpolitical spheres, but in earlier days, such would-be senators—men like Mark Hanna, for example—would have had to pay earlier party dues. As the parties' role in campaigns has deteriorated, wealthy individuals like Dave Durenberger and Rudy Boschwitz of Minnesota, Howard Metzenbaum and John Glenn of Ohio, and Bill Bradley and Frank Lautenberg of New Jersey have been able to effect lateral entry into the Senate.

Gubernatorial Races. Gubernatorial challengers must also face the problem of dealing with a deficit of recognition, money, and time. As in some Senate contests, there is a class of gubernatorial races in which these deficits are never overcome; they are races that attract only weak challengers, and the outcome of the election is a foregone conclusion. In 1982, of twenty-four incumbent governors who ran for reelection, twelve won easily (with 60 percent or more of the vote), seven had a relatively close contest (getting under 60 percent), and five lost. Among the twelve challengers who lost badly, only one held, had ever held, or had previously run for a statewide position. Among the seven who gave the incumbent a hard-fought contest, three held or had held such positions. And among the five winning challengers, four met this criterion. The same rule applies in contests for open seats, in which no incumbent is running. The 1982 gubernatorial contests involved eleven open seats. Seven of the eleven winners had held previous statewide positions; none of the eleven losers had.

Thus, as with Senate races, there is a strong and positive correlation between the quality of the challengers, the statewide recognition levels they start out with, and their likelihood of success. Inexperienced or unknown gubernatorial challengers also find it difficult to get the early financial resources and free media attention that permit them to run a credible race. As consultant Vince Breglio described most challengers' early problems:

> The package for a challenger is really different because their up-front money is always, always thin. A statewide survey, for example, you're looking at $35,000. That's a potful of money for a challenger to come up with. In all the challenger statewide races I'm working on right now, we have yet to do any full-blown surveys [in March of the election year]. Maybe they're in a position to get a good piece of research by late August, early September. But it comes very late, they just don't have the dough to do it before.

Candidates who seek to make up for lack of resources with free media attention also find themselves up against the attitude of reporters like the one who observed of gubernatorial candidates: "Coverage is post-filing day. They are just average citizens until they file for office. You don't plan your coverage until the gun goes off." Even though coverage may increase after the race formally begins, it is usually too late for an unknown challenger to profit sufficiently from free media time.

Because of these problems, successful novice challengers are disproportionately wealthy individuals who can personally finance the requirements of the early internal campaign; like similar Senate challengers, they tend to run in large, competitive states with expensive media markets they can afford to dominate. Nelson Rockefeller of New York and Milton Shapp of Pennsylvania are examples of rich amateurs who pioneered this type of campaign in the 1960s; Texan William Clements was successful in 1978; and businessman Lewis Lehrman almost pulled it off in New York in 1982. Lehrman went from being an unknown to being a household word by launching a staggeringly expensive saturation media campaign beginning in January of the election year.

Not as much is known about the financing of the gubernatorial races of less wealthy challengers. Disclosure provisions and contribution limits in the states vary widely and are rarely as stringent as the federal rules. Credible challengers appear to raise their money from the same sources as incumbents: the business sector, banks, and wealthy individuals. State party organizations rarely have the financial resources to make substantial contributions, but they frequently have access to individuals and businesses that contribute heavily. The involvement of the Washington-based national party committees in gubernatorial races has traditionally been limited or nonexistent. Although the Republicans are expanding their commitments to governors' races, the emphasis remains on Washington. The Democratic committees can afford only the most minimal involvement in such races.

Challengers for all offices face the need to achieve credibility—by demonstrating widespread support through fundraising, organization, or both. At the lower levels—in legislative and congressional races—organization can sometimes substitute for money. At the statewide level, where paid media advertising is mandatory for gaining recognition, substantial fundraising is essential. The compression of time and the complexity of statewide races make the hiring of experienced consultants unavoidable. In the final section of this chapter, we look at how a variety of challengers "put it together"—or failed to.

Examining Some Challenger Campaigns _____

Let us consider several challengers, potential and actual, who ran, or plan to run, for seats in the House and Senate and for governorships. Each case illustrates how the points we have discussed interact to produce success or failure.

A Congressional Race

Of the offices we are considering, congressional candidates run in the smallest constituencies. Congressional campaigns vary widely in their professionalism and cost, but they are simply different in kind from Senate races. A Senate candidate who had previously served exactly the same constituency as his state's single at-large House member made this point: "This is the first time we've ever had any paid campaign organization. . . . We will spend three times as much as we did on our House races. I ran [for the House] on a budget of $100,000-$125,000. We'll spend at least $450,000, $250,000 of it on media." [25]

A surprise Democratic House winner in 1982 was South Carolina's Robin Tallon, whose campaign illustrates many of the ingredients of a successful challenger effort. Until 1980, Tallon, a successful entrepreneur who had built up a chain of clothing stores, was not involved in politics. That year, he decided to run for the state legislature and was successful. At about the same time, the district's incumbent representative, John Jenrette, was indicted and ultimately convicted for his role in the Abscam scandal. So heavily Democratic was the district that Jenrette, alone among the Abscam defendants, almost retained his seat, losing by a 52 to 48 percent margin to John Napier, a former aide to South Carolina's long term-governor and senator, Strom Thurmond. Napier, who almost tripled Jenrette's spending in 1978, was a beneficiary of NRCC largesse, which was back to support his marginal seat in 1982. Napier also had the support of the district's wealthy tobacco farmers and the business community in the district's largest city. Democratic support was based substantially, although not entirely, among the 41 percent of the district's residents who were black and mostly poor.

Tallon was urged to run by blacks and whites who had supported Jenrette and who were looking for an attractive candidate who was "above reproach." He did not finally decide to enter the race until the spring of 1982. Facing a bruising multicandidate primary, a runoff two weeks later, and the general election in the fall, Tallon, not well known, would have to fight, win, and finance three separate elections in the space of six months. The support of the Jenrette organization, and

Tallon's own energetic efforts to cultivate the black community, primarily through black churches, gave him a sizable base, but not one large enough to win either the runoff or general elections. Tallon dealt with this gap by hiring experienced consultants to poll, organize a direct mail and telephone effort, and do radio and television advertising—including Jerry Rafshoon for media, one of whose previous clients had been President Jimmy Carter. The primary media campaign concentrated on introducing Tallon—as a person, a successful businessman, and a state legislator—to the district. The candidate eventually prevailed by two to one in the primary and three to one in the runoff election.

Tallon was able to achieve these results in the primary because of his ability to provide his own early money—personally contributing almost $200,000 to create an instant professional organization and fairly extensive media campaign. It was therefore something of a shock, as a campaign staffer remembered it, when the candidate, now facing the well-financed Republican incumbent John Napier in the general election, announced: "Not a red cent is coming down for the general election. Go out and raise it." The staffer continued, "Everybody with money thought Napier had it wrapped. Our poll immediately after the runoff showed Tallon was ahead, but nobody believed that poll." Tallon's fundraising problems illustrate several difficulties common to challengers. The first is inexperience and lack of information. Sandy Maisel, a political scientist and a one-time congressional candidate, commented, "Candidates make decisions on what a campaign will cost, on how much can be raised, and on how much personal investment will be necessary with an incredible dearth of information." Maisel recalls a telephone conversation with one of his primary opponents:

> At one point I asked him what he thought the primary would cost. "About $50,000 more or less." "That's just about what I'm budgeting too." I had no idea where I would raise the money or how I would allocate it, but in that brief conversation, nearly a year before the primary, my budget was set.[26]

Similarly, a Tallon staffer explained the candidate's behavior as "straight naïveté. He did not realize what was involved. He told me if he had known it was going to take that kind of money he would never have done it."

A second point illustrated by Tallon's experience is the difficulty candidates have in convincing contributors that they can actually defeat a well-financed incumbent. This is a particularly difficult proposition for a Democrat, who does not have a national party committee well financed enough to take a major gamble and, as in Tallon's case, does not have a substantial fundraising base within the district. The candidate's own polls, although conducted by a recognized professional, were not sufficient. Tallon was rescued from this dilemma by a fortuitous event. Early in the fall, a company doing market research in the area decided to ask a question about the congressional race. It showed Tallon ahead. Labor and liberal PACs finally responded. "It just ripped through the press and through Washington. Tallon is real. And money starts coming to town. Not a whole lot, but enough to pay for election day and a little bit of TV. That 150-interview poll did it for him."

Robin Tallon, outspent three to one in the general election campaign by incumbent Napier, eventually won by a margin of 5 percent. His victory illustrates a third point: like many Democratic challengers, he could get by with less money largely because of an organizational base in his district—in this case, the black church network.

Preparations for a Senate Race

Statewide candidates, with a larger and more complex constituency, must begin planning their campaign earlier; although the problems of achieving credibility, raising money, and setting up an organization are similar to those of a House contestant, the effort must be much greater.

Successful Senate challengers must start building up credibility and recognition a long time before they actually announce for office. An aspirant who already holds statewide office, such as the governorship, or a representative from a state with few congressional districts, may already have closed the recognition gap. Members of Congress in larger states who harbor senatorial ambitions must engage in activities that will make them well known elsewhere in the state. A top-ranking aide to a Republican House member who is often mentioned as a future senatorial candidate discusses what the representative is doing in advance of a likely Senate bid that is still several years away:

> We have three goals. There's a goal in the district, and that is to re-vise the image, so that people don't think we're writing a blank check to the Pentagon. We want to be a little tighter on the environment too. In the state, we want to be the heir apparent, we want to be as popular as Jack Kemp. We're doing a lot of things—top positions in the president's campaign, in the governor's campaign.
>
> I actively solicit engagements from all over the state, almost to the detriment of the district. At Lincoln Day dinners, we're out of the district. Our third goal is the national goal, to become an expert on national defense. We're going to stick with it. We've made the judgment that our future is in Washington, so we're not concerned with competing on state issues with the guys who want to be governor.

This potential candidate is positioning himself so that when the anticipated opportunity to run for the Senate arrives, he will be as well known and highly regarded as possible. The representative has already employed nationally known polling and media consultants who regularly work in senatorial races in his state. For his last campaign, he raised almost $600,000, about 50 percent more than the average Republican congressional incumbent. Although the services of the consultants and his fundraising may seem excessive for a safe district, which he regularly carries by two-to-one margins, they contribute to the "heir apparent" image he cultivates. His key campaign people have been with him since his first congressional race; his manager has since run a successful gubernatorial campaign in the state. The candidate's experienced core strategy group regard their hired consultants as "technicians for us." When the time comes to run, he will be almost as prepared as the Senate incumbent, because substantial inroads have been made in the challenges of time, recognition, and money.

Two Senate Challenger Races

Bearing in mind the financial and organizational requirements of Senate campaigns, we may compare this representative we have just described with a colleague in the same state who ran for the Senate as an early favorite but ultimately lost. This candidate had won several congressional races easily, but with volunteer-based "friends and neighbors" campaigns in which a consultant had never been used. The candidate's personal appearances were the key to the congressional campaigns; there was no paid advertising except some brochure mailings. Money was not a major consideration; the candidate had never raised more than $60,000 to win overwhelming victories.

Old friends began to think about the Senate race a year and a half in advance, but the candidate, according to a member of the steering committee, was vacillating. When the decision was finally made, in January of election year, the staff was in a desperate scramble for support outside the congressional district.

The campaign steering committee, which faced a spring primary, included no one who had ever worked in a statewide campaign. Because the candidate's previous campaign manager and administrative assistant was now working for another senator, the candidate's recently appointed administrative assistant, with no campaign experience, was named manager. The manager struggled, without complete success, to assume unquestioned control of the campaign. While he felt he had been promised final authority, the steering committee continued to rely on his predecessor for authorization of proposed campaign strategies.

Organizational difficulties infused every part of the campaign. Although nationally recognized consultants were hired early, their relationship with the local campaign got off to a bad start. The consultants were never sure to whom they should be reporting. The members of the steering committee worried about the costs of the early polls and media; they felt that the consultants were making strategic errors in media themes and placement, but with no authoritative figure to sign off on such decisions, and a lack of experience, "we went along with it because they were the media experts. There were all these people coming out of the woodwork. We ended up with so much input we began to question our own ability to make decisions."

The consultants themselves were frustrated. As one recalled after the campaign:

> The most persuasive reason to have the administrative assistant as campaign manager was that the candidate liked him and trusted him. They never considered if he was competent or not. They had to protect the candidate from the big bad consultants who were trying to steal money, were trying to steal the limelight. To me it was bizarre.

To make matters worse, the campaign had fundraising problems. Because the candidate had never had to raise large sums for congressional races, there was no pool of contributors on which to draw. Time pressures precluded a major direct mail drive for early money, the finance director was the candidate's personal lawyer and had no experience with political fundraising, and the candidate had made a decision not to accept PAC funds.

Thus, as the internal campaign phase ended, this challenger campaign, like many others, began with organizational disunity, a struggling fundraising effort, and inexperience at the top. Although the candidate's recognition levels were at this point much higher than the opponent's, the infrastructure to capitalize on it was not in place. If it had been faced with an opposition campaign with its own serious problems, the candidate might have won despite the setbacks. But the opposition was well organized and better financed. As the external campaign began in the fall, no one anticipated that this candidate would lose, but the campaign carried within it seeds of its own destruction and eventually sustained an upset defeat—outspent and outorganized because of its early weaknesses in the internal campaign. This illustration also points out the lack of experience many challengers, even at the statewide level, have with such campaigns, and the crucial role that paid consultants can play in providing such experience.

Frank Lautenberg's 1982 senatorial campaign in New Jersey demonstrates how a political unknown with enough money can put together the kind of early internal campaign that can lead to victory. When Democrat Lautenberg entered the June ten-candidate primary, which included two former members of Congress, he was totally unknown. A successful businessman who had built one of the nation's largest computer companies from the ground up, Lautenberg knew how to recruit talent. By spending $2 million, largely on television advertising, he managed to narrowly defeat the two representatives, who ran second and third, and win the primary with 26 percent of the vote. By August, he had a campaign strategy group that included Peter Hart, perhaps the best-known Democratic pollster, and Robert Squier, a nationally prominent media consultant. His campaign manager, Tim Ridley, had been a key figure in the 1980 Carter-Mondale campaign in Maryland (one of the six states they carried) and in Charles Robb's successful campaign for governor of Virginia in 1981—the first Democratic gubernatorial victory in that state in sixteen years.

Hart, Squier, and Ridley had worked together successfully in Virginia and functioned smoothly as a team. Hart was familiar with New Jersey; he had previously polled for the state's other senator and the recently retired two-term governor. Further, Lautenberg was prepared to spend another $3 million on the general election; in the end, he personally contributed over $4 million of the more than $5 million that was spent on his primary and general election efforts.

Thus this campaign was in an excellent position to deal with two key challenger problems, money and time. The almost inexhaustible supply of money bought an instant organization with expertise and knowledge about the state. It also solved another key challenger problem—recognition. The Lautenberg advertising campaign, which began in August, stressed the candidate's experience as the founder of a major high-tech company and his lifelong roots in New Jersey. The early task of the campaign was to set up Lautenberg as a credible alternative. All the planning took cognizance of this, and the race was ultimately successful.

Two Gubernatorial Races

The two Senate races we described show how challengers for the upper house build recognition, raise sufficient money, and deal with time constraints—or fail to. Gubernatorial challenger campaigns also face these problems, but differ in three ways. They are more likely to revolve around themes of competence and leadership and must incorporate whatever organizational and financial resources the state party has to offer. And the press, which takes gubernatorial campaigns more seriously and covers them more intensively, is a more important consideration. The similarities and differences come out in an examination of two gubernatorial efforts. The first is the 1982 campaign of Republican Lewis Rome, who was unsuccessful in unseating the incumbent Democratic governor of Connecticut. The second is the 1981 contest for an open seat in Virginia, which was ultimately won by the Democrat, Charles Robb.

Lewis Rome, the Republican nominee for governor of Connecticut, had held a leadership role in the State Senate and had run unsuccessfully for lieutenant governor four years earlier. He had a strong position in the state party, in a state where parties mattered. In Connecticut, nominees for office are selected at summer party conventions; primaries are held only if a losing candidate receives 20 percent of the convention vote and opts to challenge in a primary. Given the strength of the party organizations, few choose this route.

The need to gain support in the party convention means that candidates concentrate their time and resources almost entirely on the party regulars until only a few months before the general election, and therefore have little opportunity to make an impact on the electorate at large. As Thomas J. Collamore, a ranking staffer in the Rome campaign, described it:

> The candidates run around to all 169 towns in Connecticut and court these delegates to the convention. It's always the same damn people every year—Lew knew every one of them by name from the last campaign. You're spending all your time and money and resources courting these delegates when what you really ought to be doing is being in the newspapers talking about what you can do for Connecticut. It's a silent campaign within the party.

A poll done for Rome the winter before the convention made the dimensions of his problem clear. Although he was comfortably in front among Republicans, it also "showed him in horrible shape in name recognition. Among those who knew, he was going to get elected. Among the general public, he was going to get slaughtered because no one knew who he was." Another poll in August, seven months later and after the convention, showed virtually no improvement—"a feature of the Connecticut system, so inside-oriented until the final days." Rome, running against a moderately conservative Democratic incumbent who was the former party chair and who had good relationships with the Connecticut business community, was going to have to mount a massive media campaign to become known quickly. Because a substantial portion of Republican and independent voters in Connecticut live in the New York City media market, this is a particularly expensive proposition for a relatively small state. Rome needed to raise a lot of money very quickly.

But the money was not easily come by. Unlike Senate and House races, gubernatorial campaigns are not heavily supported by the national Republican party. The Rome campaign had good ties to the Republican Washington establishment; the deputy chair of the Republican National Committee was from Connecticut, and Vice President George Bush had longstanding family ties to the state. Although Rome received more national party money than any other Republican gubernatorial candidate that year, it still amounted to only about $90,000, less than half the party contribution to the Republican Senate incumbent running at the same time. Nor was it easy to raise money within the state. Fiscally speaking, the Democrats in Connecticut state government have always been at least as conservative as the Republicans. Connecticut is one of the few states without an income tax, and the Democratic governor, like his predecessors, saw no reason to change that. Moreover, his position on regulation of the insurance industry, many of whose national headquarters are in the state capital, was more flexible than Rome's. Connecticut's economy, dependent primarily on white collar jobs, was relatively healthy. The result for the Rome campaign was that "we never really had a finance chairman. Nobody wanted the job. The business community had a great thing going, they had a governor who will do what they tell him to do, and they decided they liked that."

Without enough money, the early paid media campaign was minimal. There was no television advertising before September, and there would never be any on New York City stations—it was simply too expensive.

Finally, there was the possibility of free coverage in the media, but here too, Rome ran into roadblocks. First, Rome's difficulties in raising money and the discouraging early polls were, as we have seen, exactly the signals that convince the media to ignore a race. Second, they had a much more exciting race to cover—the Senate race between incumbent Republican Lowell Weicker and challenger Toby Moffett. During the summer, when Rome desperately needed the coverage, Weicker was facing both the threat of a primary challenge from the vice president's brother, Prescott Bush, and a $200,000 negative media blitz by NCPAC. Both of these colorful events drew the press' attention heavily to the Senate race. The perceived closeness of the Senate race kept the attention on it through the early fall. Finally, Rome most needed free media play in the New York outlets to reach the vote-rich and generally Republican Connecticut suburbs there. It was impossible to get.

> The New York stations made a conscious effort to focus only on Weicker and Moffett because of the early polls, and to write the governor's race off. They told us that. We went to their studios for interviews and they didn't use them. It was a major problem and we couldn't surmount it. They wrote the campaign off.

With everyone else "writing the campaign off," the party activists in Connecticut followed.

> We had a meeting with all the town [Republican leaders] right after the convention and laid it on the line. We said we can't do it alone, we have to rely on your organizations, it has to be a grassroots campaign.... A lot of people chose to focus on the Senate race, and a lot of people thought the race wasn't winnable.

Additionally, the campaign had severe organizational problems. All the most experienced state campaign veterans had gone to Washington to take positions in the Reagan administration. Collamore, who took leave from his position in the Commerce Department and came back at the time of the July party convention, recalled:

> I got there and nothing had been done. He was in the headlines every day, on Connecticut TV every day, and he was in danger of blowing the convention because of horrible organization. The delegate vote was extremely close. All the really top talent had left town. He didn't even have a campaign manager until after the convention.

Thus Lewis Rome, a highly competent candidate, had a campaign that was in serious trouble by Labor Day. His eventual loss by a margin of four points in November raises the question of who would have been elected governor had Rome been able to run a well-financed and well-organized campaign early in the year.

Charles Robb's Virginia gubernatorial campaign differs sharply from the Rome campaign. In this race, both Robb and his opponent were very well known to the voters, both state parties took the race seriously, and both campaigns were adequately financed. Robb was the incumbent lieutenant governor; his opponent was the state's attorney general. Robb's deputy campaign manager recalled: "They had been running against each other for the past four years. This was the match of the titans. The benchmark poll in March had both of them in the 90's on name recognition. They both only had negatives of about 5 or 6 percent."

On the surface, things did not look promising for Robb. The Virginia Democratic party had gone into serious decline because of the split between old-line conservatives, on the one hand, and blacks and other liberals on the other. The split was symbolized by the decision of long-time conservative senator Harry Byrd to stand for reelection as an independent beginning in 1970 to avoid the internecine warfare of a Democratic primary. Aside from Byrd, Republicans had dominated races for statewide offices all through the 1970s. Democrats had been unable to carry the state for a presidential, gubernatorial, or senatorial candidate; by 1980 only one Democratic representative remained in the Virginia delegation. An analysis of the state's politics at the time of the gubernatorial election concluded, "In no other state in recent years have Democrats experienced such a political famine." [27]

Charles Robb, the only Democratic elected statewide official at the time, was to the left of the Byrd Democrats on some social issues such as race, but otherwise culturally and fiscally conservative. As a campaign operative described him, "He looks like a marine, he talks like a marine, he *is* a marine." He was not the ideal candidate of either wing of the Democratic party, but he was not entirely unacceptable to either. With Byrd removed, Democratic party candidates had come from the liberal end of the spectrum, and had, in the words of David Doak, Robb's campaign manager, "developed a methodology of losing." Robb had demonstrated he could win statewide, and the Democrats were desperate. As Doak's deputy remembered, "I got there and everybody said if we don't win this there won't be a party. If they didn't win they were through. Whether you were liberal, black, the whole left wing of the party said, fine, we're all going with you."

The Byrd wing similarly fell into line. Robb's opponent had run against a Byrd Democrat and beat him in the attorney general's race, and they would not forgive him or support him. The local inner circle of the Robb campaign contained every element among Virginia Democrats. A lawyer and a state senator were his preeminent fundraisers in the "conservative Democratic establishment, which is where all the money comes from." The other key local advisers were the head of the Coalition—the Byrd Democrats—who had not backed a Democratic candidate in ten years, a state senator who was a leader among white liberals, and the head of the Virginia Black Caucus, "who held that part of the coalition through some difficult times." Well financed, with the total support of all elements of his party, and with a free hand to run the kind of campaign he wanted to, Robb could organize early and well. David Doak notes: "We had eight months to put the campaign together. It took about three months to gain true control of the campaign, establish our people in key positions. The last five months we were a well-oiled machine, everybody working together, understanding each other." By early fall, Robb could not have been in a better position to embark upon the external campaign.

The Challenger: A Summary

As we observed at the start of this chapter, most challengers face serious deficits of time, money, organization, and recognition. If they do not make up these deficits quickly, they have likely lost the contest long before election day. Although it is not enough by itself, sufficient money is usually the key to solving the other problems. If challengers do not have the kind of track record that will convince PACs, party organizations, and frequent individual contributors that their races are good investments, heavy personal spending is probably necessary.

The challengers who surmount these hurdles can then go on the next stage of electoral contests—the need to set the agenda of the campaign and seize control of its dialogue. We examine that phase of a campaign in the next chapter.

Notes

1. Mario M. Cuomo, *Diaries of Mario M. Cuomo: The Campaign for Governor* (New York: Random House, 1984), 71.
2. See the discussion of career paths in Larry Sabato, *Goodbye to Good-time Charlie: The American Governorship Transformed*, 2d ed. (Washington, D.C.: CQ Press, 1983), 33-45.
3. David Rohde, "Risk-Bearing and Progressive Ambition: The Case of Members of the U.S. House of Representatives," *American Journal of Political Science* 23 (February 1979): 1-26.
4. Richard F. Fenno, Jr., *The United States Senate: A Bicameral Perspective* (Washington, D.C.: American Enterprise Institute, 1982), 43.
5. Gary C. Jacobson and Samuel Kernell, *Strategy and Choice in Congressional Elections* (New Haven: Yale University Press, 1981). See also Robert J. Huckshorn and Robert C. Spencer, *The Politics of Defeat: Campaigning for Congress* (Amherst: University of Massachusetts Press, 1971).
6. Although by definition, challengers win all open seats, in absolute terms more new representatives arrive by defeating incumbents. Of the total of fifty-three close House races in 1984, forty-five, or 85 percent, involved incumbents. Many open seats are safe for the party of the member vacating them. Of the twenty-three open seats in 1984, only nine, or 39 percent, were decided by 10 percent or less. Among the forty-three new representatives of 1984, twenty-seven were open-seat victors, as compared with sixteen who upset incumbents. However, in 1982, twenty-three victors defeated incumbents and only eight took open seats. The figures for 1980 are thirty and eleven, respectively.
7. Peter Clarke and Susan H. Evans: *Covering Campaigns: Journalism in Congressional Elections* (Stanford, Calif.: Stanford University Press, 1983), 32.
8. Cuomo, *Diaries*, 153.
9. Ibid., 153-54.
10. Malcolm L. Jewell, *Representation in State Legislatures* (Lexington: University Press of Kentucky, 1982), 29.
11. In a presentation at the Eagleton Institute of Politics, Rutgers University, New Brunswick, New Jersey, September 20, 1982.
12. Quoted in Alan Clem, *The Making of Congressmen: Seven Campaigns of 1974* (North Scituate, Mass.: Duxbury Press, 1976), 140.
13. See Lorene Hanley Duquin, "Door to Door Campaigning: How to Get the Most Out of Your Pedometer," *Campaigns and Elections* 3 (Spring 1982): 15-24.

14. For example, Larry J. Sabato, *The Rise of Political Consultants: New Ways of Winning Elections* (New York: Basic Books, 1981), chapter 4.

15. "C & E Direct Mail Fundraising Roundtable: The Pros Speak," *Campaigns and Elections* 3 (Fall 1980). See chapter 8 for further discussion of this point.

16. Hank Parkinson, "How to Get Elected to Your State Legislature," *Campaigns and Elections* 1 (Summer 1980): 50.

17. Michael Barone and Grant Ujifusa, *Almanac of American Politics 1984* (Washington, D.C.: National Journal, 1983), 446.

18. Barone and Ujifusa, *Almanac of American Politics 1984*, 1335. This list apparently inadvertently omits successful Virginia Democratic challenger Norman Sisisky; see ibid., 1217.

19. Everett C. Ladd with Charles D. Hadley, *Transformations of the American Party System*, 2d ed. (New York: Norton, 1978), 377, 377n.

20. *Congressional Quarterly Weekly Report*, July 2, 1983, 1351.

21. Thomas E. Mann and Norman J. Ornstein, eds., *The American Elections of 1982* (Washington: D.C.: American Enterprise Institute), 64-65; *New York Times*, December 4, 1984, A29.

22. Mark C. Westlye, "Competitiveness of Senate Seats and Voting Behavior in Senate Elections," *American Journal of Political Science* 27 (May 1983): 253. Low key races were defined as those in which the challenger trailed at least two to one in fundraising and which the preelection issue of *Congressional Quarterly Weekly Report* judged as noncompetitive.

23. John R. Hibbing and Sara L. Brandes, "State Population and the Electoral Success of U.S. Senators," *American Journal of Political Science* 27 (November 1983), 817.

24. See Barone and Ujifusa, *Almanac of American Politics 1984*, 1335; and Richard P. Conlon, "Solving the PAC Problem Without a PAC Limit," paper presented at the Annual Meeting of the American Political Science Association, Washington, D.C., August 30-September 2, 1984.

25. Fenno, *The United States Senate*, 21.

26. Louis Sandy Maisel, *From Obscurity to Oblivion: Running in the Congressional Primary* (Knoxville: University of Tennessee Press, 1982), 60.

27. Alan Ehrenhalt, ed., *Politics in America 1982* (Washington, D.C.: Congressional Quarterly Inc., 1983), 1225.

Setting the Agenda: Campaign Themes

6

You have to define the race. Find those issue differences where the public agrees with your side. And your opponent is doing the same thing. And the secret to it is that your issues are the important issues.

—David Doak, political consultant

When campaigns go public and enter their external phase, their key task is to communicate a message that will convince a majority of the electorate to vote for one candidate rather than another. To be successful, a candidate must now *set the agenda* of the campaign. Setting the agenda means advancing a set of themes or issues that the electorate will find more convincing than the opponent's. Jeff Greenfield, who used to work in campaigns and now writes and broadcasts about them, described it this way:

> We are talking about what the undergraduates at Princeton once labeled "megacepts," essential themes which knit the entire campaign, from speeches to advertising to slogan to press interviews, together.... The choice of such a theme is extremely difficult, because it depends on a specific mix of the candidate and the political atmosphere. The same megacept which crashes on takeoff in one election year can take a candidate to victory in the next.[1]

Agenda-setting in a campaign is pursued through all the means of mass communication—those that the candidate controls entirely (all forms of advertising, including direct mail) and those over which less influence can be exercised—the news media, partially controlled by print and broadcast journalists. Political consultants generally refer to these communication channels as *paid media* and *free media*; they are discussed in detail in chapter 7. In this chapter, we will analyze the themes candidates put forward and consider what influences their choice and what contributes to the selection of a persuasive theme.

The Nature of the Campaign Theme

Choosing a thematic emphasis is the most fundamental decision candidates and their organizations make. As Greenfield writes: "Your first task in mapping out a campaign is to put aside all thought of alliances, marketing strategy, and makeup artists and figure out *what your campaign is all about. What is the premise on which you run for office?"* [2] Setting out these basic assumptions or themes is the foundation of a campaign's grand strategy. Without a theme a campaign is likely to founder. It is no wonder, then, that most successful campaigns have clear and convincing themes.

Selecting the Theme: The Role of Issues

It is important to understand how campaign themes are related to issues. The ideal model of democratic elections assumes that candidates advance a set of detailed issue positions that give voters clear alternatives, that voters understand the alternatives being offered to them, and that they make their choices on that basis. Scholars discovered long ago that this situation never holds true. Even in the current information-rich environment, recent surveys have shown, two out of five voters cannot correctly identify the issue positions of both presidential candidates, and four out of five cannot do the same for congressional candidates. [3]

This does not mean that issues are irrelevant. In the era of strong party identification, the party banner under which candidates ran served as a shorthand for a set of issue positions, although "Democrat" might have signified very different concepts to voters in the rural South and in the urban North, as "Republican" did in the urban East and the rural Midwest. Today issues can themselves play a role in cuing voters, but not in the sense posited by democratic theorists. Although a candidate may have detailed position papers on a whole range of issues, campaigns cannot be waged on all of them. Voters have neither the time nor the interest to weigh every issue carefully. Moreover, they are likely to agree with a given candidate on some issues and not on others. Campaigns have now taken on the role of substantially determining *which* issues voters choose to think about.

Candidates use issues not only to appeal to voters who agree with them on policy but to convey messages about their personal qualities. Candidates cannot directly say to voters that they are competent, compassionate, or trustworthy, but they can suggest these qualities through the way they talk about issues. As a Republican consultant told a group of hopeful challengers at a party candidate training school, "Issues are a vehicle to build images." [4] Campaigns emphasize a limited range of issues with which they hope to identify a candidate to his or her benefit: "Issues are like chips that get moved around a board, the means but not the ends of political life." [5]

When a campaign organization surveys the issue context in which an election occurs, there is an almost limitléss number of possibilities from which to choose. All issues fall into two basic types, however. One is the substantive, positional issue. Where does the candidate stand on tax reform, national defense, foreign policy, or domestic programs? The other type focuses on personal qualities. Does the candidate convey leadership, compassion, empathy, integrity, trustworthiness?

Almost all personal themes are based on what political scientists call "valance" issues, or, in common speech, "motherhood and apple pie" issues—everyone is for and not "against" qualities like trustworthiness or leadership. When elections revolve around valance issues, the campaign agenda becomes "Which candidate is more effective in demonstrating the desirable qualities?" Some substantive questions appear to be positional but, depending on how they are presented, can also be valance issues. If candidates treat a substantive issue as one they are better equipped to handle than their opponent because of their personal qualities rather than because of any programmatic solutions they may have, then positional issues become valance issues. Democratic media consultant Tony Schwartz says of a substantive issue often treated in this fashion: "I don't think inflation is an issue. Who's *for* it? . . . The real issue is which of the two candidates would best be able to deal with [it]." [6] Genuine positional issues, in contrast, have two sides, and the candidates are perceived as taking opposing views. The challenge for campaigns that turn on positional issues is to select the ones that capture public imagination and garner public approval. If the issue is strong enough, it may come to be what Democratic pollster Bill Hamilton called a "referendum issue." In other words, the agenda of the campaign becomes a yes-or-no vote on candidates based on their positions on the issue.

Selecting the Theme:
The Role of Polls and Pollsters

The substance of campaign themes varies widely, but to be persuasive, they must be carefully tailored to the given candidate, to his or her opponent, to the constituency, and to the current political environment.

To use an analogy from marketing, the choice of a theme has to do with "product positioning" and the identification of a "comparative advantage." Comparative advantages are "the unique characteristics that differentiate a candidate from his competitors, which give his supporters a reason to prefer him over the competition." [7] A given candidate cannot pick a seemingly attractive theme out of the air and expect it to work. The theme must be credible coming from that candidate; it must fit the constituency, and it must be more convincing than the opponent's theme. The information that strategists need to determine appropriate campaign themes now comes from polls.

The most certain indicator of a state-of-the-art campaign is the presence of technologically sophisticated consultants—pollsters and media advisers. The two work together closely, for it is the pollster's findings that determine the message that media consultants design. Their functions have always been a part of American campaigns. The media adviser who produces elaborate television commercials is the direct descendant of the nineteenth-century writer of partisan newspaper articles and political tracts. Although the modern campaign's forebears did not have scientific sampling techniques or elaborate data analysis, the straw poll has a lineage that stretches back to the early 1800s. [8] What distinguishes the modern consultants is their autonomy of action, the technology available to them, and, in the most recent years, the growing role of pollsters in shaping the message that media consultants convey. We will elaborate on each of these developments.

In the days of party-line voting and party-directed campaigns, party leaders shaped the media message and directed the canvassing activities. It was Mark Hanna's party minions who produced the McKinley pamphlets pouring out of Republican headquarters in 1896, and the public relations director of the Republican National Committee who worked with his former colleagues in the advertising agencies who produced the first campaign television commercials for Eisenhower in 1952. Similarly, parties directed the canvassing efforts that predated polls. In the early twentieth century, workers in New York's Tammany Hall machine would fan out to key locations across the city, asking people their voting choices: "Thus, Tammany had what it regarded as a reliable day-to-day reading of the election situation during the campaign period." [9]

As the party organizations declined, campaigns turned to media consultants—first in advertising agencies and then in the political firms that sprang up—to devise thematic messages. Scientific polling began as an arcane specialty with a limited number of practitioners. It had to await the spread of the computer and the growth in the number of specialists before it became a staple of campaigns below the presidential level. This occurred in the late 1960s and early 1970s, fortuitously coterminous with the rise in the number of independent and ticket-splitting voters. Then the pollster was ready to step into the shoes of the party organization. Democratic pollster Bill Hamilton noted that "as political bosses trail off, it's natural that the pollster delivers where the campaign is going. The bosses, opinion leaders, and labor people used to suggest how to get their people. Now the pollsters do. They have the data."

Some media consultants responded to the increased importance of polling by creating their own polling organizations. More commonly, however, media consultants interact with, and even take direction from, independent pollsters. Republican consultant Vince Breglio, who began as a pollster, described the changes in the relationship:

> The media person's role has changed. It used to be that campaigns would go to their media person and ask for strategy. Now they ask their pollster. The pollster translates those numbers into the strategic recommendations that identify who your voter should be, what is of greatest concern to those who should be voting for you, and how you can best influence those groups. The media person becomes more of a technician . . . more of an implementer [who] gets marching orders from the pollster: "Now come back with several scripts so we can determine if you're on target or not."

The Polling Package. Pollsters have developed a fairly standard package for statewide races, consisting of benchmark, trend, and tracking polls. A *benchmark poll* gives a campaign information about the voting preferences and issue concerns of different groups in the electorate and a detailed reading of the images voters have of the candidates in the race—information that dictates a campaign's allocation of resources in a variety of important ways. It tells the campaign how and where to schedule the candidate, what issues to stress, and how to convey them. It suggests the theme and content of broadcast advertising, and where it should be placed.

Ideally, a benchmark poll is done early in the winter of election year.[10] It is followed by three or four fairly detailed *trend polls* from spring to early fall to determine the success of the campaigns in altering candidate images and voting preferences. By early October, a campaign begins its *tracking* polls by taking short nightly interviews of a smaller number of respondents, keyed to the variables that have assumed importance in the campaign. Combining a few nights of tracking polls into *rolling averages* provides a larger and more reliable sample for general strategic assessment.[11] For reasons of cost, speed, and efficiency, almost all political surveys are done by telephone rather than as face-to-face interviews. Ideally, the polling program for campaigns below the statewide level should follow the same format. Most of them, however, cannot afford such an elaborate undertaking.

A typical benchmark poll for a statewide candidate begins with "screening questions" to ask respondents if they are registered, how they have voted in the past, and whether they are likely to vote in the coming election. Interviews with those deemed unlikely to vote are terminated. Because in most statewide elections half or fewer of eligible adults actually vote, effective screening questions to assess who those voters will be are crucial.

The survey goes on to ask respondents to give their opinion of all the potential candidates in the race ("favorable, unfavorable, or one of the best"). Respondents are then asked to rate their perceptions of each candidate's credibility and compassion ("doesn't care about people like me" versus "cares about people like me," for example) and of each candidate's performance in office ("he's done a lot to hold down taxes," or "he's grown a lot in office"), and to answer a large number of questions about issues—both the respondents' view of them and their perceptions of the candidates' views. These questions are followed by a number of head-to-head voting choices.

At the time most benchmark polls are done, before state primaries, there may be a number of potential candidates, and different combinations of candidates usually produce different potential electoral outcomes. Surveys may also include questions in which a candidate is matched against a hypothetical rival whom the campaign assumes would give their candidate the toughest race—a form of "worst case" analysis. If a candidate can defeat a "perfect" opponent, he or she can defeat anyone. Conversely, if a "perfect" opponent can win, it is the campaign's job to ensure that the real opponent is not seen as that "perfect" contender.

If a candidate has any personal or political weaknesses that could become an issue in the campaign, respondents may be asked how such shortcomings—including brushes with the law, marital problems, and real or rumored scandals—would affect their choice. Polls also often test the credibility of possible explanations or rationalizations of the candidate's difficulties.

Surveys then go on to test a variety of themes that the campaign is considering. Such themes, about both the candidate and an opponent, are presented to the respondent as "scenarios" or "editorials." In a survey for an experienced challenger, the "best case scenario" read like this:

> X was a great governor. He held down government spending, kept taxes low, and ran the state like a business. He never turned his back on basic human needs. He fought for money for highways, fought for

money for education, and he did a lot to help poor people. He would be a great senator.

In contrast, the "worst case scenario" argued:

> X was a governor who put the needs of business ahead of the needs of people. He turned his back on the needs of poor people. He put the needs of business ahead of the need to protect the environment. He did a very poor job of running the state. He would not make a good United States senator.

After each scenario is presented, respondents are asked to give their overall reaction to the statement, to indicate whether they think the assertions are true, and to weigh the strength of their agreement or disagreement with each charge in the two statements. Similar scenarios are presented for the candidate's opponent, and corresponding assessments are done. When "scenario" probes are taken, respondents are often reasked the head-to-head questions to see if the information provided has changed their voting choices, on the assumption that this is the dialogue that will take place during the campaign.

Such fine-grained examination of the impact of different campaign themes is the greatest difference between private campaign polls and public polls done by newspapers, television stations, and academic researchers. Public polls are retrospective—they try to find explanations of why the public holds its particular opinions at a particular moment. Campaign polls have a prospective orientation—they examine how the public will react to different messages and themes. And there is no doubt that this testing of alternative themes and strategies can have an enormous effect.

For example, at the beginning of the 1982 New Jersey Senate race between Representative Millicent Fenwick, a Republican, and businessman Frank Lautenberg, both the public polls and the candidates' own polls showed Lautenberg trailing Fenwick by more than 20 points. The Lautenberg forces tested a variety of themes in their benchmark poll taken in the late summer. Lautenberg's manager described the results: "At the beginning of the poll, it was 27-52 in favor of Fenwick. By the end—we were introducing this information—by the end, we were ahead 39-38. We knew what information, which strategies would work and which ones wouldn't. The benchmark gave us some precision in terms of where we were going."

The actual outcome of this race was a narrow victory for Lautenberg, substantially achieved by a multimillion-dollar media campaign that sent the messages the pollsters predicted would be effective. The Lautenberg campaign was aided by external political events and discord in the Fenwick campaign organization. Nevertheless, the artful use of polling was strongly influential in turning an unknown candidate into a winner.

The final components of a typical questionnaire deal with the wider political environment in which the campaign takes place, like the job rating and performance of the president and voter demographics, such as party identification, age, occupation, education, marital status, religion, ethnicity, and race. It may also include questions about respondents' media habits to assist campaigns in determining where to place print and broadcast messages.

Good pollsters are careful to tailor a survey to each candidate and to make the campaign staff feel that whatever their other commitments, they are sensitive to the race at hand. Surveys that ask the same questions whatever the race—known as "canned" or "packaged" polls— miss the idiosyncracies peculiar to an individual contest. The campaign issues director for an experienced Senate incumbent explains why they chose one national pollster over another:

> X had a feel for the region, and Y was too intellectual, too set. He had a campaign and poll strategy that he ran in every campaign, that was not tailored, or not sensitive to, specific factors in the campaign. He also would have too many candidates and not enough time to devote to us— that was a major concern of the senator.

Interpreting Polls. In addition to being sensitive to the particular circumstances of a given campaign, a mark of the good pollster is the ability to read what practitioners call the *internals* of polling results. Experienced pollsters know that an early strong or weak showing is often more apparent than real. It is the pollster's job to go beneath the numbers and tell the candidate what they really mean. In some cases, this means being the messenger who brings the bad news. Unsuccessful congressional challenger Sandy Maisel recounts his pollster's summary of benchmark results: his incumbent opponent had the highest positive evaluation the firm had ever recorded among voters in the opposition party; "no strategy for a November election appears feasible." [12] Even worse is having to tell an apparently strong leader that he or she has serious problems. As one national pollster says: "There are lots of cases where an incumbent has a high job rating, but with a little higher than normal negatives, with the wrong words being said about him. We sort of know that a year later, with the right campaign against him, that guy is really in trouble."

Both the greatest satisfaction and the greatest frustration come when a pollster sees the promise in overtly discouraging results. A candidate like Frank Lautenberg, who can see the potential in the internals and is willing and able to commit resources to a "hopeless" race, is the pollster's joy and not the rare exception. The needlessly cowardly candidate is ubiquitous as well, however. As Bill Hamilton explained it:

> As much as the pollster says "your opponent's vote is soft ... because they generally like you, as this segment makes up its mind, they are going to move in your direction," you have candidates start thinking about getting out of the race. The pollster's got to be strong enough to make them understand a more sophisticated analysis than they can make of the data.
>
> I've had a candidate get out of the race. The poll showed him thirteen down, but also that the incumbent's support was very soft. I fought, and he still got out. His administrative assistant decided to run using that poll—never did any more polling—and he became a United States senator. Candidates get it in their heads about where they want to be when you do a poll, and if they're not there, they're not sophisticated enough to look underneath.

Some examples reveal the kinds of advice that pollsters can give to shore up the seemingly invincible candidate with feet of clay or the apparently hopeless case who has genuine potential. One gubernatorial incumbent running for reelection had an extremely high job rating in his benchmark poll and easily defeated his likely opponents in head-to-head questions. However, his benchmark also showed that half of the electorate had specific issue-related complaints about him and that he could garner only a bare 50 percent in a head-to-head question against a hypothetical strong opponent. His pollster recommended a summer media initiative aimed directly at responding to the troublesome issues. The trend polls conducted later showed increasing strength and fewer complaints; the incumbent eventually went on to win two to one.

On the other hand, Edward King of Massachusetts was not discouraged when his February 1978 benchmark showed him with 11 percent of the Democratic primary vote for governor, in contrast to the 64 percent who favored his incumbent opponent, Michael Dukakis. The survey's internals showed that large percentages of Democratic primary voters said that "under no circumstances" would they support a candidate who opposed minimum jail sentences for violent crimes, opposed the death penalty, or favored abortion—all positions taken by Dukakis. King's campaign manager said of these findings, "That's when we discovered we could get significant defections from Dukakis if we could let people know where he stood and where we stood on the issues." [13] After a primary campaign highlighting Dukakis's stand on these social issues, King defeated Dukakis by a 9 percent margin.

These two examples—in one, the incumbent's record was made the focus of the campaign; in the other, social issues were stressed— illustrate thematic strategies that, with local twists, have been used in a large number of contests. Good pollsters are also adept, however, at lifting from obscurity peculiarly local issues with the potential to become powerful themes. Such a strategy almost won the 1984 Democratic senatorial nomination in Texas for Representative Kent Hance.

Hance was running in the Democratic primary against a well-known state legislator, Lloyd Doggett, and a former member of Congress and previous senatorial candidate, Bob Krueger. The race ended in a virtual three-way dead heat, with Hance winning a place in a runoff contest by only a few hundred votes. Less than a month before the election, however, Hance had been in third place, trailing badly. His pollster described the events of the last few weeks:

> I was called into the Hance campaign twenty-five days before the primary election. The poll we took showed Hance at 7 [percent], Doggett at 23, and Krueger at 61. Hance's staff gave me twenty issues where he differed with at least one of his opponents. We narrowed that down to four on which he differed with both. Three were too narrow, but immigration really cut across the whole spectrum.
> We ran one TV spot, essentially, for three weeks, as much as we could. For three weeks, that was all that was on, every day. It hit on amnesty for illegal aliens. "If amnesty for illegal aliens is approved, within five years, two million people would be eligible for welfare." PAUSE. "Think about it." PAUSE. "Kent Hance is opposed to it. Lloyd Doggett and Bob Krueger are in favor of it." We put in a lot of pauses so that people could conjure up their own reasons for not wanting an amnesty. In twenty-five days, Hance went from 7 to 32, Krueger went from 61 to 32, and Doggett went from 23 to 32. It moved people dramatically and in a very short period of time.

For this particular candidate in this particular race, immigration was a powerful local issue. The House of Representatives was nearing the end of a widely publicized debate on immigration legislation, which included among its provisions amnesty for all illegal aliens who had entered the country prior to 1982. It was an especially sensitive issue in Texas, where the long border with Mexico provides many crossing points for illegal aliens, and which must absorb large numbers of immigrants, legal and illegal. Hance actively opposed amnesty in the House debate. In the end, the amnesty provision was approved and Hance narrowly lost to Doggett in the runoff. Without the issue, Hance was a candidate without a chance; with it, he narrowly missed victory.

Thus good benchmark and trend polling help campaigns identify potential themes. Successful campaigns are those that choose the most effective themes, based in part on their judgment of what the theme and responses of the opposition campaign will be. This varies with each individual contest.

Some Winning and Losing Campaign Themes

We next examine a number of campaigns, to capture the variations in themes and extract what few general rules apply to all campaigns in selecting a theme.

Valance Issue as Theme. Sometimes the major issue in a campaign is judged by both sides to be so compelling that the two candidates will have essentially the same theme. The campaign debate then revolves around which candidate can deal better with the overriding problem—what we described near the start of this chapter as a valance issue. Consider two recent Republican Senate candidates, Millicent Fenwick in New Jersey (who lost) and John Chafee in Rhode Island (who won). Both ran for election at a time when unemployment had reached its highest level since the Great Depression. Thus each made jobs a central campaign theme. The theme worked for Chafee, but backfired for Fenwick. A closer look at the candidates, their opponents, and the campaign environment shows why.

Fenwick was a member of the House of Representatives, serving on the Committee on Foreign Affairs. She was widely admired for her independence and integrity and had been called the conscience of the Congress for her opposition to special-interest legislation and to an increase in congressional salaries at the height of a severe recession. She was running for the Senate seat vacated by Democrat Harrison Williams, who had recently been convicted in the Abscam scandal.

Fenwick's strong reputation for honesty was a plus in New Jersey, whose citizens were disgusted with the aura of corruption that had long surrounded many of the state's politicians. The absence of long-term incumbent Williams at election time reminded voters what a different image of the state Fenwick would bring to the rest of the country. "Ethics in government" was a particularly powerful theme for this candidate in this state.

New Jerseyans were also very concerned about the state of the economy, as were most other Americans. Also, like the country at large, they were then split down the middle on whether President Reagan's economic program would hinder or promote economic recovery. In the polls, a very narrow majority sided with the president.

Along with a number of other northeastern Republican legislators, Fenwick expressed mixed feelings about the Reagan program. A firm belief in the value of a balanced budget led her to support the president frequently. On the other hand, her concern for the genuinely downtrodden and her suspicion about the worth of some expensive weapons programs made her a less than ardent presidential supporter on some important issues.

Integrity and an economic program to combat unemployment thus became the major thematic options for the Fenwick campaign. Although the campaign did not ignore the former, the candidate herself, against the advice of some of her staff, chose to wage the battle primarily on the latter. In her announcement of candidacy, she declared, "The issue is jobs, jobs, jobs."

But Fenwick did not have a clear and strong record of *leadership* in tackling unemployment. In fact, she had openly opposed the two largest recent job-creation projects in New Jersey—the building of a major sports complex (because of environmental concerns) and the development of Atlantic City as a gambling resort (because of her opposition to legalized gambling). In contrast, her opponent, Frank Lautenberg, was a political newcomer whose computer corporation had created many jobs. Lautenberg was successful in characterizing Fenwick's positions not as primarily "pro-environment" or "anti-gambling" but rather as "anti-jobs." Without a record of public service, he had only one strong suit— which was the argument that as a businessman he had created jobs and knew how to do it. As Robert Squier, Lautenberg's media adviser, said after the election, the challenger's staff was delighted when Fenwick announced at the outset that the chief issue in the campaign was " 'jobs, jobs, jobs.' We were afraid she would say it was 'character, character, character.' "

Fenwick chose as her dominant theme the one that gave her opponent the comparative advantage, instead of the one that would have given it to her. Alternatively, she might have contrasted her support for some aspects of President Reagan's program with Lautenberg's support for the unpopular Jimmy Carter, an argument that the polls on both sides showed was also convincing to the New Jersey electorate. As Lautenberg's campaign manager commented, "If, in September, they had started to try to raise the fiscal issues, that would have been very interesting." Instead, in the words of a strategist in the Fenwick campaign who had severe misgivings about the focus on jobs, "Lautenberg took her theme away from her."

John Chafee, on the other hand, was a senior member of the Senate Finance Committee and chairman of its subcommittee on Savings, Pension, and Investment Policy. He had a record of opposing President Reagan on economic issues and "offering the best organized challenge to the first round of Reagan budget cuts." [14] This was a popular position in Rhode Island, which had given the president only 37 percent of its vote in 1980, his smallest share in any state. Nor was Chafee suddenly adopting a stance out of character with his political record. As a three-term governor of Rhode Island before election to the Senate, he had pushed for increases in state spending for social and welfare programs, calling for a "state version of the Great Society." In addition to having an economic record attractive to many Democrats, Chafee was a hero to some for his work on the Senate Environment Committee and had a good record on women's issues. Thus, as his press secretary, Cleve Corlett, commented, "Chafee went into that campaign with constituencies which in most states should have belonged to a Democratic candidate—Council for a Livable World, the environmentalists, the Rhode Island Women's Political Caucus."

Chafee's opponent, Julius Michaelson, was the attorney for the state AFL-CIO, an apparently good base in a heavily blue-collar and unionized state. It was natural for him to choose jobs, and an attack on Chafee as a "Reagan robot," as the theme of his campaign. However, the "Reagan robot" charge was a difficult one to substantiate. Chafee's record demonstrated that he had supported Jimmy Carter's legislative program more strongly than Reagan's. He had voted against funds for the B-1 bomber, against the constitutional amendment for a balanced budget, against deleting funds for public works jobs, and for federal subsidy of home mortgage rates—all key votes against the president's positions. Chafee had the credentials that Millicent Fenwick lacked. As Chafee's press secretary described it:

> The agenda was largely jobs. Chafee figured out early that irrespective of the national economy, Rhode Island has severe economic problems. One of the major themes of his legislation and everything else had been jobs. He was instrumental in solving a dispute between the Navy and Electric Boat, which is the state's biggest employer. We solved that, took the credit for it. Despite Michaelson's labor connections, we got 40 percent of the labor vote. He staked out jobs and had a legislative record to back it up.

Issue and Image Themes. Not every political race is like the New Jersey and the Rhode Island contests, in both of which the two candidates fought to attain the high ground on the same valance issue. In some races the competitors stress different themes, hoping that the one they have chosen will prove more convincing. Candidates may highlight different issues, they may present contrasting personal images of themselves and their opponents, or one candidate may emphasize a specific issue while the other contender bases the campaign on personal images.

Three campaigns in the 1980s illustrate each of these cases. The 1982 gubernatorial race in New York was fought on opposing issues. Voters, narrowly rejecting Lewis Lehrman's call for greatly reduced state spending and taxing, opted for Mario Cuomo's view of the state as a "family" with obligations to the needy. On the other hand, in the 1981 Virginia gubernatorial race, neither Republican Marshall Coleman nor

Democrat Charles Robb offered voters a heavy dose of issue specifics; rather, they presented a choice of competing, relatively amorphous images. Coleman's central theme was that voters should solidify their shift to the philosophy of the Republican party. He campaigned in the shadow of sixteen years of Republican governors and of President Reagan's clear 1980 victory in the state with the slogan "Keep a good thing going." Robb, conversely, wished to direct the voters' attention to his position to the right of prior Democratic candidates; his was a candidacy of the relatively conservative element of the Democratic party, which had controlled the state for a century before the Republican rise in the late 1960s, but with more enlightened racial attitudes. This message was encapsulated in his slogan, "For a Virginia future worthy of her past."

The third variation occurred in the 1980 Senate race in Indiana. Challenger Dan Quayle ran successfully on a clearly defined platform emphasizing three interrelated issues: the need to lower taxes, to reduce spending, and to speed deregulation. Incumbent Birch Bayh chose instead to stress his image strengths as a long-term incumbent who could deliver for the state and who knew and understood its citizens. With the slogan "Birch Bayh fighting for Indiana," local ads showed Bayh talking informally with coal miners in the southern part of the state about energy concerns, with auto workers in the northern part of the state about fair trade, and with farmers in central Indiana about agricultural policy and gasohol. The ads were less about Bayh's issue positions than about his warm and caring nature and his lengthy service to the people of Indiana.

Themes and Credibility. Whatever theme a candidate chooses, it is critical that he or she follow a key precept: *"Do not offend reality."* [15] Offending reality can mean depicting a candidate in a way that is not persuasive to voters, or depicting the opponent in a negative way that is not convincing to them either. In Indiana, Bayh found it difficult to persuade voters that his major concern was "fighting for Indiana" when he had spent the past eight years running for president and leading the fight on controversial national issues, most of which were very unpopular in his state. A long-time staffer recalled:

> Birch is the classic example of how a presidential campaign can change a Senator's image at home. In 1962 he sold himself to Indiana as the all-American boy. In 1968 he sold himself as the all-American Senator. He was not into controversial issues at the time. He did not have a highly partisan image out there.
>
> With the coming of the presidential campaign you had your nice young Senator turning into a partisan, anti-Nixon, anti-Republican guy.... A lot of his supporters were horrified at their new profile Senator. [16]

Another staffer concurred:

> There was a very definite feeling on the part of a significant number of people that he was too liberal, too associated with Eastern-ers, that his staff was not from Indiana anymore, that he had lost touch personally with his constituents. Bayh's strength in Indiana was primarily due to the fact that people liked him and felt he really cared about them and their problems. And he did. But it was hard to sustain that image given his presidential campaign.[17]

Bayh had barely survived his 1974 race (with 51 percent of the vote) with a campaign based on local issues and concern for the voters—and the help of the Watergate backlash against Republicans. But by 1980, he had run hard for president once more, lost embarrassingly, and was caught in a national trend uncongenial to liberal Democrats. This time his themes were unpersuasive, and he lost his Senate seat.

In the Virginia gubernatorial campaign Marshall Coleman ran into problems similar to Bayh's. Although Coleman was running as a strong supporter of President Reagan and a successor to several conservative Republican governors, he had campaigned in his previous race for state attorney general as a relatively liberal Republican and "was suspected of progressive tendencies."[18] A strategist for his successful opponent recalls, "It was a real issue of trust and character, that he was one way four years ago and now he's this way. Who is the real Marshall Coleman?"

Attacks on opponents also fail when the electorate does not find them credible. Although "attack themes" vary widely depending upon the candidates and the constituency, two that are frequently used, and almost as frequently found unconvincing, are assertions that an opponent is less experienced or less qualified and that a personally wealthy opponent is trying to "buy the election." Mario Cuomo of New York combined these attacks in his campaign against the free-spending Lewis Lehrman, with the slogan "Lieutenant Governor Mario Cuomo for Governor—Experience Money Can't Buy." Cuomo got 51 percent of the vote, a much narrower margin than expected, given his commanding early lead in the polls and a good year for Democrats.

The problem with the experience strategy is that it can often be easily deflected. The presumed value of political experience is that it makes an officeholder more competent to do his or her job. But if the candidate being attacked can demonstrate that he or she is likely to be a competent officeholder, the experience factor loses its punch. Democratic strategist Tim Ridley comments, "I would never run a candidate on an experience stand, because all the other candidate has to do is stand up and appear competent, and the experience qualification doesn't catch." Just such a development occurred in the 1982 Texas gubernatorial race between incumbent William Clements and the challenger, state attorney general Mark White. As White's campaign manager recalled: "Clements had gone around the state for two months, citing legal cases, saying Mark White was incompetent. Mark is a very intelligent, articulate man. You get him in a debate, and it's Clements's burden to prove he's incompetent. That's very difficult to do."

Ronald Reagan is another candidate who successfully deflected charges, in election after election, about his lack of experience. He first ran for the governorship of California in 1966 against two-term incumbent Pat Brown. Brown's theme was his officeholding experience, as opposed to Reagan's career as a movie actor. Brown's political commercials featured a montage of Reagan in various film roles and as an advertising pitchman. Each ad ended with the tag line, "Vote for a real governor, not an acting one"; or, "Over the years Ronald Reagan has played many roles. This year he wants to play governor. Are you willing to pay the price of admission?" Reagan's advertising, on the other hand, featured the simple, issue-based themes that would characterize all his campaigns: the cost of government, morality in government, and the need for a change. Reagan billed himself as a citizen politician, whose interests, concerns, and attitudes were not those of a distant, cynical politician but were the same as those of other citizens. As a media consultant later analyzed the campaign, "Brown's strong cards were the three to two Democratic registration and his record in office. His weakest card was his image comparison with the pure image of Ronald Reagan. He played his weakest card. And he lost." [19]

Thus the experience factor works only if the candidate being attacked is widely perceived as wavering and ineffectual. It can even have a jujitsu effect if the opponent not only manages to deflect the charge but also pokes holes in the "experienced" candidate's record. Millicent Fenwick's claims of experience were no help when challenger Lautenberg convinced voters that her experience included opposing job creation and his included nurturing it.

Similarly, charges that a wealthy opponent is buying an election with his or her own money often fall on deaf ears. As we saw in chapter 4, financial chicanery is frequently enough to cause a candidate to be rejected at the polls. But the legal, above-board use of the candidate's own money rarely is an effective campaign issue. Voters in New York, Arkansas, and West Virginia elected Nelson, Winthrop, and Jay Rockefeller to the governorships of their respective states despite charges in every election that they were spending too freely. In Jay Rockefeller's 1984 race for a West Virginia Senate seat against Republican businessman John Raese, Raese once again trotted out the spending charge, asserting that Rockefeller should "hang his head in shame" for spending

$24 million on his various West Virginia campaigns while the state regularly led the nation in unemployment. Rockefeller countered with advertisements citing his service to West Virginia over almost two decades and picturing a campaign button that said, "John Raese. Inexperience West Virginia can't afford." This play on words deflected the election-buying charge, although the relative unpersuasiveness of the inexperience strategy may have contributed to the decline in Rockefeller's lead from 63 percent in early October polls to his eventual 52 percent victory on election day.[20] Constituents generally seem to believe that if politicians are independently wealthy, there is at least some assurance that they will not become beholden to other nefarious interests.

In short, the dominant themes that candidates use must fit the context and participants in a particular contest, and they must be believable. There are no all-purpose themes that will work in any situation, although some common ones like inexperience and election buying should be avoided. Certain factors do influence the general tenor of particular candidates' themes, however, and we will consider them in the next section.

What Shapes Campaign Themes?

Three factors play an important role in shaping campaign themes. First is the candidate's status as a challenger or incumbent. Second is the office for which the candidate is running. Finally, there is the role of broad national trends. We will analyze each of these in turn.

Candidate Status and the Theme

In most contests, one candidate is the incumbent and the other is a challenger for that office. In such races, the organizing construct for both campaigns is the incumbent's record. The incumbent advances that record as the principal reason why he or she should be reelected, while the challenger attempts to frame it as the reason to replace the current officeholder. This organizing principle often holds true even in races where there is no incumbent. One or both candidates may have prior political experience that becomes the major theme. Even challengers without political experience promote or defend their past records if their activities have brought them public recognition.

Incumbents. Typically, incumbents must trumpet the attractive aspects of their records to reinforce the electoral base that brought them victory in the past. But more important, as we briefly discussed in chapter 4, wise incumbents will do a painstaking job of "negative research" on themselves, preparing to confront possible weaknesses early by inoculating voters against charges that are sure to be made by the challenger. James Blanchard, elected governor of Michigan in 1982, did this with unusual openness when he described his opponent as "a guy who is willing to give fetuses rights in the U.S. Constitution that he is not willing to give women"; he explained to a reporter "that he had to bring these social issues into the open to avoid a last minute 'Pearl Harbor' by right-to-life and Moral Majority groups. He noted 'that way the abortion issue will come out a wash, and, on the ERA issue, I end up a winner.' " [21]

Incumbents can neutralize an attack in a variety of ways. One is to incorporate a potential weakness into the basic theme of the campaign in a positive way, communicating to voters almost subliminally, without appearing even to recognize the problem. In his campaign for reelection as mayor of New York City in 1969, the slogan and thematic thrust of John Lindsay's message to voters was "It's the second toughest job in America." Voters were meant to sympathize with the crushing burdens of the office, to perceive that some of the city's problems were intractable, and that, despite the mayor's performance, he was not to blame for them. Enough voters accepted the argument to reelect Lindsay.

In another election, this one an open-seat primary race for the governorship of Kentucky, John Y. Brown's strategists identified a potential problem with the candidate's divorce and remarriage to television personality Phyllis George. Brown, although not an incumbent, was well known as the chief executive of the Kentucky Fried Chicken chain, as an active participant in national Democratic politics, and as the constant companion of George. Media consultant Robert Squier explained how the campaign approached the issue:

> John had been married once before, and his former wife is a charming woman who is very popular in the state. And that was a kind of a question mark—would Kentucky reach out and accept Phyllis? It was my feeling that we had to go ahead and say: "Here she is—we think you'll find Phyllis, as we find her, a very charming, very bright, very nice lady." So we did a five-minute film first, that had as much or more of Phyllis in it as it did of John. . . . We really wanted to make sure that the people of Kentucky were comfortable with her in this new role and comfortable with her as John's wife. Once we got into the campaign, we reduced the amount of Phyllis's involvement in the rest of the primary media.[22]

Thus the campaign sought to establish an image of the Browns as the state's "first couple" before the opposition could paint a different picture of the candidate's domestic life. Phyllis George Brown became a distinct asset rather than a liability, and her husband went on to be elected governor of Kentucky.

A second method of dealing with a potential liability is to turn a negative into a positive. Ronald Reagan's conversion of his inexperience in office from a minus to a plus when he first ran for governor of California is one example. When Nelson Rockefeller ran for reelection as governor of New York in 1970, research showed that voters perceived him as "arrogant." As Rockefeller strategist William Ronan remembered, "we flipped that over to the positive. The positive of arrogance is leadership." [23] A massive media campaign detailed the achievements of the Rockefeller administration with "conceptual" advertising that did not picture the personally unpopular Rockefeller but rather showed miles of new state highways and cartoons of fish discussing their joy at being freed from the bane of polluted water. Rockefeller won handily.

A third strategy is to educate voters about the validity of an apparently unpopular policy. Senator William Cohen of Maine took on the nuclear freeze issue in his 1984 reelection contest. Cohen opposed the popular freeze, instead supporting the Reagan administration's "build-down" proposal. Discussing the problem, Cohen's media strategist explained:

> Bill Cohen is a member of the Senate Armed Services Committee and supported most of President Reagan's military initiatives. Anyone who would run against him would try to capitalize on the profreeze sentiment in Maine and paint him as a militarist. We'll respond by educating the [people] whose tendency is to support the freeze, to show them that it's not in the best interests of the United States to have a unilateral freeze; and your senator, Bill Cohen, has taken the leadership in coming up with a responsible arms control proposal that has bipartisan support.

In an extensive advertising campaign, Cohen coupled his argument of responsible leadership on arms control with a reminder that he also had a strong record of constituency service, exemplified in his campaign slogan, "A senator for Maine and America."

Cohen's strategy for dealing with a difficult foreign policy issue differed from that of Frank Church, the four-term incumbent senator from Idaho, who lost by 4,000 votes in 1980. A Church staffer believes things might have been different if the campaign had launched a major educational effort to explain Church's leadership, as chairman of the Senate Foreign Relations Committee, in passage of the Panama Canal treaties—a most unpopular position in his home state. The staffer observed:

> It would have been far smarter had we recognized the emotional impact of the Panama Canal treaties earlier and dealt with them. By the time it was clear that a significant percentage of the voters was using

that as a major reason to cast their vote, it was really too late. In '79 and '80 it wouldn't go away. We completely ignored Panama strategically. We answered the mail, but we never affirmatively made the case. We never did an ad on it until the very end.

Echoing this Church staffer, Republican consultant David Murray observed: "I don't think you skirt an issue. If it's there, it'll come back and haunt you, no matter what." Thus, for a candidate with a record to defend—most often the incumbent—it is not enough merely to make the positive case. Weaknesses, inconsistencies, and liabilities in the incumbent's record must be faced honestly and responded to forcefully, if there is any sign that such charges are getting through to the voter.

Challengers. Challengers face a different situation. Most challengers must simultaneously erode the favorable reputation of the incumbent and build a positive case for themselves. As one consultant put it:

In order to defeat an incumbent, you have to give people a compelling reason to vote that incumbent out. Half of the reason is the positive things about your candidate, but another dimension is where the incumbent is lacking. What has that incumbent done that's wrong? You've got to give people that compelling reason to oust the incumbent, or they're going to take the attitude, "If it ain't broke, don't fix it."

Thus, in the Lautenberg-Fenwick New Jersey Senate campaign, we observed that the two prongs of Lautenberg's theme were that Fenwick could not deal with the state's economic problems *and* that Lautenberg, as an experienced businessman, could. Similarly, in the Robb-Coleman gubernatorial campaign in Virginia, Robb argued that Coleman was a "flipflopper" whose character and integrity were suspect *and* that Robb was consistent and above reproach.

Challengers whose campaign themes portray only a negative picture of their opponents, or only a positive picture of themselves, are likely to lose. In the 1984 Maine Senate race, unsuccessful Democratic challenger Libby Mitchell unrelentingly attacked William Cohen for his support of nuclear weapons programs and opposition to the nuclear freeze, but never gave voters a reason to choose her as a replacement for the affable and popular incumbent. As a Maine publicity specialist observed of Mitchell's advertisements: "Negative campaigns like this almost never work. I can't think of an example of a challenger winning with a negative campaign." A colleague added, "She raises questions about Cohen, but we don't ever find out what she is for besides the freeze." [24]

However, challengers who don't make the case against their opponents, and only present the positive argument for themselves, are not likely to fare any better, because they give voters no reason to remove the "known-quantity" incumbent. Connecticut gubernatorial challenger

Lewis Rome discovered this in his 1982 contest with incumbent William O'Neill. Although the governor was never accused of any wrongdoing, charges of scandal dogged his administration, and one of his state commissioners was forced to resign late in the campaign. Rome, determined to run a positive campaign, stressed only his own competence and integrity and, in his media advertising, never attacked the governor directly until the last week. Speaking of corruption and influence-peddling, a Rome staffer observed, "That was the issue and it was not played right by us. We didn't succeed in convincing the public that was the issue." In the campaign's final days, one TV advertisement was run that detailed rising taxes, a state budget deficit, and indictments of administration officials. A voiceover said of the governor, who had been silent about the charges, "What does Bill O'Neill have to say? He has no comment." The Rome aide recalled, "We got the reaction we wanted. That certainly busted O'Neill out of his shell." Although it was too late to put the incumbent on the defensive, O'Neill won a narrower than expected victory. A campaign that drew the comparison between challenger and incumbent earlier might well have succeeded for Rome.

While Republican Rome was losing in Connecticut against a Democratic incumbent, the Republican gubernatorial challenger in nearby New Hampshire, John Sununu, successfully ousted Democratic incumbent Hugh Gallen. After setting up a picture of Sununu in the public mind as a smart businessman who knew how to balance a budget, the Sununu campaign ran ads attacking Gallen:

> People have been attracted to New Hampshire over the years because of our environment, both natural and economic. Hugh Gallen is doing his best to ruin all that. As governor, Hugh Gallen managed to turn a $34 million surplus into a $30 million deficit. Our taxes are higher than ever. If Gallen's reelected, we'll get a sales or income tax for sure.... We need a change. John Sununu for governor.

By giving voters a reason for both rejecting Gallen and preferring him— Sununu—the challenger eked out a narrow victory as the only Republican to defeat an incumbent Democratic governor in 1982.

Thus the themes employed by successful incumbents and challengers are mirror images. Successful incumbents run proudly on a record, taking care to preempt negative charges the opposition may raise. Successful challengers make a compelling case against the incumbent, while at the same time giving voters reasons to prefer the challenger.

The Office Sought and the Theme

Another factor influencing the choice of a theme is the office sought. Most notable is the difference in themes between candidates for an executive position and those for a legislative position. Candidates for executive office, like governors, pick themes that stress leadership and competence and focus on issues that emphasize these qualities. Candidates for legislative office, like senators and representatives, stress their command of national policy, particularly as it relates to their constituents. Senators, especially when they have national reputations, are inclined to emphasize thoughtful consideration of "big issues" like the economy or foreign policy. Representatives, with a more parochial orientation, concentrate more often on the hard work they do for constituents and on their success in using legislation to "bring home the bacon."

We return again to the need for incumbents to defend their records, and for challengers to be on the attack, because the character of both affirmative and attack themes is strongly influenced by the office sought. We elaborate on this below.

Affirmative Themes. The range of issues for executive candidates is rather narrow. In the majority of cases, gubernatorial campaigns are waged over who can better manage the state's economy—a valance issue of leadership. This translates into discussions about taxes, spending, and the programs on which state money is spent—highways, education, social welfare, and crime. In 1982 in New York, as noted earlier, gubernatorial candidate Lewis Lehrman advanced the theme that state taxes were too high—that they drove out business and stifled job creation. A typical Lehrman ad pictured the candidate walking through an abandoned plant while an on-screen graphic proclaimed, "Lew Lehrman: A Leader to Make New York Work Again." Lehrman then turned to the camera and told his viewers:

> Three hundred people used to work in this factory. But now those jobs are in New Jersey. People decide it's just too hard to make it in New York anymore—taxes are just too high, 50 percent above the national average. Our taxes drive out jobs. I'm Lew Lehrman. As an independent businessman, I helped create jobs all over New York State. . . . Job-creating incentives mean lower tax rates on middle-income families and business. Strong leadership in Albany and a good business climate can make New York competitive again. And that will mean more jobs and hope in the future.

In neighboring Pennsylvania, Governor Richard Thornburgh, in addition to defending his fiscal record, used another leadership theme that surfaces in governors' races: an executive's ability to deal with unanticipated crises. Early in Thornburgh's first term, a near-disaster of historic proportions occurred in his state in the form of the malfunction at the Three Mile Island nuclear power plant. For days, the country waited fearfully to learn if radiation would escape from the plant. Governor Thornburgh naturally played a major role in this event, and his 1982 campaign advertising, in his successful bid for reelection, drove home his leadership role in the Three Mile Island episode:

NARRATOR: In the life or death nuclear crisis at Three Mile Island, for ten days, the world watches Pennsylvania. Dick Thornburgh displays cool, competent leadership.
THORNBURGH: The reactor core is stable.
NARRATOR: Disaster is averted.
FILM OF PRESIDENT CARTER: I want to congratulate you, Governor Thornburgh, and thank you on behalf of our nation. You made us very proud.
NARRATOR: You hope these things never happen, but when they do, it's good to know there's a steady leader you can depend on—Governor Dick Thornburgh.

In contrast to the stress that executives place on leadership and competence, senators emphasize their comprehension and command of national policy. A theme of Pennsylvania senator John Heinz's campaign was his sponsorship of major legislation on a vital issue. One typical ad entitled "Trade" showed him speaking in front of a factory:

It's no secret that American business, like this Pennsylvania steel plant, is having trouble competing with foreign competition. That's why I've helped rewrite the laws to combat unfair trade practices by other nations. And why I'm sponsoring legislation to give our president power to act against countries which erect trade barriers against U.S. products. And to help small business exports, by forming trading companies the way Japan and West Germany have done. We can put Americans back to work at home, by putting America back in business.

Concentration on national issues, often with a local twist, is the traditional sort of appeal that senatorial candidates make. But because of a growing need to defend against challengers' charges that they are distant and out of touch, incumbent senators are also adopting a thematic style that stresses the more parochial concerns that usually characterize congressional campaigns. Another Heinz ad conveyed this theme. Standing in front of a clearly Pennsylvanian backdrop, Heinz tells the camera:

When most people think of the United States Senate, they think of Washington, but I believe that the key to doing a good job as a senator is to listen and learn from the people back home. I recognized that in 1976, when I promised to be accessible and accountable to the people of Pennsylvania. I've held town meetings across the state, answered your letters, and given assistance to citizens who've had problems with some branch of government. Because doing something about the problems of Pennsylvania is my first priority in the United States Senate.

As we noted, this ad is very similar to the thematic appeals that incumbent representatives are likely to make. These officeholders concentrate almost exclusively on the favors they have done for their constituents, either in bringing federal help to their districts or in cutting government red tape. The closeness of representatives to their districts and their hard work are also emphasized. All these themes are present in this advertisement for Representative Jim Coyne of Pennsylvania, which featured brief statements by "typical" citizens:

> I think that Congressman Coyne is really for the people.
> Jim Coyne's responsive——
> He went to bat for us——
> If it hadn't been for him, I doubt I'd have a business today.
> Jim Coyne works for the average guy and he's willing to fight for you.
> And he jumped right in and helped me and saved the day for our family.
> I don't know what I would have done without him.
> He is not just talking, he is doing the job.
> I believe that Jim Coyne is there to help the individual.

Attack Themes. Candidates challenging incumbents, as we have discussed, must make a negative portrayal of the incumbent an important part of their theme. The nature of the attack is also conditioned by the office for which the challenger runs. A consultant who works for gubernatorial and senatorial candidates in both parties summarized the differences between executive and legislative races that affect the criticisms their challengers can make:

> It is my view that voters are well informed about the bad news concerning a governor. Since he is in the newspaper every day, people follow his activities intimately over the years. By contrast, most voters know little about the performance of their senators or congressmen. Since voting records are hardly reported at all by the local press, a senator or congressman can have an image removed from the reality of his performance in Washington. Since there is not always a clear voting record as governor it is hard to target specific positives or negatives.
> With senators and congressmen, a great deal of new information can be introduced, since they each cast thousands of votes, adding up to a portrait that can be very carefully sketched to suit needs as an election progresses.
> I have always found that when voters find out important new facts about a candidate when they thought they knew the candidate, they tend to blame the candidate for lying to them, which then impugns his credibility as well as his popularity.

The result of these differences is that criticism of gubernatorial incumbents frequently takes the form of generalized attacks on their leadership ability or competence—often tied to their management of the state's economy. When successful Democratic challenger Bob Kerrey of Nebraska ran against incumbent Charles Thone in 1982, he made his theme the deteriorating nature of the economy and Thone's mild-mannered and rather passive stewardship. Kerrey's slogan was "A *Decisive* New Leader for Nebraska." In Pennsylvania, Representative Alan Ertel, who was running against incumbent governor Thornburgh, charged, in his advertising, that Thornburgh had not dealt successfully with Pennsylvania's economic problems:

> Why is Richard Thornburgh afraid to debate his opponent? And why is he now running a negative, low-road campaign? Maybe it's because he doesn't want to talk about his own record—higher taxes, higher unemployment, and higher utility rates. Now Richard Thornburgh is even afraid to talk to people. He walked away from an unemployed woman who tried to tell him how hard it is to feed her family. His excuse—things are tough all over. Well, things didn't have to be this tough. On Tuesday, elect new leadership. Elect Alan Ertel governor.

If an incumbent governor has some notable failure that can be targeted, it may become, as we described in chapter 4, a "referendum issue"—an issue on which the incumbent will stand or fall irrespective of almost anything else. We have already described how John Sununu made his opposition to a broad-based tax in New Hampshire, and the incumbent's support for it, a referendum issue that worked for the challenger.

Attacking legislative incumbents' leadership is more difficult, since lawmakers can rarely be held personally responsible for state or federal programs. The few exceptions are congressional committee chairmen who become closely identified with unpopular national policies under the purview of their committees. One example, as we noted earlier in this chapter, is the campaign against Senate Foreign Relations Committee chairman Frank Church of Idaho, in which the opposition tied him to the Panama Canal treaties. Another is Illinois Democratic challenger Paul Simon's successful 1984 campaign against Charles Percy, Church's successor as Senate Foreign Relations Committee chairman. Percy campaigned with the slogan "The Illinois Advantage," arguing that Illinois' extensive foreign trade profited from his chairmanship. Simon took another tack, charging in his commercials that Percy voted for tax breaks to American corporations that "take our jobs overseas." With a picture of the Eiffel Tower in the background, an announcer says, "Illinois may be hurting, but somewhere in the world Charles Percy has made someone very happy." Another announcer, speaking in French, adds, "Thank you, Mr. Percy."

For the same reason, it is also difficult to use a referendum issue in legislative races, except for challengers who are lucky enough to find a national concern on which their position is clearly distinguishable from their opponent's and which is powerful enough to move sizable numbers of voters. As we described earlier in this chapter, Representative Kent Hance almost succeeded in doing this in his 1984 Texas Democratic primary contest.

Much more common in legislative contests than competence or referendum themes, especially in Senate races, is the characterization of the incumbent as too distant from the problems of constituents. A related strategy is to paint the incumbent as ideologically out of tune with constituents. Both these charges are accompanied by a procedure known as "vote-shopping"—the challenger's staff sifts through the hundreds or thousands of votes cast by the incumbent to find some that are calculated to surprise and enrage constituents. In the Fenwick-Lautenberg Senate race, for example, Lautenberg honed in on Fenwick's few votes that could be considered "anti-jobs," ignoring the many others that were "pro-jobs." Her negative votes could be rationally explained by setting them in the context in which they were cast, but the necessarily complicated explanations, sometimes involving arcane points of parliamentary procedure, put Fenwick on the defensive and took control of the campaign's debate away from her.

The "ideologically out of step" theme is considered particularly effective against representatives and senators who, in the view of their challengers, build up positive reputations in their districts through constituency service and pork barrel legislation, but who vote the "wrong" way on less locally visible issues. In his ultimately unsuccessful campaign against New York representative Richard Ottinger, Republican challenger Jon Fossel tried to make the point, in his paid advertising, that Ottinger's favorable image was deceptive:

> Richard Ottinger has earned a reputation as a hard-working liberal congressman. But do you know how liberal Richard Ottinger really is? He voted for forced busing, admission quotas on higher education, and an $18,500 tax break for himself. It's not enough for a congressman to work hard. He has to vote right. That's why we need Jon Fossel in Congress. Jon Fossel—a great congressman for Westchester.

It can often be of assistance to the challenger if some outside, disinterested party will make the case against the opponent, leaving the candidate free to take the positive, high road. Since 1978 the National Conservative Political Action Committee has financed extensive media advertising critical of liberal senators. A NCPAC staffer described the way the political action committee sees its function:

> There was no one playing NCPAC's role of attacking the incumbent. The candidate challenging an entrenched incumbent has to work to build up his own name recognition, his own issues, his own image. NCPAC gets into a race to say, "Your senator is duping you, He does one thing in Washington and talks another way back home."

In 1980, NCPAC claimed a lion's share of the credit for the defeat of four of five of the senators it targeted, but in 1982, and to a lesser extent in 1984, it was not as successful. In 1984, it threw heavy resources into positive independent campaigns for President Reagan and North Carolina senator Jesse Helms, one of its early champions; both defeated their challengers. Negative campaigns that it waged against two Democratic senatorial candidates, John Kerry of Massachusetts and Tom Harkin of Iowa, were unsuccessful, as were most of the House candidacies with which it was involved. Among the reasons why NCPAC's theme was less convincing in 1982 was that voters, reacting to a weak economy, were less responsive to the conservative arguments of Republicans, particularly in the states that had liberal incumbents up for reelection. This observation brings us to a third factor that may overwhelm an otherwise credible campaign theme—the trends of the time.

Trends of the Time and the Theme

National trends, even when they are very strong, have a major impact on only a limited number of incumbents. State-level officeholders, like governors, can insulate themselves from national trends so long as they have their state house in order. Representatives, who build electoral coalitions based on constituency service, trust, and attention to their districts, are also not easily dislodged by national swings. Representatives who regularly win two-thirds or more of the vote can afford the few points' difference that a national swing in the vote may produce in their own districts. The representatives at risk when national tides are running are the relatively few first-termers from marginal districts who, in the previous election, were swept in narrowly on the coattails of a popular issue or well-liked presidential candidate. They have only a short time to consolidate their bases before the next election, when the trends may not be in their favor.[25]

Incumbent senators are the most vulnerable to national trends. The nature of the office makes them more closely identified with major issues. They are more likely to face well-financed challengers who can "educate" the voters about their records on significant legislation through paid mass media, particularly television. However, national trends alone are not enough to defeat most senators. Some of the other factors that make senators vulnerable must also be present to defeat an incumbent. One is marginality—a history of close elections—which can play a role even when no major policy questions are at stake. Another is advancing age or tenure. Senate incumbents who lose are disproportionately in their late sixties or older, or vying for their fourth term.[26] Finally, the incumbent's opponent must represent a clearly different ideological and issue stance, and one which is more in tune with the times It is only in such a situation that voters tend to opt strongly for the candidate riding these trends.[27] Most of the twelve Democratic senators defeated in 1980 suffered from one or more of these conditions, while the Democrats who were successful did not. Birch Bayh, for example, was seeking his fourth term after three close races, in a state that had never elected a senator to a fourth term. Herman Talmadge of Georgia was involved in a financial scandal. Warren Magnusen of Washington State was in his late seventies, and so on. These liabilities *combined with* being on the wrong side of national trends brought them defeat.

On the other hand, not only were eleven of the twelve Democratic incumbents running in the Republican landslide presidential election year of 1984 victorious, but seven of them won by greater margins than Ronald Reagan did in their states. All but one were first elected in 1972 or 1978, both difficult years for Democratic candidates. Few were identified with the left wing of their party. Victors like Bill Bradley of New Jersey and Joseph Biden of Delaware were well known "neoliberals"; Georgia senator Sam Nunn was a leading proponent of a strong military; David Boren of Oklahoma, J. J. Exon of Nebraska, and Howell Heflin of Alabama, among others, were some of the most conservative members of their party in the Senate.

Thus the candidates' status and record, the office they seek, and, to a lesser extent, the trends of the times all influence their choice of theme and its chance of success. We now go on to consider more fully how these themes are communicated to voters through the mass media.

Notes _____

1. Jeff Greenfield, *Running to Win* (New York: Simon & Schuster, 1980), 75.
2. Ibid., 74-75.
3. Paul R. Abramson, John H. Aldrich, and David W. Rohde, *Continuity and Change in the 1980 Elections* (Washington, D.C.: CQ Press, 1982), 129, 215.
4. *Bill Moyers' Journal*, "Campaign Report #4," WNET transcript, October 3, 1980, 17.
5. Xandra Kayden, *Campaign Organization* (Lexington, Mass.: D. C. Heath, 1978), 158.
6. "Tony Schwartz: Radio's Responsive Chord—A C & E Interview," *Campaigns and Elections* 2 (Spring 1981): 23.
7. Gary A. Mauser, *Political Marketing: An Approach to Campaign Strategy* (New York: Praeger, 1983), 12. See also Philip Kotler and Neil Kotler, "Business

Marketing for Political Candidates," *Campaigns and Elections* 2 (Summer 1981): 24-33.

8. See Charles W. Roll and Albert H. Cantril, *Polls: Their Use and Misuse in Politics* (Cabin John, Md.: Seven Locks Press, 1980), chapter 1.

9. Ibid., 9.

10. As we discuss in chapter 4, incumbents increasingly conduct trend polling throughout their terms. Their benchmark polls thus explore problems and opportunities identified in the earlier trend polling during their terms in office.

11. A *rolling average* consists of the results of a few consecutive nights of tracking polls (usually three), to decrease the margin of error in the smaller daily tracking samples.

12. Louis Sandy Maisel, *From Obscurity to Oblivion: Running in the Congressional Primary* (Knoxville: University of Tennessee Press, 1982), 50.

13. John K. White, "All in the Family: The 1978 Gubernatorial Primary in Massachusetts," *Polity* 14 (Summer 1982): 648.

14. Alan Ehrenhalt, ed., *Politics in America 1984* (Washington, D.C.: Congressional Quarterly, 1983), 1351.

15. Greenfield, *Running to Win,* 191.

16. Eve Lubalin, "Presidential Ambition and Senatorial Behavior: The Impact of Ambition on the Behavior of Incumbent Politicians," Ph.D. diss., Johns Hopkins University, 1981, 608.

17. Ibid., 609.

18. Larry Sabato, *Goodbye to Good-time Charlie: The American Governorship Transformed,* 2d ed. (Washington, D.C.: CQ Press, 1983), 135.

19. Gene Wyckoff, *The Image Candidates: American Politics in the Age of Television* (New York: Macmillan, 1968), 236.

20. See Raese's charges as reported in the *Charleston Gazette,* October 17, 1984, 3A; the *Gazette Poll,* October 9, 1984, 1A; and the two full-page advertisements placed in the *Gazette* by the Rockefeller campaign on November 4, 1984, 12C and 17B.

21. *Detroit Free Press,* September 23, 1982.

22. "Robert Squier's Media Miracles in Dixie: An Exclusive C & E Interview," *Campaigns and Elections* 1 (Summer 1980): 31.

23. James M. Perry, *The New Politics* (New York: Clarkson N. Potter, 1968), 124.

24. As quoted in the *Portland Press-Herald,* October 25, 1984, 8.

25. See the discussion of the roles of issues, marginality, and seniority in John L. Sullivan and Eric M. Uslaner, "Congressional Behavior and Electoral Marginality," *American Journal of Political Science* 22 (August 1978): 536-53; also John R. Hibbing and John R. Alford, "The Electoral Impact of Economic Conditions: Who Is Held Responsible," *American Journal of Political Science* 25 (August 1981): 423-39; Alan I. Abramowitz, "National Issues, Strategic Politicians, and Voting Behavior in the 1980 and 1982 Congressional Elections," *American Journal of Political Science* 28 (November 1984): 710-21.

26. Warren Kostroski, "The Effect of Number of Terms on the Reelection of Senators, 1920-1970," *Journal of Politics* 40 (May 1978): 497.

27. Alan I. Abramowitz, "Choices and Echoes in the 1978 U.S. Senate Elections: A Research Note," *American Journal of Political Science* 25 (February 1981): 112-18.

Mass Media In Campaigns

7

If you're not on television, you don't exist.

—Gubernatorial candidate

The information the electorate receives about campaigns comes from both paid media and free media. *Paid media* are the advertising messages controlled by campaigns; they are disseminated on television and radio and through print journalism and direct mail. The scope, range, and content of these messages are limited only by legal standards, ethics and taste, and the money available to pay for them. *Free media* are news stories, analysis, editorial comment, interviews, and debates. Although campaign organizations obviously have considerably less influence over unpaid media, nonetheless they seek to shape news coverage as well.

The themes a campaign devises must be transmitted effectively if a candidate is to set its agenda. A good media program advances a campaign's themes clearly and repetitiously. It should have the effect that one strategist credited to an opponent's advertising: "When I looked at his billboards, I heard his television ads." Additionally, the candidate's activities, as reported in free media, should complement what he or she is saying in paid media. In this chapter, we will examine the factors that help determine which media a campaign will select, and how it transmits its themes through paid and free media.

Which Paid Media Are Used

Television and radio advertising and direct mail are the primary forms of paid media. Although many candidates use print advertising, it has less impact than the other forms of mass communication. Fewer people read newspapers than watch television or listen to radio, and print ads are easier to ignore. Several interrelated factors affect which media are preferred: the audience sought; the office sought; the size, cost, and number of media markets in the candidate's constituency; and the amount of money available. We now examine how statewide and congressional contestants decide which paid media to use.

Statewide Contests

Television is the most effective medium for generating quick recognition, and it is now virtually impossible to run an effective statewide campaign without heavy reliance on television advertising. On average, television advertising absorbs about two-thirds of the budget of a statewide campaign. However, because of the peculiarities of media markets in various states, the cost of the same amount of television advertising for the same office varies enormously.

Television forces campaigns to think of their constituencies not simply in terms of geography but in terms of *DMAs—designated marketing areas.* In many areas, media market boundaries ignore state lines. Advertising charges are based on cost per thousand viewers. Thus, running for office in a state with a large population, or one with multiple media markets, can be vastly more expensive than running for the same office in a lightly populated state or one with few media markets.

For example, the populations of Rhode Island and Idaho are almost exactly the same—about a million people. Yet Senator John Chafee of Rhode Island spent only half as much in 1982 as Senator Frank Church of Idaho spent in 1980, although both contests were close and hard fought, and costs had escalated dramatically between 1980 and 1982. The major reason is that the entire compact state of Rhode Island is reached by a single media market in the state capital and largest city, Providence. Idaho, much larger and less densely populated, has four media markets within the state, and a significant proportion of its population is served by stations in Spokane, Washington, and Salt Lake City, Utah.

Another way to illustrate the difference in the price of advertising is to consider the varying costs of placing a thirty-second local ad on CBS's popular *60 Minutes,* a program highly favored by media buyers because of its large audience of politically attentive and independent voters. How much the spot costs depends on where it is aired. In 1984 the ad would have cost $1,000 in Des Moines, Iowa; $2,000 in Tulsa, Oklahoma; $3,750 in Hartford, Connecticut; and $9,000 in New York City.[1]

From a candidate's point of view, New Jersey has the country's worst media environment. New Jersey not only does not have a single network station within its boundaries (and until 1984 had no commercial stations at all) but is served by the New York and Philadelphia markets, which are the first and fourth largest and most expensive in the country. In other instances, the number of markets is less important than the cost. States like Pennsylvania, Tennessee, and Virginia have a large number of markets, but many of them reach small populations and are relatively inexpensive. On the other hand, many of the numerous markets in states like California and Texas cover large populations and are very expensive to penetrate. The name recognition of gubernatorial challenger Mark White in Texas had reached only 50 percent after he won a hard-fought three-way Democratic primary, served as state attorney general for four years, and spent more than a million dollars on radio and television to get himself known.

The differences in the 1980 and 1982 activities of NCPAC—which sponsors independent advertising campaigns against liberal senators—were also partly attributable to costs in different media markets. NCPAC scored some of its greatest 1980 successes in states like Frank Church's Idaho and George McGovern's South Dakota. The states' small populations and relatively cheap television costs permitted NCPAC to run saturation advertising campaigns against the senators for a long period of time. In contrast, some of NCPAC's 1982 targets—Edward Kennedy of Massachusetts, Daniel Patrick Moynihan of New York, Lloyd Bentsen of Texas, and Paul Sarbanes of Maryland—represented states with some of the most expensive media markets in the country.

These considerations led NCPAC to make a strategic decision to abandon efforts against Moynihan and Bentsen and concentrate its resources in Maryland and Massachusetts. This decision had little to do with either NCPAC's relative distaste for the senators involved or the likelihood of their defeat. It was predicated, first, on the less expensive rates in the Maryland and Massachusetts markets and, second, on NCPAC's own cost-benefit ratio. As a NCPAC staffer explained it: "One of the main problems with New York was that the state is too expensive. With all the problems the Republicans were having in '82, how much chance did we have of beating Moynihan versus the awesome cost of media in New York State?"

Sarbanes seemed vulnerable early in the election year. But more important, much of the negative advertising against him ran in the Washington, D.C., market, where it would be seen by other lawmakers and political movers and shakers in the nation's capital. NCPAC seized this opportunity to impress political insiders and frighten other targets. In the case of Kennedy, the group had few illusions that he could be defeated. But the large expenditures were justified for other reasons:

> If we target a flaming liberal, nationally known bad guy like Teddy Kennedy, that's going to cost us 400 grand, but how much money did it raise for us—800, a million? Fundraising is a factor as well. When we send our contributors a list—"Should we target Teddy Kennedy?"— they send it back—"Yeah!" Check it off, mail it back in with $20. Multiply that by thousands. We need to target more bad guys to raise more money to beat more bad guys.

Thus the size and cost of various media markets is an important factor in both planning campaign strategy and in accounting for the variations in campaign expenditures in different states for the same office.

House Contests

In congressional campaigns the use of television varies according to the media market situation, but in most cases is less important than in statewide campaigns. A study of congressional primary campaigns found broad regional differences associated with the media markets in the candidates' locality. Almost three-quarters of the candidates in the Southwest, where television is relatively inexpensive and markets correspond more closely to districts, bought television advertising, as opposed to a quarter of the candidates on the West Coast and 16 percent of those in the Middle Atlantic region. A study of congressional general election races yielded similar findings. Less than half—44 percent—of all candidates used television advertising. The cost efficiency (certainty of reaching only viewers in the candidate's district) and the market potential (the number of reachable households divided by the cost of an average advertisement) were much greater in rural districts than in urban districts, and in midwestern, southern, and border states than in New England and the West.[2]

Vulnerable congressional incumbents, contestants for open seats, and serious challengers all saw personal contact, radio, and direct mail as more important communication channels.[3] These approaches are preferred because they are all more susceptible to audience targeting than is television. Radio is the least targeted of the three, but is less expensive than television, and some stations do have fairly well-defined geographic and demographic audiences, such as particular minority groups or age groups. Direct mail's major virtue is the very high ability to target—not only by mailing just to voters in the candidate's district, but also by devising specific messages for specific groups. Direct mail is especially important in urban congressional districts, where no other mass media are as cost-efficient. John Simms, a Washington direct mail consultant who works on many congressional campaigns, explained:

In the expensive media markets, they don't have an opportunity to put much on the tube. They may do some radio. There's a lot of political advertising on all the media at that time; it's hard for them to be heard. So they spend a lot more money on list development and direct mail and voter contact. A lot of those campaigns may easily spend as much as $150-200,000 with an organization such as mine.

For little-known congressional challengers, campaign strategists see direct mail, and even radio and television, as adjuncts to heavy personal voter contact—preferably by the candidate, or by surrogates if necessary. In Arizona, for example, John McCain won his first election in the state's solidly Republican First Congressional District by defeating three other candidates in the all-important primary. McCain had moved to the district only a year before and embarked on his primary campaign with virtually no recognition. Much of the almost $600,000 he spent on his primary and general election races was devoted to television. His district, which encompassed only the city of Phoenix, was appropriate for a television campaign to make McCain known quickly. The television advertising was accompanied by heavy door-to-door campaigning, however. His media adviser, Jay Smith, described the combination of tactics:

> He wound up knocking on 15,000 Republican household doors in Arizona, where the summer temperature is about 115 degrees in the shade. I remember distinctly being out there when the first TV ads hit, and he came back and said it was night and day in terms of the response on the street. It was a combination. He couldn't have done it with just the TV advertising.

On the other hand, when New Jersey Republican representative Jim Courter was redistricted into a new, heavily Republican constituency and faced a difficult primary, he used no television at all. Messages in the New York City market would have been extraordinarily expensive and beamed to an audience of which his constituents made up less than 5 percent. Courter instead relied on several waves of direct mail to likely primary voters. His exurban and rural district was ill-suited to heavy door-to-door campaigning, so instead the candidate took to the telephone. An aide recalled: "Courter would call 500 people a day. We'd have five phones going at once. They'd keypunch the addresses that night, and a letter would go out the next day."

It is in the area of direct mail and personal contact that statewide races, except in the smallest states, differ from congressional contests. Consultant Vince Breglio discussed the reelection campaign of Senator Orrin Hatch of Utah:

> When Orrin would come into the state, we'd put him in front of a five-button phone, and have five people calling into a neighborhood. They

would call and say, "Senator Hatch is here and wants to say hello." By pre-identification we would know if they supported him. In twenty seconds, he'd give them a little spiel. The word of mouth was incredible.

However, Breglio noted, this type of technique is less effective in larger states:

When you're in a state with big numbers, personal contact and direct mail can help if you can identify a reasonably small subgroup, but for some reason direct mail loses its impact with four million pieces. It's a tool that works best with 40-50,000 households. If you're talking New York or California or even New Jersey or Florida, you have a much heavier dependence on electronic media.

In sum, therefore, statewide campaigns usually rely to a greater degree on broadcast advertising, while those for lesser office place more reliance on direct voter contact—in person and by mail and telephone.

Types of Paid Messages

The messages that candidates transmit in their paid media fall into four general categories: positive messages about themselves, negative messages about their opponents, comparisons of the candidates, and responses to charges by opponents. Which type of message a candidate sends is affected by the stage of the campaign, the status of the candidate, and the competitiveness of the race. Almost all candidates begin their campaigns with positive messages that present their experience, credentials, and accomplishments. Negative or comparative messages, if they are used, generally come later. Voters react to negative messages with hostility, unless the candidates disseminating them have first drawn a positive picture of themselves to which criticism of an opponent can be compared.

The conventional wisdom of campaign strategists used to be that only challengers should use negative messages, in their efforts to paint incumbents as unworthy of reelection. A much better known incumbent was thought to be giving an opponent free publicity by mentioning his or her name, even in an attack. The thinking now is that only incumbents who face *weak* challengers whose charges against them never penetrate (either because the challenger lacks the money to publicize them or because they are completely unconvincing) can afford to take the high road—sticking to a positive campaign and ignoring the challenger's existence. A strong challenger, on the other hand, cannot be ignored. Bob Beckel, a Democratic strategist who helped orchestrate Walter Mondale's negative campaign against Gary Hart for the 1984 Democratic presidential nomination, said:

There used to be an old adage in politics that you don't mention your opponent's name because he's somebody who isn't known. But the ridiculous thing about that is by election day, a good challenger is going to be known by most everybody who goes to the polls. Our theory is that on the way up, when the name recognition increases, you try to associate some negative notions with that name.[4]

In the next sections we will analyze positive messages, negative messages, comparative messages, and response messages to see how each is used.

Positive Messages

In a statewide campaign, the early television messages are usually positive and biographical, conveying to voters what sort of person the candidate is and stressing the high points of his or her career, as in this ad for Senator Moynihan of New York. While the camera showed pictures of Moynihan in informal poses, with his family, and in various New York locations, a narrator intoned:

> He worked the docks and shined shoes to help pay for school. He and his wife, Liz, bought their first home in Delaware County with a GI loan. And they raised three children in this state. He went to Washington as President Kennedy's assistant secretary of labor. Adviser to four presidents, ambassador to India and to the United Nations. He's smart, and thoughtful, but he can stand and fight with the best. And friend or foe will tell you, he's his own man. Our man. He's New York's Moynihan.

A challenger who lacks the type of experience in government that someone like Moynihan had must take a different approach. Since challenger Frank Lautenberg had no record of public service, his biographical ads showed his deep roots in New Jersey, his success in private life, and its relevance to his Senate bid. Here is the transcript of one of Lautenberg's early TV commercials:

> NARRATOR: What you take out, you have to put back in. Lautenberg feels that sentiment has guided his personal decision to enter public life. To pay back some of the debt he and his family owe New Jersey.
> LAUTENBERG (talking to a blue-collar worker): It's a whole different experience. I never ran for public office before. I had plenty of private office. It'll be a lot of work, but it's worth it; it's an investment in our country; it's an investment in our state. I believe in the state; it's been very good to me, the country's been great. My parents came as immigrants; I succeeded like nobody believed, so why shouldn't I give back some of that which I took?
> NARRATOR: Frank Lautenberg for New Jersey. New Jersey first.

Positive advertising also highlights the issues or images candidates want to stress. As we noted in chapter 6, some candidates use issues to transmit the central messages they want to convey about themselves. In an important sense, the issue itself is not the key message but, rather, what the issue suggests about the candidate. Other candidates focus on a generalized image that gives the voter a sense of what their approach would be to a particular issue. The contrast between "issue as image" and "image as issue" has rarely been drawn more strongly than in the 1982 gubernatorial contest in New York between Republican Lewis Lehrman and Democrat Mario Cuomo. Lehrman used proposals for cutting taxes to improve the state's business climate as the vehicle to create an image of leadership and competence, as in this message:

> New York needs 200,000 new jobs a year in the 1980s. With these new tax incentives, I'm confident we'll create new jobs and bring back business. Our people have the talent, the drive, the imagination. Now all we need is the leadership.

Cuomo's campaign, in contrast, disseminated a message that stressed the candidate's compassion and the need for a governor to care about every citizen in the state. One spot featured the candidate talking earnestly to a rapt audience:

> You must believe passionately in something. And I do. I believe in making things better even if only a little bit better. I believe nothing will ever be perfect, but that you can always improve things, and it's worth giving all your energy just to improve it this much. And I think that's what I can do as Governor.

Another pictured Mrs. Cuomo, sitting in her backyard with some of their children, telling viewers:

> The one thing Mario believes in the most is traditional values. Things like hard work, opportunity, and, of course, the family. We've been married almost thirty years, and I can tell you, he'll be the kind of governor that'll make you proud.

Lehrman, in other words, used a specific issue—a tax cut—to suggest what he would do for the state's economy. Cuomo, on the other hand, offered viewers a picture of himself as a warm-hearted, generous family man—a sort of father figure for the state. The positive-messages ads we have illustrated show how candidates use their appearances in front of the camera to make a particular statement about themselves.

Once candidates have established a positive image, it may become necessary to go on the attack. This is essential for the challenger facing a favorably regarded incumbent, but also for the incumbent whose challenger is gaining ground. Negative or attack advertising comes in two varieties—pure negatives and comparisons. We will examine both kinds.

Negative Messages

The purely negative message concentrates entirely on the opponent, only reminding the voter of the alternative at the very end. For example, a negative ad run by Senator Charles Percy's 1984 campaign against challenger Paul Simon had the following text:

> Ayatollah Khomeini orders the destruction of the American Embassy in Tehran. Fifty-three Americans are held hostage as Iranian mobs explode in hatred for the U.S. America unites against Iran, but Paul Simon writes an official letter to the ayatollah praising him as a "just and holy man." Simon labels the seizure of fifty-three American hostages as merely a misunderstanding. Is this the kind of foreign policy we want from an Illinois senator?

Viewers are then urged to reelect Percy.

Consultants agree that the most effective negative ads are those that distance the targeted candidate from the needs and feelings of the electorate while showing how concerned the attacker is about those same qualities. In the 1984 North Carolina Senate race between incumbent Republican Jesse Helms and his challenger, outgoing governor James B. Hunt, Helms's massive paid media campaign featured particularly strong negative messages against Hunt such as, "I voted against the Martin Luther King holiday. Where do you stand, Jim?" and "I wouldn't vote for Walter Mondale or Jesse Jackson for president. Where do you stand, Jim?" Hunt's press secretary saw Helms's strategy as an effort to focus the campaign not on himself but on "this politician who's supported by gays, Commies, Ted Kennedy, Julian Bond, and the ultra-liberal media."[5] While it is not clear to what extent Helms's victory can be attributed to his negative campaign, it did focus the debate on the differences between them.

Comparative Messages

As exemplified by the Helms ads, increasingly, campaigns are moving away from purely negative attack ads to "comparatives," which consultants believe are more convincing and less distasteful to voters than blunt negatives. Comparatives examine the record of the two candidates, to the benefit of one of them. After airing numerous positive ads detailing his plans for bringing New York more jobs, 1982 gubernatorial challenger Lewis Lehrman pointed up the difference between his positions and those of his opponent, Democratic lieutenant governor Mario Cuomo, and of the outgoing Democratic governor, Hugh Carey:

> Who can create more jobs for New York: Lew Lehrman or Mario Cuomo? Mario Cuomo is a lawyer, and under Carey and Cuomo, New

York now ranks forty-ninth in creating new jobs. Lew Lehrman is an independent businessman. As president of Rite-Aid Stores, Lew Lehrman created thousands of real jobs in New York State. In addition, Lehrman is the only candidate who has presented a concrete plan for creating 200,000 more jobs a year. Lew Lehrman has the experience of creating real jobs. Elect Lew Lehrman governor.

Response Messages

The fourth type of message candidates transmit in their paid media is the response—answers to an opponent's attacks. When campaigns react to each other in this way, they become "electronic debates," in which candidates are commenting on the validity of each other's themes and arguments. We will enlarge on this final stage of a campaign in the next chapter. Before going on to the debate stage of campaigns, let us consider the role of the unpaid, or free, media in the early stage of campaigns, when candidates attempt to set their themes and seize control of the agenda.

The Role of Free Media

To understand the role of print and electronic journalism in political campaigns and the way campaigns relate to free media, it is necessary to keep in mind several distinguishing characteristics of the journalists who are assigned to campaigns and of the press coverage that candidates receive during campaigns. These traits include: journalists' preference for covering politics rather than policy; the greater coverage given to incumbent or better-known candidates; and the differences between print and electronic journalism. Additionally, there are important differences in the coverage of nonpresidential and presidential campaigns.

Political Journalists and Journalism

The central finding of every study of political journalists and of their coverage of campaigns is that the press treats campaigns as "horse races" (who is ahead and who is behind?) and as strategic exercises rather than as debates about issues.[6] There are three interrelated reasons for this: reporters' definition of what is news, reporters' stress on objectivity, and political reporters' backgrounds.

News, for the reporter, is something that *happens*. Michael Robinson and Margaret Sheehan explain the importance of this apparently trite observation: " 'Horse races' happen; 'horse races' are themselves filled with specific actions. Policy issues, on the other hand, do not happen;

they merely exist. Substance has no events; issues generally remain static." [7] Once a candidate's position on the issues is reported, it is not news unless it changes. On the other hand, candidate appearances, charges against other candidates—whatever their merits—new poll results, discord within the campaign organization, and the like are all events that merit reporting as news. They will thus get more coverage than discussion about issues.

Second, reporters' adherence to the canon of objectivity means that they do not see the evaluation of policy positions as part of their job, except in rare investigative pieces or in analysis columns or editorials. A well-thought-out policy position on a complicated issue implies an ideological or philosophical construct, a certain way of looking at the world. News reporters do not consider it the job of an objective press to make value judgments about the validity of a candidate's philosophy. Reporters know that the factual elements of the horse-race aspects of the campaign—the crowds that candidates draw, their standings in polls, the amount of money they raise, the endorsements they garner—can be measured, whereas issue positions cannot be so easily reduced to statistics. Reporters' interest in issues thus takes on a strategic quality. One reporter described the attitude of the press toward candidates' position papers: "Everybody knows they're bullshit. But if you don't do it, you'll get criticized for having a vacuous campaign. If you do do it, they won't get written about, but you won't be criticized."

Issues become important to political reporters when they take on a dynamic quality that can be written about as events. Two common examples are reporting of inconsistencies and gaffes or factual errors. If candidates make the slightest alterations in positions without a convincing rationale, or make the smallest error in fact, reporters are likely to pounce. Such slips are seen as illustrative of candidate incompetence, or of conflict within a campaign about what strategic positions to take, and are factual, colorful, and interesting—in short, news.

Third, since most reporters working on major campaigns are specialists in covering politics, they often do not know very much about the major issues. Because of their previous experience and own interests, they are more comfortable describing the day-to-day events of a campaign: "Political reporters tend to be fascinated by the process, the mechanics of politics. They are not particularly interested in, or knowledgeable about, policy issues. Issues tend to be covered by other reporters—specialists on economics or foreign policy or what have you—in the relatively large news organizations where full-time political reporters work." [8] Reporters' own interests and skills direct them away from issues and toward evaluation of campaign strategy and its success.

Coverage of Incumbents

Second only to the preference of campaign reporters for covering politics rather than policy is the tendency to cover incumbents rather than challengers. This emphasis stretches from presidential campaigns down to congressional campaigns. An analysis of 1980 presidential campaign coverage by CBS Television News and one of the leading wire services, UPI, found that fully three-quarters of all stories about presidential candidates in the ten months preceding the election featured then-incumbent Jimmy Carter—many of them about Carter in his "official" role as president rather than a candidate.[9] Similarly, a study of 1978 congressional races found that, on average, incumbent representatives received over 50 percent more coverage than did their challengers in the last six weeks of the campaign. Even in the last week, incumbents' names were mentioned in 88 percent of the campaign stories, whereas the challengers' names were mentioned only 52 percent of the time.[10]

Incumbents get more attention from the press simply because they are easier to cover. Their official activities would be reported anyway, and they have an established relationship with the press. Reporters "want to simplify and regularize their work load. Given a choice they stick to the most accessible ways to gather news. . . . Like other occupations, newspaper work is more habitual than innovative. Habits favor the status quo—incumbents more than challengers."[11] However, greater coverage of incumbents is also a function of the reporter's assumption, correct in a majority of cases, that the incumbent is the front-runner and likely winner. Thus, "unless or until they exceed public expectations at the polls or in the polls, hopeless cases get hopeless coverage."[12]

Differences Between Print and Electronic Journalism

A third factor of importance to campaigns is the difference between print and electronic journalism. First, given the length of television newscasts, a political story will receive somewhere between thirty seconds and two minutes of coverage. The written text of all the news presented on an evening network broadcast would not fill the front page of the *New York Times*. Thus, even if television reporters wished to present an in-depth story on a candidate on a given day, time constraints make it virtually impossible. Second, because television is a visual medium, any substantial story, to hold viewers' attention, must have an interesting visual background. The way the story looks is as important as how it sounds. If a campaign event isn't graphically appealing, it is likely to be ignored.

The stepchild of electronic journalism, radio, presents a different situation. The news departments at music or talk stations are starved for funds and attention. Many are "rip and read" operations—tearing copy off a wire service machine and presenting it as the news. Radio stations are much more likely than major market television stations to use political press releases exactly as they are written by a campaign staff, or to feature "actualities"—comments taped by candidates on issues of their own choosing and offered to stations for free play. (The sophisticated media production facilities of both national party organizations have made it possible to offer video actualities via satellite to local TV stations as well.) Because of the difficulty that many candidates for office below the statewide level have in getting free TV and newspaper attention, alert campaign staffers may take advantage of the availability of radio air time. This opportunity is further described near the end of the next section.

Coverage of Nonpresidential Campaigns

Beyond these general precepts about campaign reporting, there are significant differences between the coverage given to nonpresidential and to presidential campaigns. The two most important distinctions are the volume of coverage and the extent to which candidates are subjected to critical analysis.

Presidential campaign coverage begins as much as two years before the election and becomes the subject of daily reporting by January of the election year. The winter and spring caucuses and primaries are events that become a "handle" for the coverage. In contrast, one reporter estimated that daily newspaper coverage of gubernatorial races does not start until Labor Day and that Senate races are not covered extensively until Columbus Day—less than a month before the election. Another reporter said: "There used to be a tradition that you'd write a story on Labor Day kicking off the campaign. We do that later and later now. Even though in some respects the candidates are getting ready earlier than they ever did, I don't think the public awareness is; we have to wait a little bit to grab them."

Furthermore, nonpresidential candidates receive less critical scrutiny. In news stories, as opposed to commentary or editorials, network television reporting of presidential campaigns is analytic, thematic, and critical: "The networks consider film of the candidate's words as record enough, and their job is to analyze and criticize what the candidate's words really mean." [13]

This is much less true of television coverage of nonpresidential candidates, however. Network news essentially does not report on nonpresidential candidates. In the ten months prior to the 1980 election, CBS ran one ten-second story about a governor's race, and all House and Senate races combined got 2 percent of CBS's newstime. Much of that dealt with the members of Congress enmeshed in the Abscam scandal and with the activities of NCPAC in targeting liberal senators.[14] What media coverage nonpresidential candidates do receive is on local television and in local newspapers, and it is rarely critical or analytic, particularly of candidates for federal rather than state office.

The differences in press attention occur for two reasons. First, unlike presidential candidates, senatorial and congressional candidates do not travel with a press entourage; they have no campaign bus or plane. When candidates come to a local media market, reporters who have not otherwise been following them are assigned to cover their appearance. With only a remote idea of the details of a story they may not cover again for weeks, if ever, they are unlikely to subject the candidate to a searching analysis.

Second, reporters who *do have* political beats are usually based at the statehouse. A Senate campaign manager explained, "You have a state press corps that is highly conversant with state issues, knows them intimately, can get in a dialogue, and suddenly they're covering a federal campaign." Statehouse reporters attach less priority to federal races. One commented: "Gubernatorial elections are inherently more interesting and important than Senate elections, and you have to go with that. The set of issues they deal with is different. One person is being asked how they would run the state and the other how they'd vote in the Senate. They're not equivalent."

Thus even senatorial candidates can find it difficult to get as much coverage as they would like. John Chafee's Senate campaign in Rhode Island had this problem, despite the single major media market in Providence. Chafee's press secretary recalled: "Television in Rhode Island almost ignored that race, almost completely. Most stations didn't show up at press conferences. The biggest station's sum total of on-scene coverage was to cover each candidate for a day; and they'd report stories off the wire, but very little."

Thus journalists' view of the office, even more than the nature of the media market, is the critical factor. The less the coverage, the more it benefits the better-known incumbent. Chafee's press aide added:

> I got very upset when the major TV station wouldn't cover a press conference when Chafee was being endorsed by the Women's Political Caucus. But the flip side is they wouldn't cover Michaelson [his opponent] either. I'd give up mine for theirs not being covered. As the

incumbent, you control a lot more. It would be far more frustrating in the challenger's shoes.

Below the statewide level, candidates' ability to get free media coverage is so limited that relations with the press are almost an afterthought. The director of the Republican campaign to get control of the New Jersey state legislature, described in chapter 5, stressed the almost total reliance on radio advertising, direct mail, and phone banks, saying, "We were assuming we would get no free media." A New Jersey political reporter for one of the state's most respected papers confirmed the correctness of this view: "We cover seven legislative districts, which means forty-two candidates for the Assembly and Senate, so no one of them is going to get a whole lot of play."

House campaigns, particularly those of incumbents, also heavily stress their paid messages and voter contact activities, and take the same view of the press. They do not expect television coverage and assign little importance to newspaper coverage. A ranking aide to an entrenched incumbent described the print coverage as minimal: "We didn't go out of our way to cultivate it. We weren't out there to do media events. There was very little coverage that wasn't our press releases. They played our releases." A staffer for another incumbent first recalled that the campaign did not have a press secretary, then remembered, "Oh, actually it was the candidate's brother, who hung around. He also did the print ads and the bumper stickers. The campaign manager didn't care."

To congressional campaigners, getting on radio news with actualities is of somewhat more interest. Because filling their news time easily and cheaply is the primary concern of most radio stations, campaigns, as noted earlier, have a good chance of getting technically decent actualities on the air, particularly in smaller markets. The actualities most likely to be picked up are those that describe events and thus resemble genuine news stories. A Michigan challenger was successful in placing this typical actuality on nine of the ten stations in his rural district:

> PRODUCER'S VOICE: This is RAM radio network. Norm Hughes, a candidate for Congressman in Michigan's eighth district, was a witness before the Republican platform hearings today. At the Detroit meeting, Hughes succeeded in placing language in the draft platform that would require foreign producers to meet the same standards for farm produce as American producers must. Hughes also discussed other moves needed to bolster the farm economy. Our report is 24 seconds long and begins on my count 3-2-1. . . .
> HUGHES: The Republican Party should take pride in the ability of the American farmer to provide our citizens with their food needs while at the same time providing the single largest balance of trade. Basically the farmers want to be able to be free to produce whatever

quantities that they can and they want the federal government to do nothing for them except help export the products of their labor.[15]

Actualities have a number of advantages over regular radio advertising. First, they are considerably less expensive. Although production costs are the same, the only other investment is for a telephone call to the station manager. Second, they are presented as news rather than as commercials and thus have the greater credibility associated with news. Third, they are targeted to events as they are occurring, and have an immediacy and relevance that paid messages may not have. Finally, they can substitute for a personal appearance by the candidate. As consultant Charles Black observes, "Granted, the candidate cannot make personal appearances in all the small towns and boroughs—but there is no reason his voice cannot." [16]

In summary, for challengers below the statewide level, free media coverage is essential to build recognition. As we have seen, however, they are unlikely to get whatever meager coverage there is unless they have raised enough money to establish a presence with their paid advertising. Reporters, along with the rest of the political community, share the view of the consultant who said, "Money is a reflection of your political support." By and large, though, the free media is a more basic concern of campaigns for statewide positions—senators and governors—and the latter more than the former.

Campaign Interaction with the News Media _____

Although nonpresidential candidates may find the news media's casual attitude toward their campaigns rather frustrating, there may be an advantage to the lackluster and tardy attention the media provide. Nonpresidential campaigns can establish their themes before the press takes an interest and devise events for reportage that reinforce the message they present in their paid advertising. This is the reverse of the situation in presidential campaigns, where, media strategists agree, "The messages each candidate communicates to viewers in the nightly news shows are far more important than the messages they convey in their ads." [17] In the following sections we will examine how campaigns respond to the challenges and opportunities offered by the news media.

Meshing the Advertising and Press Messages

For senatorial and gubernatorial candidates, the desired role of the press is coverage reflecting the theme the candidate is purveying in paid media. If the campaign is not successful in meshing the advertising and press messages, voters are unlikely to internalize the campaign's theme or to understand exactly what messages the candidate wants to send. As consultant David Garth observed, "When the paid media is conveying one message and the free media conveys another, you actually lose support." [18] Both strategists and outside observers of ultimately unsuccessful campaigns cite the disjunction of free and paid media messages as a factor in the candidate's loss. A staffer for Indiana senator Birch Bayh said: "I felt the kinds of things Quayle said on free TV were much more consistent with his campaign themes, and much more reinforcing than Bayh was. I used to try to get him to stick to two or three points and he never did. He was too complex; he wasn't a robot." Of New Jersey Senate candidate Millicent Fenwick, a strategist asked: "Was there a theme in the general election? Quite honestly, no, because of the candidate herself. It was hard to put her on track and hold her."

Exploiting Media Events

In reporting on senatorial and gubernatorial candidates, the press concentrates on the candidate's appearances—known in the trade as "media events." It is the task of a good campaign staff to coordinate speaking engagements, and other events that the press will cover, with the paid commercials for the candidate. Describing the relationship between Senator Frank Lautenberg's paid and free exposure during his campaign against Millicent Fenwick, Lautenberg's campaign manager explained:

> We wanted the free media to always be complementing what we had on the air, so when the jobs ads started running, we went on a two-day job swing through the state, to sites that pointed up some example of Mrs. Fenwick's anti-jobs record. The same thing with the Social Security advertising. We'd go to a senior citizens' home to dramatize the thrust.

Strategist Eve Lubalin, discussing Senator Birch Bayh's swings through Indiana's various media markets, said of the media events staged by the campaign, "We decided what the TV story would be, and it usually worked." One such event, designed to complement the paid media on energy concerns, had the candidate talking to some coal miners at a loading dock: "I remember being on the phone with the coal company people, talking about what it looked like—I had never seen it—basically what kind of visual it would be, what I wanted to create. Then I got some mineworkers to go over there."

Losing Control of Free Media

Because of the relative lack of interest the press has in Senate races, such strategies generally work, and campaigns can maintain good control over their press coverage. Press coverage creates problems for a Senate campaign only if the contest generates a great deal of conflict or has other elements the press can seize on as newsworthy. Such was the case confronting the liberal Democratic senators who were the victims of the first massive targeting effort by right-wing groups in 1980. Eve Lubalin described the effect of the conservative assault on Bayh:

> From the time NCPAC put us on their list, I don't think there was one story I read in an Indiana paper that didn't start off, or have parenthetically in one of the first three paragraphs, "Birch Bayh, one of the five most liberal senators targeted by conservative groups...." It began to dominate the news. Wherever Bayh went, instead of the thing being covered the way we wanted it, the story was these groups picketing him.
>
> When the oil companies demanded service station owners take down our posters, we were going to film Exxon coming in and forcing this little service station dealer to take down his Bayh poster, and Bayh talking about freedom of speech, freedom of the press. The pickets were there and the TV coverage was them heckling Bayh—we totally lost control of the event.

The inability of the senators under attack in 1980 to react quickly and effectively to the right-wing onslaught also played into the hands of the media, with their penchant for highlighting candidates' inconsistencies. The press secretary to Frank Church of Idaho, another 1980 victim, believes that "NCPAC galvanized a lot of response. The biggest problem we had in that campaign was to come to agreement, adopt a strategy to deal with the right wing, and we waffled all over the place." In 1982 and afterward, the attacks were expected, planned for in advance, and effectively deterred by most of NCPAC's targets.

A different problem confronted Senate candidate Millicent Fenwick. She was dogged not by protesting groups, but by the nonsenatorial image created by her being the nationally known model for Lacey Davenport in the popular "Doonesbury" comic strip. If every story about Birch Bayh referred to him as "one of the five most liberal senators," every story about Fenwick characterized her as "the pipe-smoking aristocratic grandmother." In its editorial endorsement of Frank Lautenberg, the *New York Times* headline read, "Horatio Alger Versus Lacey Davenport." When President Reagan visited the state on Fenwick's behalf, newspaper photos featured a protester carrying a sign reading, "73-year-old actor has lunch with 72-year-old comic strip character." Such coverage did not encourage voters to take Fenwick seriously.

Performing Well on TV
Interview Shows and Debates

Another major form of free media exposure available to Senate candidates consists of appearances on news interview programs and debates with their opponents. These have some value to candidates not because of their minuscule audiences but because short excerpts from them become "bites"—brief items on the regular news programs. Their greatest value, however, comes when a candidate performs well in the eyes of the press: "The media often take their cues about electability from a candidate's performance." [19] It is of some importance to campaigns that debate performances can influence the tone of the rest of the media coverage. When 1984 Maine Senate challenger Libby Mitchell missed her final debate with incumbent William Cohen because she was at the hairdresser's, the press coverage was immediate and savage: "She was in Vassalboro getting her hair cut. . . . We've been working on this for two months. Everyone knew about it except the Mitchell people," the state's largest paper quoted the television station manager.[20] Such stories were no help to the already staggering Mitchell campaign.

The Special Case of Gubernatorial Candidates

Because reporters attach more significance to gubernatorial races and because they receive heavier and earlier coverage than Senate contests, free media coverage plays a somewhat greater role in governors' races than it does in Senate contests. As in presidential contests, gubernatorial campaign strategists attempt to use the press to complement paid messages effectively, or even as a partial substitute for expensive advertising.

The fact that journalists arrive earlier in the campaign season, pay more attention, and are more knowledgeable about the issues can be a particular advantage for lesser-known and underfinanced challengers. In a Senate race, a challenger with little money for paid advertising, and in an uphill battle for press coverage, would be unable to get a theme out and would be well on the way to losing. A gubernatorial challenger, with some luck, can conserve funds for a last-minute advertising push and use the press to keep the campaign alive. This was the strategy of challenger Mark White in his successful Texas race against incumbent William Clements. As his manager described it:

> The strategy of the campaign was to fight a holding action until the last three weeks. We couldn't match Clements's money. We trapped Clements into a series of debates, which was his downfall. The most important part was [that] the debates would give the press something to

focus on in this intervening period while we saved up our money, something other than Clements's paid media.

However, it was not enough simply to perform well in the debates, as White did. The campaign also had to convince the press that White was a credible candidate by sustaining a paid media presence and demonstrating that the candidate had support, which, as usual, was defined as the ability to raise money. White's manager described the campaign's problems in this regard and the way the staff dealt with them:

> In the middle of August, we had about $60,000 in the bank—we were broke. That $60,000 bought about two weeks of radio at minimal levels. Everybody said, "Let's throw it on the radio and we'll try to raise the money for next week's radio tomorrow." That's the way we lived for ten weeks. We'd bring Mark off the road for a day and a half and try to raise enough money for next week. We were always about three days away from somebody in the state writing a story that we were broke.

Differences Among Media Outlets

In deciding how to approach the press, a final consideration for candidates is the difference between radio, television, and print journalism and journalists. Radio presents the fewest difficulties but offers the fewest rewards. Aside from actualities, or participating in call-in shows, there is not much of a role for radio in a campaign's free media plan. Candidates have shown increasing interest in local cable television, which is similar in many respects to radio, but its audiences are still very small.[21]

The major consideration for campaigns in planning media events is to strike a balance between the need for planned visuals, which television demands, and the cynicism with which print reporters regard media events. A staffer for a Senate campaign recalled, "If you wanted to get TV to cover the candidate, it had to be something you could cover in thirty seconds that had an interesting background, whereas with a newspaper story, you had to convince them there was a story and not just a visual there." A Senate press secretary with experience as both a print and television reporter said: "I tried to set up events that weren't insulting to the print guys for the sake of TV. Because you can create a terrible backlash of being criticized as a media-conscious campaign—which of course every campaign is. It's an awful balance." A reporter for a state news program on New Jersey public television, which is closer in behavior to print than to commercial TV, gave an example of the usual differences between the print-versus-television coverage of a media event in the campaign of Governor Thomas Kean:

Kean was campaigning with Jack Kemp in Camden. They were walking on this horrible, horrible street, talking about urban enterprise zones. We did a pretty harsh report. After all the other television crews left, we went and asked the neighbors what they thought about the visit. That was a better story than their being there. You couldn't get away with that on commercial TV. There's no action there at all. The parade's gone. All the visuals have left.

In summary, press coverage can have some effect in nonpresidential campaigns for statewide office, particularly for governors. But unlike its role in presidential campaigns, it is clearly secondary to the candidates' paid media in advancing the campaign's central arguments. As one consultant mused, "If you don't have money for media, the only way you build credibility is with the press. . . . If you don't have money, you're probably going to lose."

Much of the early fall of election years is devoted to a campaign's agenda-setting requirements. The messages that campaigns transmit in paid and free media are what permit them to set the campaign's agenda. Elections become close contests when both campaigns are successful in setting out themes that penetrate the consciousness of voters and strike enough of a chord to produce a potential winning coalition. As strategists in close contests move into the final weeks, they seek to hold their coalitions together, find appeals that will persuade undecided voters, respond to charges by their opponents, and, finally, get their supporters to the polls. In the next chapter, we look at these final weeks of a campaign.

Notes _____

1. These costs are reported in *Congressional Quarterly Weekly Report*, December 22, 1984, 3152; *Des Moines Register*, October 21, 1984, 1A.
2. Louis Sandy Maisel, *From Obscurity to Oblivion: Running in the Congressional Primary* (Knoxville: University of Tennessee Press, 1982), 111; Edie N. Goldenberg and Michael W. Traugott, *Campaigning for Congress* (Washington, D.C.: CQ Press, 1984), 116-19.
3. Goldenberg and Traugott, *Campaigning for Congress*, 116.
4. Stuart Rothenberg, *Winners and Losers* (Washington, D.C.: Free Congress Research and Education Foundation, 1983), 49.
5. Tom Wicker, "The Other Jesse," *New York Times*, April 17, 1984, A23.
6. See, for example, Jeff Greenfield, *The Real Campaign* (New York: Summit Books, 1982); John Carey, "How Media Shapes Campaigns," *Journal of Communication* 26 (1976): 50-57; Thomas E. Patterson and Robert D. McClure, *The Unseeing Eye: The Myth of Television Power in National Politics* (New York:

Putnam, 1976); Thomas E. Patterson, *The Mass Media Election: How Americans Choose Their President* (New York: Praeger, 1980); Michael J. Robinson and Margaret Sheehan, *Over the Wire and on TV* (New York: Russell Sage, 1983); Peter Clarke and Susan H. Evans, *Covering Congress: Journalism in Congressional Campaigns* (Stanford, Calif.: Stanford University Press, 1983).
7. Robinson and Sheehan, *Over the Wire and on TV*, 148.
8. Donald Matthews, "Winnowing: The News Media and the 1976 Presidential Nominations," in *Race for the Presidency: The Media and the Nominating Process*, ed. James David Barber (Englewood Cliffs, N.J.: Prentice-Hall, 1978), 66-67.
9. Robinson and Sheehan, *Over the Wire and on TV*, 6.
10. Clarke and Evans, *Covering Campaigns*, 43-46.
11. Ibid., 5.
12. Robinson and Sheehan, *Over the Wire and on TV*, 76.
13. Ibid., 233.
14. Ibid., 172-73.
15. Nedra Carpel, "Radio Airtime: Free for the Sophisticate," *Campaigns and Elections* 1 (Winter 1981): 41-42.
16. Ibid., 42.
17. Martin Schramm, "The Media Isn't the Message," *Washington Post National Weekly Edition*, April 16, 1984, 12.
18. Ibid.
19. Jeff Greenfield, *Running to Win* (New York: Simon & Schuster, 1980), 199.
20. *Portland Press-Herald*, October 20, 1984.
21. *National Journal*, April 7, 1984, 657-61.

Winning the Election 8

> *Even though we were down six points ten days before the election, I figured we were going to win because I felt we really controlled the dynamic of the races; we controlled the dialogue and the definition of what was at stake.*
> —Manager for a successful Senate challenger

As campaigns move into the final weeks before the election, their course is determined by what has gone before. If one of the candidates— usually a weak challenger—has not acquired reasonably high levels of positive recognition or has not advanced a theme that appeals to substantial segments of the electorate, the contest is effectively over, even though the balloting has not yet taken place. In some elections, however, the contest may remain spirited until the final moments.

When the race is a tossup, campaign organizations have two major tasks. The first is to continue to advance the candidate's arguments, reinforce the candidate's base, and respond to the opponent's charges. The second is to devise and implement a plan to ensure the highest possible turnout of the candidate's supporters on election day itself. In this chapter we will look at the activities in this final stage of closely fought campaigns.

The Electronic Debate

By the time a campaign reaches its final weeks, the two candidates have had the opportunity to set its agenda and assume control of its dialogue. The degree of success each campaign achieves produces one of three patterns: (1) A candidate who is far ahead will refuse to be drawn into debate. Opposition charges go unanswered, so long as there is no evidence that they are affecting the electorate. (2) A candidate who has been far ahead is put on the defensive, is on the wrong side of the momentum in the race, and is in danger of losing control of the dialogue. (3) Both candidates have advanced persuasive themes capable of mobilizing a winning coalition. In the second and third cases, campaigns take on the quality of an electronic debate—a volley of charges and countercharges on TV and radio and via direct mail. In their paid and free media, candidates must respond to compelling accusations, make appeals that will rally those still undecided, or convert weak supporters of the opposition to their cause.

The problem for a campaign is to determine what type of situation it actually faces. Volatility in the electorate has increased enormously in the past few decades. In the 1940s, more than three-quarters of the voters made up their minds about whom to support before Labor Day. This figure frequently dwindled to a third by the 1980s. Another third did not decide until the last two weeks of the campaign, or on election day itself.[1] Thus even candidates who seem safely ahead worry that some last-minute activity on the part of the rival camp or events on the national or world scene will erase an apparently secure lead. For their part, candidates who believe they are on the defensive or are locked in a close race have to deduce what appeals will swing the momentum in their direction.

All campaigns have considerable difficulty in determining exactly which voters need shoring up, what the most effective last-minute appeals will be, and where and how to communicate the messages. The uncertainty characterizing the final days can lead to strenuous efforts in all directions, with little knowledge about the effectiveness of any strategy. In Stimson Bullitt's classic formulation, "every cartridge must be fired because among the multitude of blanks one may be a bullet."[2]

The Advent of Tracking Polls

As Robert Caro has described, in the "era before the widespread use of political polling, information was a commodity very difficult for a politician to obtain. . . . A candidate might wonder—might be desperate to know—how his strategy was working, but it was hard for him to find out."[3] With the advent of reliable polling techniques, a major source of useful information became available. Campaigns that use *tracking polls*— scientific samplings of opinion taken every day during the last few weeks of a campaign—can chart the considerable ups and downs in candidates' support, identify which groups in the electorate are particularly volatile, and what issues concern the voters most. As pollster Bill Hamilton observed, "Nobody goes in with that much of a solid vote anymore. That's why tracking is so important."

Any professionally managed senatorial or gubernatorial campaign that can afford it now uses tracking polls. The usual recommendation is that the polls begin about a month before the election and continue until immediately before election day. In theory the same schedule applies to House races, but tracking is much less frequent in these contests. For all the reasons we have noted earlier—one-party dominance of many congressional districts, the lopsided margins in many races, the lower media profile—a substantial number of House races are never in doubt. In the minority that are real contests, tracking is usually too expensive. Hamilton estimated that a congressional campaign must be budgeted at no less than half a million dollars to afford tracking polls. Only about a fifth of House candidates raise this much, and many are the safest of incumbents. Further, competitive House races tend to be in the suburban areas of large population centers, where the high cost of media makes it difficult for candidates to get new information out to the voters.

No sophisticated campaign organization doubts the need for tracking polls; the problem is to pay for them. Here Republican candidates have a distinct advantage. Polling is another function increasingly performed by their national party committees. The National Republican Senatorial Committee tracks all close races for four to six weeks prior to election day. Although Federal Election Commission rules specify that the committee cannot transmit the detailed findings to campaign organizations without charging them against permissible in-kind contributions, they "*are* allowed to describe general trends and suggest remedial action—which is, of course, all any campaign really needs to know." [4]

The value of such information is seen in close races like Missouri senator John Danforth's 1982 contest against Democratic challenger Harriet Woods. In June, incumbent Danforth was ahead by about thirty points. After Woods won a surprisingly strong early August primary victory, the margin narrowed to a still very comfortable fifteen points, where it remained through the middle of October. But in the third week of October, the bottom dropped out for Danforth, as it did for many other Republican incumbent senators. Democratic challengers were increasing their media barrages, and the news was dominated by the recently announced 10 percent rate of unemployment, the first double-digit jobless figure since the Great Depression. Republican tracking polls now showed the race as even.[5] Party strategists in Washington "suggested appropriate adjustments in Danforth's media advertising cam-

paign, and Danforth was able to surge ahead in the final hours." [6]
Neither the Woods campaign nor the national Democratic party had any
similar polling system; the Woods effort, in fact, was "flying blind" in
the crucial closing days.

Danforth defeated Woods by less than two points. In a post-election
analysis, Woods's manager mused on strategies the campaign might
have utilized, concluding "What if. . . . ? We'll never know, will we?" [7]
Had the Woods effort been privy to the information the Danforth
campaign had, she might, indeed, have known.

Beginning in 1984, the National Republican Congressional Committee undertook the performance of the same function for House candidates in close races. As Republican consultant Vince Breglio said of the
defeat of fourteen Republican House incumbents in 1982:

> There were incumbents who shouldn't have lost. They lost because
> they didn't know where they were going in the last two weeks of the
> campaign. They thought they were ahead, but the data they were
> looking at was from mid-September, and things had changed dramati-
> cally enough that they needed much more in the way of media and
> much more aggressive posturing. With that in mind, the congressional
> committee is going to do some tracking in selected races.

Thus in competitive races daily polling of a volatile electorate has
become virtually a necessity in the last four weeks or so of a campaign.

Tracking Polls and Campaign Money

Tracking is important not only because of the information it gives
campaigns so they know to adjust their strategies. Reliable data
that a once-hopeless candidate has come within striking distance is
critical for raising the money that campaigns need for the final paid
advertising and get-out-the-vote efforts in a close race. In the case of
Missouri's Harriet Woods, for instance, more than half the money spent
in the general election was raised in the last two weeks of the campaign.
Much of it was "Washington money"—contributions from PACs based
in the capital and from national party committees.[8] As in Representative
Robin Tallon's campaign, described in chapter 5, the money did not flow
in from these sources until Woods could demonstrate she was indeed a
credible challenger. Democratic committees could only afford to give
Woods roughly a third of what the Republicans gave Danforth; moreover, well over half of Woods's party money did not arrive until the
final two weeks. Her support from PACs was less than half of Danforth's, and 40 percent of that also arrived in the last two weeks.
Wyoming representative Richard Cheney describes well the problems
candidates have with Washington money: "Much of the money that is

said to be available for campaigns really does not appear until after the race has already been decided." [9]

On the other hand, failure to move up in the tracking polls slows up the flow of funds coming into the campaign. Even the well-funded Republican national committees stop short of maximum efforts when tracking shows their candidates trailing substantially. The executive director of the National Republican Senatorial Committee observed: "This committee has a very strong interest in knowing exactly what's going on in each state so it can decide where to spend its dollars, where to direct supportive PACs or individuals. . . . We will be very bold and aggressive to try to make things happen, but we won't throw our money away." One Republican Senate candidate who learned this was right-to-life activist Florence Sullivan, running against incumbent Daniel Patrick Moynihan in New York in 1982. The national party committees invested $350,000 in the Sullivan campaign, primarily for television advertising. When tracking polls showed Moynihan maintaining his lead, the money was cut off. Sullivan, who personally managed to raise only $117,000, against the more than $2 million spent by the Moynihan campaign, lost by a two-to-one margin.

The importance of sufficient money for a last-minute drive was also seen in the Millicent Fenwick-Frank Lautenberg campaign in New Jersey. At the end of September, polls for both candidates showed Fenwick maintaining a twenty-point lead and also a large lead in voter recognition. Both campaigns stopped polling for two weeks. With a cash-flow problem and an apparently insurmountable lead, the Fenwick campaign decided it could postpone its planned tracking until mid-October and use its phone banks for fundraising calls rather than for tracking. The Lautenberg organization simply found the news too depressing; as the manager recalled, "I said no more polls. We started joking about running for governor in '85." Nor were any public polls taken during the first half of October, and the National Republican Senatorial Committee did not begin to track the race until mid-October either.

However, during the moratorium on polling, Lautenberg ran an extremely heavy negative media campaign against Fenwick, and unemployment figures, which hurt every Republican candidate and played directly into the theme of Lautenberg's advertising, came out. When polling resumed in mid-October, Lautenberg had cut Fenwick's lead by two-thirds, and their recognition levels were virtually even. Fenwick's pollster remembered: "We said it was a new race. The recognition difference she had was over." Another Fenwick strategist added: "We shouldn't have stopped in October. Money was a problem. We would have had an indicator to start our negative ads much earlier." The

Fenwick campaign devised a response to Lautenberg's charges, but by then her organization was even more strapped for money. As media consultant Jay Smith said of these ads, "Nobody got a chance to see them. The tracking showed we were going back up. We were able to penetrate at all because we socked what we had in radio."

The Lautenberg campaign had no such problem. Seeing possible victory at hand, the candidate himself invested another $300,000 in media for the last few days. Having already purchased the maximum amount of air time available at the lower rates for political advertising, the Lautenberg campaign now bought additional time at the much higher commercial rates. In the subjective view of Fenwick consultant Jay Smith "this man was so bent on winning, the well was so deep, that he bought additional spots at the corporate rate. He was paying the same for a thirty-second spot in prime time in New York City in the final ten days as Exxon would, which is mind-boggling. I'd never seen a candidate who could do that."

Last-minute Strategies

If candidates have good information in the last few weeks and sufficient money to implement a strategy, the question is what that strategy should be. Usually there will be a distinct intensification of the negative tone of the contest. As we have seen in chapter 6, the initial themes of almost all successful challengers, who usually start the race behind, involve attacks against the incumbent. If the attacks draw blood, they are likely to continue until the very end of the contest. However, incumbents—or any frontrunners—who find their leads diminishing must now counterattack. Only the most secure can avoid an attack strategy in the closing weeks and continue to run positive campaigns that ignore the opponent.

Senator Moynihan, in his contest with Florence Sullivan, for example, had "an overwhelming lead that did not fade in successive waves of poll figures" and "ran a campaign that—although unfailingly polite when the candidates met—virtually ignored her." [10] More common are the responses of beleaguered Senate incumbents once far ahead, like Indiana's Birch Bayh and Missouri's John Danforth. A Bayh adviser described the serious erosion of the senator's strength in October—"It was like losing Vietnam—we decided we had to go severely negative. It was extremely controversial; Bayh had never done it before." In Missouri, Danforth began with an entirely positive campaign, wishing to "win reelection as an endorsement of what he considered his affirmative record." When his opponent's attacks made the race a tossup, in the last days "Danforth went negative, accusing Woods of demagoguery and distortion." [11]

In addition to launching negative charges against the opponent, campaigns respond to accusations against them that seem to be having an impact on the electorate. Such responses must not make it seem as if the candidate is on the defensive and in fact concerned about losing. One way of avoiding a loser's image is to integrate the campaign's own theme into the response in such a way that the answer not only effectively refutes the charge but reinforces the candidate's message as well.

The themes of the Fenwick campaign, for example, had been the candidate's long years of service and her reputation for integrity. For eight weeks, her opponent had engaged in an intensive negative campaign that highlighted carefully selected aspects of Fenwick's long record and implied that the seventy-two-year-old candidate might not be in full control. A recurring question in the Lautenberg ads was, "What could be on Millicent Fenwick's *mind* down in Washington? Certainly not New Jersey." When Fenwick responded, her advertising continued to stress her experience and character, implying that her opponent might be deficient in both:

> On Tuesday, New Jersey will decide who will take the Senate seat Harrison Williams was forced to resign—Millicent Fenwick or Frank Lautenberg. Mrs. Fenwick has a long record of excellent service to New Jersey. She's been called the conscience of the Congress, and the Bergen *Record* says she's given New Jersey's image a much-needed boost. Lautenberg has no record in elective office. Given the outright lies in his campaign, he must have no conscience either. Millicent Fenwick— because New Jersey deserves a senator with integrity.

A similar attempt to integrate the candidate's theme into a response to a charge occurred in the 1982 New York gubernatorial race between conservative Republican Lewis Lehrman and liberal Democrat Mario Cuomo. Lehrman spent weeks lambasting Cuomo for his opposition to the politically popular death penalty and for his positions on criminal justice generally. One frequently played Lehrman spot asked:

> Have you taken a close look at Mario Cuomo's positions on crime? Cuomo has supported every one of Hugh Carey's six vetoes of the death penalty. If he's elected, Cuomo favors releasing some prisoners before their terms are completed, and when asked what the solution is to crime, Cuomo said, "There is none." Lew Lehrman will sign the death penalty and make criminals serve their full sentences. Lew Lehrman believes we can reduce crime.

Cuomo's response to Lehrman incorporated his theme stressing traditional values and the family; an ad showed him walking down his own middle-class New York City street, telling viewers:

Recently on this street my wife and son were mugged and robbed. Like
so many other victims, we'll never forget that experience. As governor,
I'll fight back for the things that work—more police, less plea-
bargaining, and surer, stiffer sentences. Criminals have to learn that
they'll be caught, convicted, and canned. With all of our politicians'
tough talk, they haven't done that. I'll do it, because I have to do it—for
my family and yours.

Some candidates are fortunate enough to destroy opponents'
charges by proving them false. A candidate trapped in a well-publicized
lie is extremely unlikely to win. Perhaps the most bizarre example of
this fact occurred in the Mississippi gubernatorial race of 1983. Going
into October, the state's then-attorney general, Democrat Bill Allain,
held a thirty-point lead in the polls over Republican businessman Leon
Bramlett. Although Republicans had never won a gubernatorial race in
Mississippi, one candidate had come within four points. The state had
two Republican representatives and a Republican senator, and had voted
for the Republican presidential candidate three times since 1964. A black
candidate who had previously run for the Senate, splitting the Democratic vote and permitting the Republican to win, was once again
running as an independent in the gubernatorial race. A Republican
victory by a strong candidate was, therefore, by no means out of the
question. Bramlett's organization, which had fired its campaign manager
and national consultants in September and was dominated by political
amateurs, including the candidate himself, frantically searched for a
major issue to use against Allain.

The issue they came up with led to one of the strangest and dirtiest
campaigns in recent American history. In mid-October, a Jackson
attorney appeared on Mississippi television in a paid political program
to announce, "Our investigation has established by clear and convincing
evidence, beyond a reasonable doubt, that Mr. Bill Allain has, over the
years, frequently participated in homosexual activities with male prostitutes." Interviews, which followed, were intended to show that these
alleged sexual contacts were black transvestites. With graphics identifying them as "Nicole Toy, AKA Grady Arrington" and "Davia Ross,
AKA David Holiday," the transvestites were asked such questions as
"When you say *oral sex*, did he [Allain] want you to perform oral sex
on him?" and "Is it general knowledge in the gay community that he is
dating men?" To all such questions, the interviewees replied affirmatively.

It was soon revealed that Bramlett supporters had paid the homosexuals substantial sums to make their charges. Allain's advertisements
containing his denial of the charge, while obviously necessary, were no
less astounding. His ex-wife told voters she had had a normal married
life. The candidate himself appeared, announcing, "I'm Bill Allain.

Yesterday I passed an independent lie detector test, proving that the charges against me are false." Another Allain advertisement summarized the campaign's response: "There's a new word in our campaign for governor, and the word is smear. Here is what the smear merchants would like us to believe. Three male prostitutes. Each with criminal records. Each admittedly bribed [for] $300, and $50 a day."

Despite the spectacular nature of the charges and the introduction of sexual and racial elements in one of the most conservative and racially charged electorates in the nation, Bill Allain garnered 55 percent of the vote in a three-way race. After the election, the homosexuals appearing in Bramlett's paid broadcasts confirmed the voters' opinion that the allegations were false and that none of them had ever met Allain.

In the final days of an election period, campaigns may also choose to level charges, or respond to them, in a quieter and more targeted fashion, through direct mail. Direct mail is used to reach specific audiences. For example, a Lautenberg piece sent into the New Jersey black community reminded minority citizens that a vote for Fenwick could continue Republican control of the Senate and the occupancy of important committee leadership positions by senators such as Jesse Helms, who had led the battle against making the birthday of Martin Luther King, Jr., a national holiday. Such mailings illustrate the observation of Republican direct mail strategist John Simms: "A TV message can't be very specialized. That's not true with mail. You can mail a very specialized message that has no bleed into other groups."

Thus, in the last weeks of a closely contested campaign, candidates use their advertising to level accusations against their opponents and to reply to charges made against them. At the same time, the press is stepping up its coverage of these campaigns. The interaction of campaigns with the press in this period is our next subject.

The Role of Free Media

As campaigns move into their final phase, coverage by print and television journalists intensifies but does not change in any important thematic or substantive respect. Indeed, if anything, reporters' interest in the horse race aspects increases. Sophisticated campaigns quickly learn that while the press will report the charges and countercharges that characterize this stage of the campaign, it will draw back from making any assessment of their validity or factual accuracy. Because campaign strategists are aware that independent judgments are more credible than statements by candidates or their supporters, however, they seek external confirmation of their positions from outside institutions like the media.

As we have indicated in chapter 7, however, campaigns are not likely to get it. An aide to Connecticut gubernatorial challenger Lew Rome said of the Connecticut press: "They didn't care about what we were saying about Bill O'Neill. We would make an accusation with some facts, and they would demand more instead of trying to find more themselves. They did no work on their own in terms of developing a story." The Bayh campaign had no more luck in persuading the press to look at the links they believed existed between challenger Dan Quayle and right-to-life and fundamentalist religious groups dogging Bayh—links that his campaign felt were not only politically damaging but also violated campaign finance laws. Eve Lubalin said: "The reporters refused to investigate until the last weekend, when the groups ran out of money and Quayle printed their literature with his campaign committee's name on it. It was so outrageous that the last weekend, as Quayle went around the state, he was followed and asked about it. By then it was too late." In Idaho, Senator Frank Church, under assault by NCPAC, had a similar experience. His press secretary recalled:

> I kept making a point to the largest papers—NCPAC says Church did something and you report what NCPAC says. Church says he did not. Now look, he did or he didn't. You can go to the public library and get the record. On a couple of occasions they finally did, but over the long run, no. There's inertia and lack of resources.

Nor are these observations merely sour grapes on the part of campaign organizations. Students of the media and reporters themselves confirm them. In their study of network and wire service coverage of the 1980 presidential election, Michael Robinson and Margaret Sheehan found that CBS and UPI were almost eight times as willing as other news organizations to draw explicit conclusions about presidential candidates' chances as about their leadership qualities. They concluded, "Saying nothing about the issues, beyond what others have said, strikes us as being the first commandment in campaign news coverage." A study of coverage of the 1984 presidential election yielded similar findings.[12] Similarly, an analysis of congressional campaign coverage discovered that although reporters agreed that the candidates emphasized the issues above anything else, the journalists themselves stressed personal characteristics and political attributes such as experience and name recognition in their stories.[13] A journalist for a major state newspaper described the reporter's view:

> The reporter thinks—the charge, the countercharge, and it's covered like that. The middle ground—who's correct and who's wrong—there's no time to find that out. Or someone will get dispatched to find out and

will write a Sunday story. That's the catch basin in journalism. Correct it on Sunday, but let it go wrong for six days.

Thus all the factors described in chapter 7—the journalists' lack of substantive background, the pressure to move on to the next assigned story, the premium on hard facts and events as opposed to judgments—operate as the press covers the end stages of a campaign. How, then, do campaigns act to get their stories out?

The Techniques of Charge and Countercharge

Since campaigns cannot rely on reporters to effectively press their charges and responses, they must place primary emphasis on their own paid media. Thomas Patterson and Robert McClure argue persuasively that, given press attention to campaign hoopla and the horse race, voters in fact learn more about candidates' issue positions, and criticisms of them, from political advertising than they do from political journalism.[14] In fact, dramatic new charges made in advertisements will often rate a news story. As one reporter observed, "Nowadays, if a candidate is going to start attacking, it's more likely to happen in a new series of TV ads than in a speech someplace." Candidates may call press conferences for the explicit purpose of screening new advertising waves for the press. The purveyors of the sexual charges against Mississippi governor Bill Allain, for instance, decided to buy advertising time only after they were unable to convince the leading Mississippi media to investigate. Once the ads were aired, investigation was minimal, but coverage was not.

Still, as Republican media consultant Roger Ailes said, "In the beginning, when a candidate is totally unknown, paid media tend to define a candidate's background. But then as the public gets to know the candidate, and Election Day approaches, I think the importance of the so-called free media increases and the paid media decreases."[15] Thus campaigns seek ways to get effective press coverage of the messages they want to disseminate, other than the usually ineffective strategy of giving reporters a lead to follow up. Playing on reporters' own preferences, they try to create a news story, through either a new series of advertisements or a staged event.

To be effective, strategists must keep in mind several factors which make it more likely that the press will pick the story up and that the story will be regarded as credible and persuasive by both the journalistic community and, ultimately, the public. We will examine those factors in the following sections.

Staying Off the Defensive. It is generally unwise for candidates to defend themselves personally or to make the hostile accusations against the opponent. When candidates themselves try to explain away charges that are matters of judgment rather than fact, they are usually seen as having been forced on the defensive, and the explanation will be reported that way. Perhaps the classic example of this is Richard Nixon's "I am not a crook" defense at the height of the Watergate investigation. Furthermore, candidates who themselves issue harsh evaluative judgments about the opposition run the risk of making the tone, rather than the substance, of their accusations the story. In Connecticut, when mild-mannered gubernatorial challenger Lewis Rome increased the level of his attacks on his opponent, according to a Rome aide, "the columnists began to write, 'This is not the Lew Rome we know—he's turned mean.' "

Basing the Charges on Facts. Effective charges, from the point of view of the media and the public, must be based on hard facts and not judgments. As seen in the Allain case in Mississippi, accusations based on questionable data tend to backfire on those who make them. Strategist David Doak gave an example from the Clements-White Texas gubernatorial race, in which White was using high utility rates and Clements's closeness to energy companies as a major issue.

> Clements cut a commercial saying we were demagoguing the issue, that we were lying. He seized on the fuel adjustment fee and said it was law, nothing could be done about it. Well, it wasn't law, it was regulation. His own commissioner came out and said in a statement that the governor was misinformed. We ran two former Democratic commissioners, along with his own commissioner, saying seven other states had gotten rid of this thing.

A similar event worked to the benefit of Senator John Chafee in his Rhode Island race against challenger Julius Michaelson. Michaelson told reporters that Chafee had lied when he said he would not take campaign contributions from oil company political action committees; as evidence, he pointed to a reported Chafee contribution from "Occidental." It turned out, however, that the contribution was from the Occidental Insurance Company, not from the oil corporation of the same name. As Chafee's press secretary gleefully recalled, "He got a huge headline—Michaelson Errs on Charge Against Chafee. It was a devastating story."

In both the Clements and the Michaelson cases, candidates making the charges suffered in two ways: the "facts" they tried to use against their opponents were turned against them, and as the issuers of false accusations, their own credibility suffered. In making such charges, campaign strategists must bear in mind three rules enunciated by Doak: "First, it's got to be on the record, material about the [candidate's] public life; second, it's got to be absolutely factual and have no holes in it at all; and third, it has to be a fair representation of the factual accuracy."

Using Respected Outside Figures to Accuse or Respond. The use of outside parties to deal with a charge, rather than the candidate or the campaign organization—as in the case of the public service commissioners who came to White's defense on the utility issue—is an example of a third precept campaigns must follow in making or responding to charges. Allegations or responses are always more credible when external and respected figures make them. Consultant Jay Smith illustrated this point in describing the response of the Fenwick campaign to what it considered lies and distortions by Frank Lautenberg about Fenwick's record and character:

> For Millicent Fenwick to stand up and say it isn't true—that's not news. So what we did was to bring George Bush up, the vice president of the United States. He was talking to the press, hitting our theme, [that] this man has crossed the line. At the same time we had [retiring senator] Nick Brady go up there. We brought Governor Kean into the act to do the same thing. They were all saying the same thing. We provided the scripts.

Similarly, when 1984 Senate challenger Joan Growe strongly implied in her advertising that Minnesota senator Rudy Boschwitz would not release his income tax returns because he had something to hide, Boschwitz responded by running radio and television advertisements featuring Minnesota's other Republican senator, Dave Durenberger. Durenberger charged that he had "never seen a campaign as negative and personal" as Growe's, and further quoted editorials in Minnesota newspapers that called Growe's accusations "sleazy" and "shabby innuendo." When Growe protested, a Boschwitz campaign representative replied, "All we're doing is responding by letting her know what some of the newspapers are saying." [16]

Exceptions to the Guidelines. Thus, in making or responding to accusations, candidates ideally should employ third parties and present the case on the facts. The only time the candidate should be personally involved is when that alone will make an allegation or a response credible. Bill Allain in Mississippi, for example, could not duck comment on the homosexuality charges leveled against him; at least part of a believable response had to involve the candidate himself. Allain's success in refuting the charges points up again the general rule that facts are more convincing than opinions or emotional appeals. Allain did not emotionally and defensively say, "I am not a homosexual," as Nixon had unpersuasively argued, "I am not a crook." Instead, Allain produced hard evidence—the payments made to his accusers and an "independent lie detector test," "proving that the charges against me are false." Allain was believed, whereas Nixon was not.

If personal intervention on the part of candidates is so rarely effective, why do so many of them come to their own defense? The most frequent answer is that such candidates are often underfinanced challengers who may not be experienced enough to know that this is a poor strategy or, more often, who do not have the money to get their messages out in paid media. Challengers such as Lewis Rome in Connecticut and Julius Michaelson in Rhode Island depended more extensively, and unsuccessfully, on the press because both were heavily outspent and could not afford the kind of advertising campaign they needed. Further, both had trouble marshaling the facts to support their charges. It was difficult to accuse Rome's incumbent opponent of mismanaging the state economy when Connecticut was in much better shape than the rest of the country; it was hard to paint Chafee as a "Reagan robot" when so much of Chafee's record belied it.

Eventually, time runs out for campaigns, and election day is upon them. The opportunity to attack the opponent or defend the candidate is over. Campaigns hope their arguments have carried the day and that the large volatile element of the electorate will swing in their direction. But in those races where few votes appear to separate the candidates, the get-out-the-vote (dubbed "GOTV" by campaign participants) activities on election day become crucial, as do the voter targeting activities that must precede them. We look at them now.

The Role of GOTV and Targeting ─────────────────────

Get-out-the-vote efforts are designed to do what the name implies—bring as many of a candidate's supporters as possible to the polls on election day. Most simply, this means finding out which voters support a candidate and making sure they actually vote.

The second task is relatively straightforward, but the first is fairly complicated. Voters may support candidates strongly, oppose them strongly, be undecided, or have weak preferences that could change as a result of information received during the campaign. In a competitive race, those in the last two categories decide its outcome. Devising a strategy to assess correctly who these swing voters are and implementing that strategy is a process known as *targeting*. A candidate's strong supporters must not be ignored either. As voter contact specialist Pete Curtin observed of GOTV efforts directed at strong supporters, "There's a tremendous need to do that. I've seen campaigns that lost because they took their core vote for granted."

It also bears repeating that GOTV makes a difference only in campaigns that have already created the conditions that give them a potential majority: "Identification and turnout programs presume that campaigns have created a winning strategy and implemented it by effective tactics. . . . Identifying and turning out every supporter in the district will not produce a victory unless the candidate has more backers than does his opponent." [17]

GOTV, Old Style

Historically, GOTV was the province of the political party organizations. Harold Gosnell describes the role of the dominant Democratic Chicago machine in the 1930s: "Efficient precinct captains saw that a thorough canvass was made before each general or intermediate registration, so that they could be sure that the names of all their potential supporters were on the books." [18] On election day itself, fueled with organization street money, party workers fanned out over the district to get supporters to the polls. Their degree of success in this vote pulling operation strongly influenced the subsequent award of the party's patronage resources.

Today, although party organizations still play a role, particularly in less visible, low-turnout elections at the county and municipal levels, the vast majority have become increasingly enfeebled. Consultant Curtin, a close observer of the fabled Hudson County, New Jersey, machine, which controlled state elections in the days of the legendary "Boss Hague," said:

> My sense is that the organizations don't understand that times have changed, that people with twenty or thirty years of service as county committeemen are slowing down—actually slowing down. They do have these tiny notebooks with their lists, but the list used to be fifty and now it's thirty. They can get a vote out, but it's not sufficient to win.

Another consultant who has worked closely with organization politicians in the same state agreed: "It's a function of not moving into the modern era of politics. They're still twenty years back. It's not that they don't have the resources. They still have some jobs, a lot of things you need. But in terms of mobilization, they're not very good."

How to relate to local party organizations that want to be involved during this period is a special problem. The issue rarely arises for candidates west of the Mississippi, where, as described in chapter 3, party machines never fully developed. "You've got to understand," says one strategist, "that traditionally in the West, the party is not as influential as in the East. There's really nothing west of Natchez, there never has been. It's a throwback to the Progressives."

In the East, where remnants of the party machines remain, campaign organizations are unenthusiastic about heavy dependence on party activists, who are considered unreliable and not conversant with modern techniques. In a strong but fairly typical comment, a campaign manager for a House incumbent said of the local party organization: "They weren't useful, they weren't dependable, they weren't helpful. We didn't want to rely on county organization people; they're more trouble than they're worth. They're more concerned if their name is in the right place on the invitation. They just don't produce. We don't need them."

Campaigners do not feel safe if they entirely ignore the party activists, however. When election day comes, party organizations can often supplement the campaign's own efforts in mobilizing the voters. Another campaign manager observed: "The Democratic regulars and the traditional elements of the Democratic base like labor are real utilities in the last ten days of the campaign. If they're going to make any contribution, it's getting out the vote. There's really one day when all that matters."

Moreover, strategists believe that although party activists may be of limited assistance, they can seriously damage a campaign if they turn hostile. As one adviser noted:

> Party organizations are capable of generating intense negative energy. They will just distract you for the whole race if you don't pay attention to them, if you don't court them. If you're suddenly having to deal with a county chairman who's badmouthing you to the press, or a state chair who says you're not running a good campaign, it just screws up the inside of your campaign. It gives inside people with dissent an occasion to question the whole strategy.

Another campaign staffer agreed: "How much they can help you is questionable, but how much they can hurt is documentable. People can badmouth and destroy you. If they're out in the cold, they're going to be badmouthing you. Somehow you've got to keep them separate because you don't want them mucking around."

Campaigns deal with this situation in two ways. First, they send their own paid field staff to serve as liaisons with the party organizations. One House campaign assigned paid field staff to party offices during the last three weeks of the campaign. A Senate campaign had a paid operative in every county of the state by Labor Day. This tactic gives the campaign organization information about what the party people are doing and an opportunity to offer them advice and manage crises before they get out of control. It is also part of the second and more important strategy in dealing with the party regulars: it keeps party activists happy so that they will not denigrate the campaign and will do whatever they are capable of on election day itself. A campaign manager described his "party pacification" operation:

> We would call party leaders every time we went into a county; we would call every party leader and say the candidate was coming. Not that they wanted to come, but they were offended if they didn't know. We'd call them at least once a week to give them inside gossip. The candidate would call them—he'd make a couple of hundred calls every week. At the end of the campaign, we sent them all a paperweight or something.

The aging and old-style politicians who dominate what remains of local and county organizations have become ineffective at mobilizing voters because of shrinking bases in their communities. As we discussed in detail in chapter 3, patronage jobs are fewer. Once-prized positions as precinct captains are less attractive and more difficult to fill. More voters are self-declared independents, and many partisans split their tickets. Campaign organizations thus have had to look beyond their local parties for an effective get-out-the-vote operation.

At first, volunteer canvassers, moving from house to house or calling residents listed in telephone directories, replaced or supplemented party workers. But through the early 1970s, such GOTV drives were not notably successful from the perspective of the campaigns that conducted them. It was not that the activities did not boost turnout—they did. The difficulty was that they increased turnout indiscriminately. More voters showed up at the polls if contacted by campaign organizations, but their preferences were not significantly different from those of voters on the whole. One analyst noted:

> To be effective, a canvass should concentrate on turning out the vote among voters and in neighborhoods which are likely to support the party; and it must avoid contacting opposition voters. (It is worth noting that despite the rather obvious nature of this advice, neither party is particularly successful in concentrating its efforts in this manner.) [19]

"Blanket" canvasses, another observer added, always benefited the normal majority, which probably did not even need such efforts to win.[20] Sophisticated campaign organizations understood this; but the absence of party registration in many states, the growing numbers of voters registering as independents, and the proclivity of partisan voters to split their tickets all made it difficult for campaigns to figure out how to avoid contacting and mobilizing those who in fact would not support them at the polls. In the next section we will examine how technology helped solve the problem.

The New Technology and GOTV

The advent of sophisticated data-processing techniques revolutionized the means by which campaigns could identify, contact, and mobilize the critical swing voters. Once computers permitted the analysis of large amounts of data, those data could be organized in ways that greatly increased the ability of campaigns to target the "right" voters to contact. Election districts could be classified according to party strength, propensity of voters to swing from one party to another in succeeding elections, and levels of turnout. The swings and turnout variations could be refined further: Were they related in specific ways to certain offices or types of candidates? Would higher turnout in a given district be likely to help or hurt the candidate? Analyses could be conducted not only of election districts, but of particular voters within them, to determine their voting histories—how often, and for which elections, did they turn out? Were they regular primary voters, a likely indicator of strong attachment to a party?

By the late 1970s, further refinements emerged as political consultants took up what became known as *geodemographic targeting*. Using detailed data from small, homogeneous tracts identified in the U.S. census, companies like the pioneering Claritas Corporation divided these areas into different groups, or clusters, with distinct patterns of ethnicity, race, housing style, family life cycle, and other variables. Each cluster was given an evocative name, such as "Old Melting Pot," "Bunker's Neighbors," or "Blueblood Estates." It was possible to identify by cluster type all areas of a given constituency. Polling data on opinions and attitudes could be integrated with the other information about the clusters. Based on these data, campaigns could determine the kinds of messages that would be most effective in each cluster. In his 1980 gubernatorial race in West Virginia, for example, Jay Rockefeller used Claritas to distinguish between unemployed, middle-class, and upscale coal miners to produce specialized direct mail messages for each group.[21]

Such developments increased the likelihood that campaigns could zero in on their own current and potential supporters and not end up mobilizing the opponent's as well. Studies of the new, more targeted GOTV approaches indicated that they do indeed have the desired effect. In a special election for the Washington, D.C., City Council, for instance, turnout rose 9 percent among sympathetic voters contacted by a phone bank, as compared to the turnout of a matched control group that was not contacted.[22] Some analysts argue that only in races such as this, which have little visibility in the media and low turnouts, does GOTV make a difference.[23] However, Barry Brendel, the voter contact specialist for candidate Frank Lautenberg in the 1982 New Jersey Senate race, found almost exactly the same effect on turnout as in the D.C. City Council contest. Solid Democratic precincts in New Jersey left as an uncontacted control group turned out at a rate 7 percent lower than similar precincts where Lautenberg targeting and GOTV activities had been carried out.

The richness of the new targeting information, and the variety of ways it could be organized and analyzed, meant that campaigns could adjust their targeting plans for voter identification and contact to the particular situations they faced. Some of the possible variations are apparent in an examination of the voter contact programs in several Republican House campaigns. One candidate was running in a race in which the state party assumed responsibility for calling registered Republicans; he therefore contacted only independents. Two others contacted all voters in swing districts, because in one case the state had no party registration, and in the other the Republicans were in such a minority that the candidate needed many Democratic voters, as well as independents, to put together a majority. Still another contacted only registered Republicans who had certain demographic characteristics associated with consistent party-line voting, because the district contained areas with a large number of registered Republicans who often voted Democratic.[24]

We should not conclude that the apparent precision of these techniques is foolproof, or that all campaigns use targeting as skillfully as they could. First, the quality of the data available, and the time it takes to put it in usable form, varies significantly. In some states, voters are required to register by party, and their telephone numbers as well as addresses are recorded; all this information, in one central location on computer tapes, can be purchased at a reasonable price. In states at the other extreme, there is no party registration; registration records are maintained by the individual counties; phone numbers are not recorded; and the data are not in computer-readable form. The particular situation faced by an individual campaign can substantially affect how early voter contact is started and whether it can be completed in time.

Second, the more sophisticated the targeting plan required, and the more work that needs to be done to implement it, the more expensive it will be. Campaigns may know what needs to be done organizationally but simply not have the financial resources to carry the plan out. In Indiana, the Bayh Senate campaign brought in a consultant experienced with geodemographic targeting fairly late in the race, when the tides were turning sharply against the senator, and then ran out of sufficient funds to implement the program statewide. Agreeing with Bayh, a top campaign staffer said: "He thought if we had more money, that might have won the election for us. We had evidence that it was really working for us." Challenger Harriet Woods's Missouri Senate campaign might have picked up the additional 28,000 votes she needed to defeat incumbent John Danforth with a strong voter contact program, but she could not afford it. As Woods's manager said: "Had we spent $250,000 on phone banks, as Danforth did, we would have had that much less for radio and television. Without our media campaign, we could never have gotten the snowball rolling." [25]

Bearing in mind these important caveats, we can now examine the typical organization of targeting efforts, the factors that affect them, the way they feed into the final GOTV efforts, and the kinds of activities that actually take place on election day.

The Targeting Plan

A well-done voter identification and contact effort begins in the late summer or very early fall. At that time, campaign organizations acquire the names, addresses, and telephone numbers of the groups of voters they have decided to contact. The majority of voter identification and contact is done at central telephone bank locations set up by the campaign itself, or, especially in the case of statewide races, by business concerns that specialize in telephone solicitation and interviewing. Those making the calls can be volunteers, paid workers, or a mixture. Increasingly, volunteers are used only when financial constraints make it necessary. No matter how dedicated the volunteer corps, they cannot be depended upon to staff a phone bank reliably at the right hours. Voter contact specialist Curtin explained, "We use the volunteers for other activities. No matter how large a turnout you get, it's still unpredictable. You can't do systematic voter contact work with volunteers. When you have paid workers, it's a job."

Calls initially go to whatever groups the campaign has identified as critical to its efforts, within the resources it has. In Democrat Jim Howard's 1982 New Jersey congressional race, in a district thought to be made more marginal by redistricting, professional callers phoned all of the district's registered Democrats, independents, and Republicans in areas where Howard had run well in the past, to ascertain their voting intentions in mid-September. This involved contacting almost 200,000 households. After the first call, those considered "unpersuadable" were ignored. Howard supporters and "undecideds" then received four waves of targeted mail over the next six weeks.

In the same year and the same state, Senate candidate Frank Lautenberg had to devise an effective targeting plan for the entire state, rather than for just one of its fourteen congressional districts. Brendel,

Lautenberg's voter contact specialist, first eliminated all counties considered safe for either Lautenberg or for his opponent, as well as sparsely populated areas with very few voters. In the remaining counties, each election district was identified as swing or solid. The solid districts were put aside temporarily, and the one thousand heaviest swing election districts were intensively phoned by paid workers to identify "favorables" and "persuadables," who received two waves of mail keyed to the media messages Lautenberg was conveying on radio and television. The campaign had hoped to send out more mail, but even Lautenberg's well-financed effort ran short of money. When the campaign's budget was increased in October after Lautenberg's improved standing in the polls, it was too late for any more voter identification efforts, and the phone and mail operation was competing with the need to increase the heavy television advertising still further.

Charles Robb's gubernatorial campaign in Virginia, a state that is larger in area but smaller in population than New Jersey, had paid workers at 140 phones in the major cities calling into swing precincts to identify "persuadable" and "favorable" voters. In the rest of the state, volunteers, working out of county campaign offices and friendly law firms with phones available in the evening, did the same—after training at the campaign's central office, and under careful paid supervision. As in New Jersey, solid precincts were set aside for later attention.

These examples make it clear that two factors affecting campaign targeting plans are the resources available for the effort and the office sought. The less visible the campaign is in the mass media, and the lower normal turnout tends to be, the more important targeting, telephoning, and direct mail are in the overall plan. Statewide campaigns must expend enormous resources on broadcast advertising. The sophisticated geodemographic efforts that voter contact specialists recommend for a closely contested race in a large and heterogeneous electorate are extremely costly and therefore not used as frequently as they might be. Targeting efforts are not ignored but do not loom as large in statewide campaigns as in smaller-constituency races.

Voter Registration Drives

Closely related to targeting are voter registration drives. In order to vote, a person must be registered, and more than a quarter of the potential electorate in most areas is not. Traditionally, voter registration drives have been conducted by the Democratic party and organizations sympathetic to it, since nonregistration is concentrated among groups such as low-income people and minorities who tend to be Democratic voters.[26] The usual Democratic technique is to conduct blanket registration drives in favorable areas. Republicans, whose core supporters are much more likely to be registered, have in the past generally eschewed this activity.

However, spurred by the increased turnout in 1982, which bene-fited the Democrats, the Republican National Committee and the Reagan-Bush campaign committee embarked in 1984 on a $10 million high-tech effort to find and register likely Republican voters. Be-cause they lack the solid group support that Democrats have in many areas, Republicans would not benefit from the kind of blanket drives their opponents conduct. Instead, the Republicans used what data-processing professionals call "merge and purge" to create lists of individuals to contact. In Colorado, for example, direct mail consul-tants matched the names of 2.2 million driver's license holders against those of 1.2 million registered voters, which yielded 800,000 names of persons eighteen and over who had licenses but were unregistered. They then eliminated all those living in ZIP code areas with heavy Democratic voting, reducing the list to 120,000 names. These names were then matched with phone numbers, which were available for 60,000 names.

A phone bank in Denver called these 60,000 households to ascertain whether the individuals had recently registered, whether they intended to vote in the 1984 election, and whether they were favorable to either President Reagan or incumbent Republican senator William Armstrong. Those not registered but intending to vote, and inclined toward the Republican candidates, totaled 20,000 individuals. They received a personalized letter from the state party chairman telling them where to register. The names were then transmitted to county Republican orga-nizations, which were to follow up and make sure the people got registered.

In states such as New Mexico and Florida, human intervention, in the person of phone bank workers, was entirely eliminated. Computer-dialed phone calls, when answered, activated a tape recorded message asking the respondents whether they were registered and whether they favored President Reagan.[27] Such reliance on modern-day technology is expensive, and the Republicans ended up investing as much as $7 on every new voter registered.

GOTV on Election Day

The resources and planning that go into targeting activities come to fruition on election day and on the days immediately preceding it. Over the weekend, and on Monday and Tuesday until the polls close, phone banks expand, and paid workers, volunteers, and party organizations are pressed into service to recontact the voters previously identified as favorable.

The final activities of the Howard, Lautenberg, and Robb campaigns, whose targeting activities we have described, illustrate the elements of a good GOTV effort. In the Howard congressional campaign, the fifteen phones used for the voter ID effort were increased to forty for the final four days. However, this time, although only identified supporters were called in swing districts, those districts that had been confirmed to be heavily Democratic during the initial voter contact phase were objects of what is known as a *blanket pull*—every household was contacted. In Lautenberg's Senate effort, the solid precincts that had been set aside and never phoned for identification purposes also became objects of a blanket pull. Previously identified "persuadables" in swing districts were also phoned. The Robb campaign in Virginia began blanket pulls in solid districts for the first time one week before election day. In the middle of the week, identified Robb voters in swing districts were called again. In the last thirty-six hours, blanket pull calls were resumed.

As noted earlier, campaigns also now press into service the party activists and interest groups who can get out a vote. The Howard campaign benefited from separate phone operations set up by labor unions and environmental organizations. They, along with party workers, made up a cadre of more than three hundred people who were also going door to door. The Lautenberg campaign had substantial labor help too, as well as party workers and personal organizations loyal to big-city mayors. In Virginia, the mayor of Richmond turned out two hundred teachers to work the streets. Additionally, the campaign sent out "flushing crews" to go door to door in the most solid districts—those estimated to contain at least 70 percent Democratic voters. The crews consisted of six students per car and a labor union supervisor, assigned six precincts each.

Blanket pulls by phone and door-to-door canvassing, which could potentially bring out the opposition's supporters, can be done only in the most solidly partisan localities, especially those with a history of low turnout. In the current era of split-ticket voting and mostly heterogeneous neighborhoods, heavily black districts most often fit this description. As the one easily identifiable group that still tends to be geographically concentrated and overwhelmingly Democratic, it merits special attention from Democratic candidates on election day. The orchestrator of the field operation in one urban congressional district said, "We worked the black districts down to the bone." Another Democratic strategist noted that "you don't have to persuade black voters to vote for you; you just have to persuade them to vote at all."

The machine-era "graveyard vote" and other forms of election day corruption are generally a thing of the past, disappearing in the wake of a more educated and affluent electorate and stricter reporting of campaign expenditures. Election day workers are still often paid sums ranging from $5 to $100, but in the words of one field organizer, "Every bit of it has receipts and Social Security numbers." Although there is no widespread corruption, pockets continue to exist. One Republican campaign manager reported declining an offer to see to it that elevators in a large urban housing project with a heavy Democratic vote were "out of order" on election day. Another participant in a southern campaign that attracted a large poor and rural vote described the election day GOTV effort there:

> It depends on paying off the right people at the right time with the right credibility in the right neighborhoods. A lot of bad things happen on election day, which we didn't get into too much. We paid off what we thought were the right people and let it lie. We didn't really have a strong election day operation, just a set of people we thought we could depend on.

Blanket pulls and the use of groups outside the campaign to do GOTV activities are a phenomenon almost entirely associated with Democratic campaigns, because of the dissimilar constituencies of the two parties. With the recent exception of white religious fundamentalists and organizations like the right-to-life movement, the Republican party has not had identifiable groups who could play the role that labor unions and others have played for the Democrats. As a general rule, the core Republican vote is better educated, more politically aware, and likely to turn out anyway. One Democratic strategist said: "Phones are a much more important tool for Democratic candidates than Republicans. What is the real return for Republicans? Their vote is going to come out anyway. Democrats are the ones who need to mobilize."

Republican strategists accept this assessment of their core vote, but as the minority party in most areas, the core party vote is not enough to produce victory. Republican victories often depend upon carefully identifying and bringing out independents and "persuadable" Democrats. Republican consultant David Murray explained: "If you're a Republican, the independent voter is the prize. The problem with them is they're the most difficult voters to bring out. The Democrats physically deliver their votes, working with unions and their party organizations and municipal and county employees. Republicans don't have it." Thus, precise and extensive targeting is crucial to them. In National Republican Senatorial Committee executive director Mitch Daniels's colorful analogy, "it's like the U.S.-Soviet strategic balance. The Democrats have throwweight, so we have to have accuracy. They have quantity; we have to have technical advantage." A staffer at the National Republican Congressional Committee elaborated:

> The Republican party—Republican institutions—have perfected certain things over the years—small-giver fund-raising; candidate improvement and training; the whole range of direct candidate services. The Democratic side has perfected turnout.
>
> I don't know if that's directly the Democratic party institutions; it's more prevalent in institutions such as labor. But clearly their forte is mobilizing bodies in the last three weeks. . . . That is the mandate for our party.[28]

This line of thinking among Republicans has brought about the voter registration activities we described earlier in this chapter. And as a Texas GOP strategist observed: "We are not going to pay $5 for every new Republican and then let that person stay at home on election day. We are going to check those names against our computers all day November 6, and if some guy hasn't shown up by 6:00 p.m., we'll carry him to the polls." [29]

Election day, the day of decision, finally arrives as it must. In the year or more preceding it, candidates have decided to run and sought the informational and financial resources they need for the race. Within the constraints imposed by their individual beliefs and the nature of their constituencies, they have framed the arguments that constitute a case for their election and tried to present them to the public as effectively as possible. They have made every effort to get their supporters to the polls. If they neglect these tasks, or do not do them as well as their opponents, they probably will fail in the voting booth as well. If they carry out these functions they will probably win.

In the past five chapters, we have detailed how modern-day American campaigns negotiate these hurdles. In the final two chapters, we consider what the future may hold for campaigns and candidates. We also offer some thoughts about the effects of America's candidate- and media-centered campaigns on its political culture, major political institutions, and policy processes—for ultimately, beyond the color, excitement, and human drama of political campaigns, it is because of such consequences that campaigns demand our careful and thoughtful attention.

Notes

1. See the data on this point in Stuart Rothenberg, *Winners and Losers* (Washington, D.C.: Free Congress Research and Education Foundation, 1983), 54-58.

2. Stimson Bullitt, *To Be a Politician* (Garden City, N.Y.: Doubleday, 1961), 90.
3. Robert Caro, *The Years of Lyndon Johnson: The Path to Power* (New York: Knopf, 1982), 644.
4. Larry Sabato, "Parties, PACs and Independent Groups," in *The American Elections of 1982*, ed. Thomas E. Mann and Norman J. Ornstein (Washington, D.C.: American Enterprise Institute, 1983), 106n.
5. See the data presented in Jody Newman, "Taking on an Incumbent: The Remarkable Woods-Danforth U.S. Senate Race," *Campaigns and Elections* 4 (Spring 1983): 37.
6. Sabato, "Parties, PACs and Independent Groups," 76. Woods's last poll was taken on October 23; see Newman, "Taking on an Incumbent," 37.
7. Newman, "Taking on an Incumbent," 39.
8. Ibid., 38.
9. Richard Cheney, "The Law's Impact on Presidential and Congressional Election Campaigns," in *Parties, Interest Groups and Campaign Finance Laws*, ed. Michael J. Malbin (Washington, D.C.: American Enterprise Institute, 1980).
10. *New York Times*, November 3, 1982, B5.
11. Michael Barone and Grant Ujifusa, *Almanac of American Politics, 1984* (Washington, D.C.: National Journal, 1983), 659.
12. Michael J. Robinson and Margaret Sheehan, *Over the Wire and on TV* (New York: Russell Sage, 1983), 49; Maura Clancey and Michael J. Robinson, "General Election Coverage: Part I," *Public Opinion* 7 (December-January 1985): 49-54.
13. Peter Clarke and Susan H. Evans, *Covering Campaigns: Journalism in Congressional Elections* (Stanford, Calif.: Stanford University Press, 1983), 39-41.
14. Thomas E. Patterson and Robert D. McClure, *The Unseeing Eye: The Myth of Television Power in National Politics* (New York: Putnam, 1976); see also Jeff Greenfield, *The Real Campaign* (New York: Summit Books, 1982).
15. *New York Times*, November 1, 1982, B1.
16. *Minneapolis Star-Tribune*, October 21, 1984.
17. Rothenberg, *Winners and Losers*, 89.
18. Harold Gosnell, *Machine Politics: Chicago Model*, 2d ed. (Chicago: University of Chicago Press, 1968), 81.
19. Gerald H. Kramer, "The Effects of Precinct-Level Canvassing on Voter Behavior," *Public Opinion Quarterly* 35 (Winter 1970-71): 572.
20. John C. Blydenburgh, "A Controlled Experiment to Measure the Effect of Personal Contact Campaigning," *Midwest Journal of Political Science* 15 (May 1971): 381.
21. Alan Magill, "Turning Census Data into Meaningful Information for Political Strategists," *Campaigns and Elections* 2 (Winter 1982): 4-17. See also the description of the Claritas program and its political uses in Jonathan Robbin, "Geodemographics: The New Magic," *Campaigns and Elections* 1 (Spring 1980): 24-45; Joseph Mockus, "Targeting Your Turnout," *Campaigns and Elections* 1 (Summer 1980): 55-63; Larry J. Sabato, *The Rise of Political Consultants: New Ways of Winning Elections* (New York: Basic Books, 1981). See the methodological critique of geodemographic targeting in Mark Atlas, "Gambling with Elections: The Problems of Geodemographics," *Campaigns and Elections* 2 (Fall 1981): 4-12.
22. William C. Adams and Dennis J. Smith, "Effects of Telephone Canvassing on Turnout and Preference: A Field Experiment," *Public Opinion Quarterly* 44 (Fall 1980): 389-95.

23. Blydenburgh, "A Controlled Experiment," *passim.*
24. Rothenberg, *Winners and Losers,* 85-86.
25. Newman, "Taking on an Incumbent," 39.
26. Two extensive studies of nonvoters' characteristics are Arthur T. Hadley, *The Empty Polling Booth* (Englewood Cliffs, N.J.: Prentice-Hall, 1978) and Raymond E. Wolfinger and Steven J. Rosenstone, *Who Votes?* (New Haven: Yale University Press, 1980).
27. For a full description of the program, see T. B. Edsall and Haynes Johnson, "The GOP's Search for Voters," *Washington Post National Weekly Edition,* May 7, 1984, 9-10.
28. *New York Times,* November 7, 1982, B3.
29. Edsall and Johnson, "The GOP's Search for Voters," 10.

The Play and the Players: Future Directions in Campaigns

9

The party campaign committees can be very helpful. They can also be a pain in the neck. If you're doing a race they've targeted, there's the financial advantage that's very great. But other than giving us the money, access to contributor lists, getting national speakers to do fundraising events—other than that, I don't look for them to do a damn thing.
                                        —Jay Smith, political consultant

With consultants, you have to assemble a campaign à la carte from a very expensive and unaccountable menu. There will always be a role for those people in a complex, technology-based election system. But in my judgment they are not sufficient all by themselves. The most successful campaigns will be those that are in a position to draw on a standing organization, the party, for resources, technical help, and money.
                                        —Mitch Daniels, NRSC

"There has been no greater change in American politics in recent years than the manner in which candidates run for public office. The very character of electioneering has been altered irrevocably by the revolution in campaign techniques."[1] The replacement of the traditional political party organization by technology and those who know how to use it is the crucial change that engendered this observation by political scientist Larry Sabato. The role of the party boss has been taken over by the political consultant, that of the volunteer party worker by the paid telephone bank caller. Most voters learn about candidates not at political rallies but from television advertising and computer-generated direct mail; candidates generally gather information about voters not from the ward leader but from the pollster. The money to fuel campaigns comes less from the party organizations and more from direct mail solicitation of individuals and special-interest political action committees. In short, candidates have become individual entrepreneurs, largely set free from party control or discipline.

Although the changes in campaigns have been real and vast, there are also some less obvious continuities. Campaigners have always utilized the major means of mass communication and public relations in a particular historical era. Alexander Hamilton served as the ghost writer for George Washington's farewell address. Thomas Jefferson's political success stemmed in part from his command of the written word when tracts and pamphlets were the major means of political communication, and Franklin Roosevelt was a master of the radio. Television and the computer are in an important sense only the most current incarnation of these communication techniques. Nor are the special-interest groups prominent in current American politics an entirely new phenomenon. They are direct descendants of the nineteenth-century abolitionists, prohibitionists, and suffragettes. As for business, its role in politics has been active and controversial since the founding of the country.

And there is also a continuing but changed role for political parties. The Republican national committees, which were moribund and almost bankrupt organizations not many years ago, have assumed a place of some importance in Republican campaigns. The Democratic national committees, after being stung by their defeats in 1980, have begun to follow suit. Parties now seek to shape a role consonant with their new environment. Parties in the old system provided two key resources: money and strategy. The emergence of political action committees and professional political consultants gave candidates alternatives to the party. The future role of the political parties in campaigns will therefore depend not only on what they do but also on the future roles of these other actors.

Thus we begin this chapter by looking at new developments and likely future directions in the political consultant and campaign technology industry. We then go on to examine the emerging roles of the more traditional campaign actors—special-interest groups and the parties—as they move to adapt to technologically driven and candidate-centered races.

The Institutionalization of the Campaign Industry

The last two decades have seen the emergence of a new industry—a set of people and institutions who make their living from work associated with political campaigns. The first professional consultants, as we saw in previous chapters, viewed campaigns as seasonal work, one class of clients among many for advertising agencies, public relations firms, survey research companies, or documentary filmmakers. Although the participation of such generalists in campaigns has not disappeared, political consultants are, increasingly, specialists whose livelihood depends entirely on politics. It is thus not surprising that participants in this industry would seek, as do any business executives, to expand, systematize, and rationalize their businesses. There are at least four emerging developments in the campaign industry that result from its increasing specialization and institutionalization: moves toward the reduction of seasonal business fluctuation, mergers or vertical integration, market expansion, and the generation of new products and services. We will discuss these in turn.

Reducing Seasonal Fluctuations: The Permanent Campaign

Consultants are moving in a variety of ways to ensure that they have business outside the traditional campaign period. Not only is that period itself lengthening, but consultants are successfully looking for ways to sell their products day in and day out, all year long. One development is the increasing practice of the national party organizations and certain interest groups to put consultants on annual retainers. Another is year-round business from successful candidates, especially for executive office.

Some consultants have convinced their clients, particularly governors, that there is value in paid media outside of election periods. Governors Bill Clinton of Arkansas and Mark White of Texas both bought advertising early in their terms to explain the need for tax increases. Clinton was first elected to a two-year term in 1978 with 63 percent of the vote but was narrowly defeated in 1980. Public opposition to tax increases played an important role in his defeat. Clinton's 1980 opponent, who ran against the tax increases, wound up raising taxes himself, and lost to Clinton by ten points in 1982. By then, more taxes were required for sorely needed educational programs, and Clinton faced another race in 1984. A consultant to Clinton said of the events beginning with the 1980 defeat:

> I always felt something could have been done to have prevented that. In Clinton's second term, almost the same thing was materializing. In order to get an education package through, he had to pass new taxes, and he didn't want to go down the tube again. I suggested these ads to shape the public perception of what was going on. Essentially we were

trying to explain the tradeoff between improving education and taxes. Instead of having it fixed in the public's mind that he raised taxes, we wanted it fixed in the public's mind that he improved education.

The response in Arkansas encouraged the same consultant to suggest a similar strategy to White when he guided a tax package through the Texas state legislature in 1984, midway through his four-year term. White had promised to improve education in Texas without raising taxes. This became impossible when Texas was hit hard not only by the recession, but by an unexpected drop in oil prices. The legislature declined to pass White's suggested 1 percent increase in the state sales tax, instead adopting a complicated package including so-called sin taxes on cigarettes and alcohol and increases in auto registration fees. White wanted to frame the issue to make it clear that the taxes were necessary to get the education program he had promised in his campaign. This resulted in an extensive four-week statewide advertising campaign, featuring White telling Texans:

> When I ran for governor, I made a promise to you and to myself. To give Texas first-class schools. To raise teacher pay and to toughen academic standards. But that costs money. We had to raise taxes on things like liquor, cigarettes, and beer. I had hoped we could avoid raising taxes. But times changed and the economic slowdown and the drop in oil prices forced me to choose between keeping down taxes or helping our kids. The legislators and I made a decision. Our kids come first.

Clinton was easily reelected in 1984. If initiatives like White's are successful, there is little doubt other governors will emulate them.[2] A similar event occurred in New Jersey in 1984. There, the Republican governor, Thomas Kean, and the Democratic-controlled legislature faced a politically more pleasant question: what to do with a budget surplus, generated as a result of an improving economy and tax increases the previous year. Kean wanted to send every taxpayer rebate checks (which grateful taxpayers would presumably notice were from him), while the Democratic legislative majority wanted to institute a permanent tax cut (which grateful taxpayers would presumably attribute to them). To assist the governor and help frame the debate, the Republican State Committee paid for full-page advertisements in all of the state's daily newspapers, asserting that the Democrats were refusing to let the governor rebate the money to taxpayers, and including a coupon that readers could clip and send to their state legislators, indicating their support for the governor. Astute New Jersey citizens following these events might have given some thought to the fact that the governor was likely to stand for reelection in 1985 and that Democratic legislators were among the contenders for their party's gubernatorial nomination.

This trend may be confined to executive officeholders. It serves the same purpose as the presidential press conference or the fireside chat. Other executive officers cannot command the free television time the president gets, nor would their appearances usually generate much public attention. But the thirty-second spot does not overtax viewers when inserted into some television program they are watching anyway, yet it gets a message across when repeated over a period of time.

Legislative officeholders traditionally do not have the same opportunities for extended televised appearances like the executives' press conference, speech, or televised town meeting. Television media markets, as we have seen, are often not designed to cover congressional districts well. However, House members communicate regularly, easily, and cheaply with the franked newsletter. Senators might seem likely to adopt the technique of advertising outside election periods, especially since their terms are for six years and, during that time, their constituents may forget who they are, but senators are wary. A consultant reported: "I suggested this to a senator. But he says he's not going to do it, it would be a sign of weakness. There is the problem that when a governor does it, he's clearly explaining his program. A senator doesn't have as clear a program."

Executive as opposed to legislative client-candidates increasingly generate other kinds of business for consultants outside the election season. Pollster Bill Hamilton elaborated:

> If a governor is elected, there's a lot of polling you can do in that state—whether it's special-interest groups the governor is close to, constitutional referenda, even occasionally state agencies—very legitimate stuff. A Senate campaign helps your reputation, but there's never any continuing business. You sell them once every six years. They're not executives. There's not as much of a continuing relationship with a senator as there can be with a governor.

In the consultant community, one group often still out in the cold after the campaign season is the campaign managers. Winning managers return to or land jobs on incumbents' office staffs, but this is less often possible for the talented professional manager who happens to lose. Moreover, having gone through one campaign, even successful managers are loath to take on the job again if they can avoid it. As an ex-manager described the problem, "A person who sits around a House office makes a lot more, and they don't have to kill themselves for the money." Both national party organizations recognize the manager problem and are beginning to think about solving it. A ranking Republican aide commented:

> Building a talent bank is something we haven't done adequately. The party should move into a training role—identify people early and take

them under our wing. We need to create a cadre of people who don't want to go off and be committee staff directors or consultants, which brings in more money for less accountability and headaches.

A Democratic counterpart expressed similar views:

I'd like to see the day when this party trains campaign managers, puts them in the field on an apprentice run. After the campaign we put them in a job—with a law firm, a PAC, a trade association—where they can work in the off-year, and in the campaign year we can call them back. They're tried and true and proven and they don't have to worry about being out on the street in the off-year.

Naturally, all consultants applaud any developments that will smooth out seasonal fluctuations in their business activities and prevent any of them from being out of work during the noncampaign season. Their clients are becoming more and more convinced that consultants can help them build a record in office that will serve them well when the campaign season returns. Thus both sides see value in what is increasingly becoming a permanent campaign.

Vertical Integration:
Reorganization of Consultant Services

A second recent development that is likely to intensify in the future is a change in the organization of consultant services. Most political consultants set up shop as specialists in one type of service: polling, media, organization, and the like. Now they are organizing formal or informal full-service companies. Smith and Harroff is one such firm that works on federal and gubernatorial campaigns on the Republican side. Jay Smith described the company's role:

The campaigns in which we are most successful tend to be campaigns where our control is great. We're a full service agency, involved in everything from the creation of organization to media to direct day-to-day liaison with the press. We're most successful when we're brought on at an early stage so we don't inherit mistakes and inferior personnel.

Consultants still on their own have informal relationships, working primarily with certain other specialists. The NRSC's Mitch Daniels described what he observed: "You have people integrating vertically now—polling firms buying telephone operations, media firms hiring buying services. You've got loose affiliations, quasi-joint ventures where a given consultant drags along another one."

For instance, a leading Republican pollster, Robert Teeter, is not formally affiliated with the Republican media consultants Bailey-Deardourff, but in many statewide campaigns they will be found working together. Similar arrangements occur on the Democratic side, where media specialist David Sawyer frequently works with pollster Bill Hamilton, and pollster Peter Hart is often associated with media consultant Robert Squier. David Doak, an organizational specialist who had previously hired out independently as a state director in the Carter presidential campaigns and later as the manager of two successful Democratic gubernatorial campaigns, now advises such campaigns as a principal in the multiservice Squier company.

Firms that work on lower-level campaigns, or in narrower geographical areas, have moved in the same direction. Pete Curtin, who is involved in Democratic local, legislative, and congressional campaigns, specializes in voter contact activities but, like others, prefers more participation and control: "Ideally, the campaign manager implements our plan. It involves scheduling, press, events, and fundraising. We suggest we sit in on the staff selection, or even recruit the staff so there is no question they can implement the plan." All these arrangements are examples of consultants' increasing tendency to operate not as freelancers but as part of a formal or informal organization that provides candidates with all necessary campaign services.

Market Expansion:
High-tech Campaigns at the Local Level

Companies like Pete Curtin's, which design campaigns for state legislators and local officeholders, are an example of a third trend, the adoption of high-tech campaigns at the local level. Curtin worked for the Democrats against the New Jersey Republican Legislative Campaign Committee, whose activities on behalf of a number of targeted legislative candidates we described in chapter 5. The state Democratic party and a consortium of PACs contracted for more modest but similar services from Curtin's firm.

The campaign activities of state PACs and parties more and more resemble the behavior of their national counterparts. In many state-level races, PACs are becoming an increasingly important source of campaign funds. In New Jersey, for example, political action committees contributed about 17 percent of all money spent by candidates in the 1979 legislative elections. Four years later, in 1983, they contributed about 39 percent of all funds amassed by state Assembly and Senate candidates.[3]

As we noted in chapter 3, state party activity has increased notably in recent years, but not everywhere. The state organizations in the Midwest are much stronger than those in some other areas of the country; those in the East are particularly weak. As at the national level, there is also a dramatic difference between Democrats and Republicans. A 1984 survey of state party chairs found that almost two-thirds of the state Democratic organizations, but only a quarter of the Republican units, reported annual budgets of less than $250,000. Unsurprisingly, therefore, staffing levels also varied widely by party—two-fifths of Democratic state organizations had two or fewer paid staff, while a similar proportion of their Republican counterparts employed seven or more staffers.

The Republican state organizations benefit heavily from assistance provided by their strong and wealthy national committee. As a Republican national staffer explains, "While we have these limits on federal expenditures, the next logical place to go with our dollars is to build stronger state parties beneath these campaigns. Those transfers are not limited."

The national Republican party provides, to at least two-thirds of the state affiliates, direct financial aid for both the parties and their individual candidates; assistance in fundraising, polling, and data processing; and candidate recruitment and training. A quarter or less of the state Democratic organizations get such assistance from their relatively impoverished national committees. Averaging across the country, approximately two-thirds of the Republican state party funds come to them from their national committees. The state Democratic parties, with much lower average budgets, receive only a third of their money from the Washington committees.

Despite having much less money, the Democrats do fairly well at providing some services to their state legislative candidates. Although 90 percent or more of the state Republican parties contribute money to candidates, assist them with fundraising, and run campaign seminars, two-thirds or more of the Democratic organizations also offer these services. About three-quarters of the Republican state organizations offer some polling and media consulting, but so do half of the Democratic organizations. Although there is little Washington money to contribute, national consultants friendly to the party often volunteer to advise local campaigns when they are in the area working with other clients. As we saw in the case of the New Jersey Legislative Campaign Committee, receiving party money from the national level has not required candidates to espouse particular positions, but to spend the money in ways the party committees deem wise—generally, sophisticated voter contact activities. As at the federal level, such assistance does not buy fealty from legislative officeholders. Less than a third in both parties are considered "very active in state party affairs." [4]

New Products and Services:
Increased 'Narrowcasting'

A final likely trend of future campaigns is proportionally less "broadcasting" and more "narrowcasting." Rather than sending general messages to entire constituencies, candidates are likely to send increasingly specialized messages to identifiable constituency groups. As television costs consume an ever-larger share of the campaign budget, and are entirely out of reach for many candidates, less expensive alternatives are becoming both more available and more effective. The future is likely to bring less broadcast advertising and more use of telephones, specialized targeting techniques, and specialized direct mail. If the compartmentalized audiences of cable television grow, another method of transmitting specialized media messages will be available. Already, cable has been credited with substantially assisting Massachusetts representative Barney Frank in his defeat of Margaret Heckler (later a Reagan cabinet secretary) when redistricting put them in opposition. Thus, technology will simultaneously play an increasing role in the smaller political units and make larger political units approachable in a more targeted way.

The Changing Role of
Special-interest Groups

Along with consultants, special-interest groups and their associated political action committees have come to play a major role in candidate-centered campaigns. In this section, we look more closely at their activities.

It is important to recall the differences in the campaign activities of business, labor, and independent, or nonconnected, political action committees, as discussed in chapter 3. Corporate PACs, which dominate in both numbers and in amounts of money given, have confined their activities to contributions to campaigns, rather than in-kind expenditures for services. In the most recent election cycles, though, some trade PACs have made modest forays into other areas. The National Association of Realtors set up a telephone bank operation for Montana senator John Melcher in 1982, and the American Medical Association's AMPAC has done some print advertising for candidates and made their own polls available to them. There is much discussion of increasing in-kind expenditures on the part of business PACs, but the actual activities are still scattered and modest.[5]

Many of the business committees have their hearts with the Republicans and maintain closer ties to the Republican party committees. But they contribute to Democratic incumbents on key legislative committees unless they sense which pro-business Republican challengers are in strong positions to defeat such incumbents. Richard Conlon, executive director of the Democratic Study Group, bitterly calls this strategy "the game of Shoot the Sick: A business PAC behaves normally by buying access to a Democratic incumbent as long as the incumbent is likely to continue holding office. If there is a good chance the Member can or will be defeated, then the business PACs switch over to help the Republican challenger." [6] Representative Leon Panetta, a California Democrat concurs with Conlon: "In the 1980 election, we could see that a Republican challenger had the ability to get two or three hundred thousand dollars in the last weeks of the campaign and knock off the incumbent." [7]

Labor PACs, as we have seen, customarily engage in other activities beneficial to Democrats besides making contributions to campaigns. Much of it involves direct communication to their members, urging them to support a given candidate (almost always Democratic), and telephone bank and similar operations aimed at getting out the vote. Labor unions, however, do not participate in other campaign communication to reach the electorate at large—they do not make independent media expenditures for or against candidates; nor have they figured as the directors, rather than the shock troops, of organizational efforts.

Although some business and labor groups have issue agendas beyond their economic interests, material benefits are their priority. But interest groups with primarily nontangible concerns also have a long-standing record of political participation. As we noted earlier, abolitionists, suffragettes and prohibitionists flourished in the nineteenth century. Recent examples include the Vietnam-era antiwar movement, the right-to-life organizations, and pro- and anti-gun-control lobbies. Such groups arise when an issue generates passion and its champions believe that the political parties are not dealing with it. Some of them fade as the issue is resolved, is adopted by one of the two major parties, or loses its capacity to mobilize substantial numbers. Other groups coalesce around issues that never entirely go away, such as environmental concerns, traditional morality, or disarmament, but which ebb and flow in salience depending upon current events.

The influence of nonmaterial or ideological groups on campaigns, and on politics in general, has been greatly heightened by technological developments and by changes in the campaign finance laws. Before the advent of the computer and television, it was difficult for the geographically dispersed proponents of a given cause to communicate and to organize. Virtually the only national political groups were the parties. Party organizations sheltered many subgroups, and party leaders could adjudicate and mediate disputes among them. In the last few decades, the picture has changed. Now, for instance, television and radio preachers rally those disturbed about the "new morality," and anti-abortion or pro-choice activists are knit together through direct mail. At the same time, the establishment of the political action committee, which can make campaign contributions and engage in its own activities on behalf of candidates, has provided a convenient vehicle for organizing like-minded activists.

Thus the crucial development is "not the proliferation of single-issue institutions—which have always existed and attempted to influence the political process—but rather a precipitous decline in the capacity of party elites to resist, channel, accommodate, or limit the demands of these groups." [8] Before the introduction of the direct primary, television, computerized mailing lists, and political action committees, representatives of special-interest groups might have run unsuccessfully as fringe party candidates. Now with the help of technology and the direct primary, they can get elected with a major party label.

The social upheaval of the 1960s spawned interest groups on both sides of the ideological spectrum. In the next two sections we will describe, first, the rise of left-wing organizations and then consider the right-wing response.

The Rise of Liberal Ideological Groups

The Vietnam antiwar movement, which was concentrated on university campuses, evolved in 1970 into the Movement for a New Congress. It was committed to electing legislators who shared MNC's goals. When George McGovern ran for president in 1972, he inherited many MNC activists and their mailing lists. McGovern raised large sums through direct mail and television appeals, but when the war ended and McGovern left the national scene, there were no political action committees to serve as a locus for the other interests of the peace activists.

Other issue-oriented liberal groups organized in the 1960s. The civil rights movement generated a number, including the Southern Christian Leadership Conference, whose leader was the Reverend Martin Luther King, Jr., and among whose lieutenants was the young minister Jesse Jackson. Feminists founded the National Organization for Women. Consumer activists and good-government proponents banded together in Ralph Nader's Public Interest Research Group and the citizens' lobby Common Cause. These organizations had more lasting agendas than the antiwar groups, but Great Society legislation and Supreme Court decisions of the 1960s and 1970s on issues like busing and abortion satisfied some of their most pressing demands. The groups on the left subsided into relative quiescence. In important ways, their agendas had become the social status quo.

The Conservative Reaction

In reaction to the social changes brought about partly by the political activity on the left, the disaffected could increasingly be found on the right. Conservatives became alarmed, sometimes enraged, at the successive Supreme Court decisions banning school prayer, promoting busing, legalizing abortion, and restricting capital punishment. The broad social movements for progressive education, feminism and gay rights were also highly disturbing to these people. Foreign affairs were another area of concern. The withdrawal from Vietnam, détente with the Soviets, and the ceding of the Panama Canal were all seen as lowering the international status of the United States. Many of the demands of the disaffected on the right were first expressed in the unsuccessful presidential candidacies of George Wallace in 1968 and 1972. When Wallace failed and the demands remained unfulfilled, however, the opponents of these policies, unlike the left before them, soon had the fully developed resources of direct mail and the instrument of the political action committee.

Many umbrella "New Right" groups (as they were soon styled) sprang up in the late 1970s, often as the creations of political entrepreneurs, such as John T. (Terry) Dolan's National Conservative Political Action Committee (NCPAC), Paul Weyrich's Committee for the Survival of a Free Congress (CSFC), Gary Jarmin's Christian Voice, and Gregg Hilton's Conservative Victory Fund. They were fueled by direct mail appeals designed by the Viguerie Company. Richard Viguerie's organization got its start in politics in the Wallace campaigns and was unequaled in its development of conservative mailing lists. The fundraising powers of several of the umbrella organizations were impressive. In 1978 the CSFC spent $400,000 on campaign-related activities; four years later the figure was $2.3 million. NCPAC spent $700,000 in 1978; four years later, more than $10 million.[9] Unlike other PACs, which expended most of their funds on direct contributions to campaigns, groups like CSFC and NCPAC specialized in providing in-kind services—polling, campaign schools, campaign managers, and field staff—and in making independent expenditures, such as for direct mail pieces and radio and television advertising, whose content was controlled by them rather than by candidates' campaign organizations.

Specialization of techniques emerged among the groups. The CSFC stressed targeting, organization, and GOTV activities, while NCPAC did mostly polling, direct mail, and media. The CSFC worked mostly in favor of particular candidates, while most of NCPAC's efforts were directed at negative campaigns against liberal incumbents. The various organizations informally pooled data at frequent luncheon meetings of the Kingston Group, named for a hotel meeting room in which they had first convened.

Although the New Right leaders claimed to be studiously nonpartisan and interested merely in electing "real conservatives," the chief beneficiaries of their largesse were conservative Republicans who shared their agenda. However, many New Right figures made it clear that they were even more hostile to the Republican and corporate establishment than to the Democrats. The Democrats, at least, were what they said they were. The Republicans and business groups, in the New Right's view, often talked conservative but sold out to the moderates and liberals, expediently abandoning principle for short-term gains. As Weyrich said of the business community:

> I would put many of the business PACs on the top of my list of enemies when it comes to practical political operation. The extent to which we have made any contribution in helping to elect people is the extent to which we have opposed business PACs in primary elections. . . . It was up to ideological PACs such as ours to help these harder-line candidates win the primary elections, many times fighting the business community all the way.[10]

Nor were Weyrich and his colleagues enamored of the Republican party establishment and the party committees. The Kingston Group discussed legal action against the Republican National Committee when the RNC raised $700,000 from a direct mail appeal to conservatives, asking for help in defeating the Panama Canal treaties, but refused to donate $50,000 to support a New Right-sponsored congressional "truth squad" traveling the country to oppose the treaties.[11]

The New Right establishment moved as vigorously against moderate Republican candidates as it did against similarly erring Democrats. In 1982, NCPAC spent $200,000 on an unsuccessful negative campaign against Lowell Weicker of Connecticut, the most liberal member of the Republican Senate delegation. They also supported an independent candidate in the race, hoping that the few votes he garnered would help throw the election to Weicker's opponent. Two years later, they moved against Illinois Republican senator Charles Percy, chairman of the Foreign Relations Committee and another supporter of the canal treaties—first endorsing his liberal Democratic opponent, Paul Simon, as the lesser of two evils and, subsequently, a third-party candidate. The vote this candidate received was only about 4,000 less than Simon's narrow margin.

What distinguishes the New Right from other issue-based protest groups is the breadth and scope of its activities. In many ways, it has the characteristics of a full-fledged political party—a geographically broad base, an issue agenda that is more far-reaching and specific than that of the Democratic and Republican parties, a determination, eventually, without sacrificing principle, to gain control of the government, and an ability to provide all the services that a party can provide.

Discussion of formally organizing a conservative party picked up steam as New Right leaders perceived an even stronger shift away from their favored issues among Democrats and became increasingly pessimistic about remolding the Republican party in their image. Richard Viguerie, who had previously believed "Democratic and Republican politicians have written national and state laws in such a way that it's almost impossible to start a new party," [12] had changed his position by 1984: "I've come to realize in the last few years that the big business community . . . has its hooks so solidly into the Republican party that I'm not sure you can really make the Republican party a vehicle. . . . The only way we are going to get our issues dealt with is to have a new party." [13] He thus joined the CSFC's Paul Weyrich, who has long favored such a party:

> The country could be governed much more easily if various single-interest groups formed a more-or-less permanent coalition. . . . We feel that if there were a real second party in this country, the nation would be better off. . . . I think that the only way such a new force will come about is through a coalition of the conservative parts of both parties, allied with the special groups. . . . Such a coalition can eventually become the dominant party and win elections.[14]

Since a new major party has not emerged in the United States in well over a hundred years, this dream is probably unattainable. How long the idea percolates depends on a number of imponderable factors, including the direction and success of the Republican party after Ronald Reagan, the staying power of the issues that brought the New Right to prominence, and the possibility of future changes in the campaign finance laws that would weaken the position of PACs. Moreover, some of the original leaders of the organizations seem to be tiring. Charles Black and Roger Stone, who, along with Terry Dolan, had been among the original founders of NCPAC, left to form a consulting firm whose clients include some Republican candidates of whom the New Right does not approve. Dolan himself announced that he would retire from active involvement in NCPAC after the 1984 elections.

Although PACs have contributed about five times more money to campaigns than parties have since 1980 (due in considerable part to the limits placed on parties by the new campaign finance laws), the political parties have grown very much stronger in the past few years and perform many other functions for campaigns besides contributing money to them. Their recent activities are the subject of the next section.

Revival of the Party Role in Campaigns _____

When modern technology first became an important factor in campaigns with the advent of television in the presidential contests of the 1950s, it was, as we saw in chapter 3, at party initiative. The Republican National Committee commissioned and paid for Eisenhower's advertising. However, party control of the technological delivery of campaign messages had a short history and one that ended just as campaign technology was fully flowering. In 1968, the Nixon campaign set up the first technology-based campaign organization independent of the party structure. By the early 1970s, the limits on contributions built into the new campaign finance laws made it rational for other candidates for federal office to follow the Nixon campaign's lead. It is only since the mid-1970s that the American political parties have attempted to leap on the technology bandwagon and thus reenter campaigns in a significant way.

An observer in the mid-1970s might reasonably have concluded that American political parties were one of the lesser-noticed casualties of the preceding cataclysmic decade. In little more than ten years, the United States had witnessed three political assassinations, decisively lost a major military engagement for the first time, saw destruction of major elements of the social order in the civil rights and women's movements, watched its economy brought to the brink by a handful of "unimportant" oil-producing countries, and suffered through a far-reaching political scandal in the Watergate affair. These events engendered strong feelings of cynicism and alienation that affected all major political institutions, including the parties. Americans relied less on the parties for voting cues, and, helped along by technology, the candidates depended less upon them as well.

Both parties' national committees were moribund. Organizational weakness at the top soon worked its way downward. The Democratic party was struggling to pay off a multimillion dollar debt it assumed from Hubert Humphrey's campaign in 1968. The Republican National Committee could raise only $300,000 toward its $2.3 million budget in 1975. Ideological activists in both parties launched serious attacks on organization-favored presidential candidates. After unseating the Illinois delegation loyal to the consummate organizational pol, Chicago mayor Richard Daley, at the 1968 Democratic National Convention, left-wing activists succeeded in nominating George McGovern in 1972. Former governor Jimmy Carter of Georgia, running as an outsider, bested "regular" Democrats like Washington senator Henry Jackson in the 1976 nomination race. Despite party attempts to make outsider campaigns more difficult in 1984, two more consummate outsiders, Gary Hart and Jesse Jackson, garnered between them more than half the votes in Democratic primaries that year.

On the Republican side, right-wing activists, rising from the ashes of the 1964 Goldwater debacle, almost succeeded in nominating their hero, former California governor Ronald Reagan, in 1976 and toppling incumbent president Gerald Ford, another party organization stalwart. In 1980 their triumph at the presidential level was complete, and in 1984 they dictated the writing of the Republican platform and turned back attempts to dilute their strength by changing the rules regarding representation in the 1988 national convention.

Senate, House, and gubernatorial candidates increasingly engaged in candidate-centered campaigns, ignoring the parties, and triumphed in primaries through their own efforts. Whereas state party organizations had reported recruiting for an average of 3.5 offices in the early 1960s, this figure had declined to 2.6 in the late 1970s.[15] Federal candidates saw little utility in either the state committees or the congressional and senatorial committees in Washington. A Democratic Congressional Campaign Committee staffer said: "The congressional committee frankly didn't have a lot of visibility or credibility with members of Congress. They didn't think the committee had to be alive, alert, energetic, or involved." A National Republican Senatorial Committee aide described the committee as "a sleepy, inconspicuous one-horse operation" in the early and mid-1970s. Observing that thirty-two of the states had no provision for party endorsement of gubernatorial candidates and that such endorsement played little role in most of the others, Sarah McCally Morehouse noted that in two-thirds of the states, candidates "enter the governor's office as self-made tribunes who got where they are under their own power."[16]

Changing Roles for the Parties

However, the events of the 1970s and early 1980s pushed the parties in new and revitalizing directions relevant to campaigns. In some ways the developments were similar for the two parties; in others, different. One similarity was that candidates and campaigns both turned to their parties as a result of defeat. For the Republicans, there were devastating losses in the House and in the states as a fallout from the Watergate affair of the early 1970s, although the picture was not as grim at the presidential level. While Republicans were heavily outnumbered in state governments and in Congress, they had won three of the four presidential contests between 1968 and 1980, two of them in landslides. For the Democrats, the situation was the obverse: although they maintained their majorities in both houses of the national legislature and in the majority of states, there was discord, and serious weakness, at the presidential level. Not until their losses of 1980 did Democratic Senate and House candidates show much interest in a possible role for the party.

A second similarity, and one with important implications for American politics generally, was the increasing nationalization and centralization of the parties. For a century or more, the distinguishing feature of American politics was decentralization. The lifeblood of the political parties was their state and local organizations. The national committees were little more than an organizing locus for the state and local chieftains, who met every four years to nominate a president. The strength of the local parties was rooted in control of political patronage and nominations. Gradually, as we have seen, both died out. Conversely, the increasingly important and expensive role of technology in campaigns argued for the centralization of expertise and the growth of a national clearinghouse function for the parties. The old flow of communications and influence had been from the local to the national party organizations; centralization reversed its direction.

The homogenizing of national politics by television was another factor that contributed to party centralization. Unlike the pre-television era, when northern blacks and southern segregationists could co-exist in the Democratic party, as could eastern internationalists and midwestern isolationists in the Republican party, national television resulted in "Democrats" and "Republicans" all over the country sharing similar views and attitudes, and made a vigorous national party role possible for the first time. The increasingly well-defined view of each party gave rise to a substantial amount of party-switching by officeholders, particularly after the victory of the conservative Goldwaterites at the 1964 Republican National Convention and again after the Reagan triumph in 1980.

In the earlier period, well-known politicians such as South Carolina's Strom Thurmond and Texas's John Connally moved from the Democratic party to the Republicans, while New York City mayor John Lindsay and Michigan senator Don Riegle went in the other direction. In the later period, Democratic House members in Florida, Pennsylvania, Arizona, and Texas became Republicans, and numerous southern Democrats decided to make runs for office as Republicans. Representatives who found themselves in the "wrong" party, based on their policy views and voting habits, even acquired well-known nicknames. The liberal or moderate Republicans, concentrated in the Northeast, became known as "gypsy moths," and the conservative Democrats, centered in the South, were styled "boll weevils."

A third similarity between the parties was a stress on electability over ideology in choosing which candidates to support. Unlike the other two developments, this was a carryover from earlier periods. Despite the increasing homogeneity of both parties, the gypsy moths and boll weevils were a fact of life, and even greater diversity continued to exist among the party delegations in the Senate and among governors.

A Democratic Congressional Campaign Committee staffer said: "This committee is not ideological at all. We want to make sure those folks are representing the district, not us." In explaining why the national party committees intervened for the first time in 1984 Senate primary contests, the NRSC executive director dismissed ideology and stressed electability and its importance for the Republicans in maintaining their control of the Senate: "In this particular election, we are not going to tie our hands. It's the first time the majority hangs by a hair. For us to take a fastidious hands-off policy would be very short-sighted if we can influence the nomination of somebody who can win and might be our fifty-first seat. Our first mission is to win a majority." By emphasizing local issues, the Democrats, who had been practically shut out of federal representation in states like Idaho, Kansas, Nebraska, and Arizona, were able to elect governors somewhat to the right of the popular perception of the national party. Conversely heavily Democratic states like Maryland and Rhode Island sometimes chose moderate or liberal Republicans as statewide officeholders.

These phenomena—efforts to reinvigorate the parties because of the need to deal with serious defeats, the shift in the locus of the party away from its subnational to its national units, and the emphasis on electability—characterize both parties. In other ways, however, their activities related to candidates and campaigns have become very different. The success and strength of parties may be judged in two different ways: "expressively" or "competitively." [17] Expressiveness deals with the extent to which parties accurately and fairly represent the strength and ideas of their constituents, while competitiveness stresses their ability to win elections. Although the two national party organizations paid some heed to both of these criteria as they sought to reassert themselves, their particular strengths and weaknesses led the Democrats to emphasize the expressive function and the Republicans to stress the competitive function.

The Democratic party's primarily expressive response was shaped by its majority status, its greater diversity, and its ties to organized constituency groups. Conversely, the Republican party's primarily competitive response was determined by its minority status and its greater degree of homogeneity and cohesion. The differences these contexts produced in the parties' relations to campaigns and candidates are our next focus.

The Democrats: Procedural Reforms

The Democratic party, as we have repeatedly observed, has been the majority party in the United States since the early 1930s. Even in the face of more and more self-identified independent voters (now numbering roughly a third of the electorate) and the 1984 Reagan landslide, the Democrats continued to maintain a narrow lead over the Republicans among party adherents nationally. Their position with the electorate, according to Gallup polls, was no worse than it had been during the Eisenhower period. Until 1980, the Democrats controlled both houses of the Congress every year but four since Franklin Roosevelt's first election in 1932.

In the early years of the party's domination, most strong local machines were Democratic. The era of the New Deal, in the 1930s and 1940s, was the time of greatest strength for the Democrats' most important group allies, organized labor. Before the campaign finance reforms of the mid-1970s, in practice only trade unions had been permitted to form political action committees that could contribute to campaigns. Union workers were also a large and easily mobilized force for canvassing, election day activities, and the like. Consequently, Democratic candidates fell into a pattern, largely successful, of relying on their local organizations and labor as the bedrock of their campaigns. Candidate recruitment was not a problem. With so many offices that Democrats could count on winning, many local officeholders and state legislators waited in line to try for election to the House, Senate, and governorships.

The decline of Democratic party organizations, the rise of liberal issue activists, the advent of the new campaign finance laws, and the growing importance of contributions from business political action committees still did not seriously affect Democratic campaigns. Local officeholders continued to stream into campaigns for higher office. The new-style issue activist officeholders usually were not unfriendly to the labor agenda, and labor continued to support them financially and organizationally. Even a Democrat like Gary Hart, who voted wrong more often than right from labor's point of view, was able to collect almost $150,000 from labor PACs for his 1980 Senate campaign.

Democratic incumbents who controlled important committees in Congress and policy in the states could garner their share of financial contributions from businesses more interested in access, government contracts, and favorable regulatory decisions than in ideological purity. But the labor movement remained the bedrock. While business PACs split their contributions, better than 90 percent of labor PAC money went to Democrats. Corporations could not produce telephone banks and election day workers; labor could. Xandra Kayden observes of the relationship between Democrats and organized labor: "The historical alliance between the two groups has been of tremendous advantage to Democratic candidates and has operated efficiently enough to enable the central Democratic party structure to remain in what might be called 'arrested development.' " [18] Christopher Arterton comments: "Labor has, in effect, made it too easy for the Democrats." [19]

Other extra-party groups took on tasks that might have been the province of the party. Liberal House members formed the Democratic Study Group (DSG), which, until 1981, was in effect supported by the taxpayers, since it was financed out of the members' staff allowances. In addition to legislation-related activities, DSG staff performed campaign-related functions, such as the compilation of voting analyses and opponent research. The National Committee for an Effective Congress (NCEC), an independent PAC committed to the election of liberal representatives and senators and therefore mainly Democrats, provided a variety of services but became especially noted for its targeting analyses. Its director asserted that it saw itself as a substitute for the Democratic National Committee, which "provides almost no services to candidates." [20] Another independent PAC, Democrats for the Eighties, specialized in issue materials.

Short of money and with such groups performing what might have been party functions, the Democratic senatorial and congressional committees remained barely active. The Democratic National Committee occupied itself with attempts to cope with its difficulties at the presidential level. A series of party commissions, wrestling with the rules governing primaries and delegate selection for the national party conventions, tried to make the process more open and participatory, to accommodate the liberal activists who had made their influence felt beginning in 1968. Because Democrats controlled many of the state legislatures, which set some of these rules in the individual states, and because the Republicans remained uninterested in these questions, the Democrats exerted influence on the presidential selection procedures in both parties. Aside from instructing state parties about the dates of their national convention delegate selection, delegation composition (various commissions issued changing edicts about representation of such groups as party officials, minorities, women, and young people), and the like, the national committee had little contact with the state committees, which in most cases were mere shells anyway.[21]

The Democrats' defeat in 1980, when they lost control of the presidency and the Senate, and effective control much of the time in the House, persuaded Democratic federal officeholders to take the potential role of their national committees more seriously. For the first time, there was a need to think about the party's competitive function as well as its expressive one. As a national staffer described it: "It finally dawned on some folks in the House that the Republicans and their congressional committee were doing a tremendous amount of in-kind services for one-third what our incumbents had to pay for the same services. The votes that Reagan was getting in the House kind of pushed it along." The national committee's 1984 delegate selection rules gave less weight to satisfaction of constituency wants than in the past, and more weight to the role of the party regulars. With the appointment of Representative Tony Coehlo of California as chairman, the congressional campaign committee moved aggressively to raise money through direct mail and to plow much of what was garnered not into campaign-related expenditures, but into further direct mail fundraising appeals. The congressional committee donor base grew from 3,000 contributors in 1978 to more than 100,000 in 1984. The committee's staff increased from eight to about thirty.

Democratic congressional candidates at first looked askance at how the newly flush congressional committee was spending its money. The manager for a Democratic committee chairman recalled: "I was one of the campaigns bitching and moaning in '82 that when we needed an extra check or an in-kind service they were tight as could be. This congressman went out and raised $150,000 for the DCCC." However, the strategy by and large paid off. By 1984, the Democrats had opened a media center that could produce low-cost advertising spots for candidates. The almost nonexistent formal communication with PACs was much improved. The committee also maintained a list of approved consultants, managers, and field staff. However, the requirement that party-paid candidate mailings be designed, written, printed, and mailed by the committee was still a more expensive proposition than the DCCC could afford. In fact, the RNC's 1983 postage bill of $7.5 million was about twice as much as the total amount raised by the DCCC that year.[22]

The Republicans: Organizational Reform

The candidate-related services on which the Democratic party finally embarked after 1980 were modeled on the efforts of the Republicans, who had begun highly successful direct mail fundraising a decade earlier. All of the services the Democrats could finally offer their candidates were already available to Republican candidates, and on a much larger scale, as we discussed in earlier chapters. The Republicans moved beyond the simple establishment of a media center to produce low-cost, high-quality advertising for many candidates and the national party, and on to sophisticated testing of advertising messages. The Republicans did not merely produce PAC lists; they frequently met with PAC representatives, mailed them material on targeted races, and hosted receptions for candidates to meet PAC personnel. Paid mailings for their candidates flooded out of party headquarters.

The Republican party conducted hundreds of polls and actively recruited candidates. Its computers maintained voting record histories and accessed indexes to the nation's leading newspapers and magazines. State parties could tie in to the national party's data-processing facilities. Regional field and finance directors assisted the state parties, which became increasingly better financed and staffed, particularly in comparison with the Democrats. If the Republicans did not pioneer any given electoral technology, they soon acquired it. Money was a problem only to the extent of figuring out how to spend all that was available. Moreover, because the Republican national committees were such large patrons of professional phone bank operations, direct mail houses, and other private vendors, they could even prevail on some of them to offer discount rates to individual candidates' campaigns.

The Republican strategy was driven by the party's minority status. By the mid-1970s, it was clear to the top personnel at the national committees that widespread Republican victory could be achieved only by intensive attention to campaign technology. The party was aided by a greater degree of homogeneity among its officeholders but, even more, by the shared interest in shedding the minority position. The competitive rather than expressive function was what animated the Republicans. Unlike the heterogeneous and often feuding Democrats, who until recently had little incentive to band together as a party, the Republicans did unite. A staffer who switched to a Republican Senate office after the defeat of his former Democratic employer described the difference between the parties:

> Republican campaigns tend to be more structured, more thoroughly planned. Democrats tend to go off and hire a pollster there and a media adviser here. There's more of a Republican network where the various

campaigns work well together, meshing with the national organizations. The Senate campaign committee is very good at sharing. Consultants use it as a clearinghouse. The Democratic party is all over the place. You get nothing out of your committees. It's not just the cohesive structure Republicans have. It's not just money. It's an attitude. The Republicans, despite the ideological differences from a Weicker to a Chafee to a Helms—there still tends to be an attitude that "we're all in this together." The Democrats just don't have it.

On the surface, the developments in the Republican party would seem to be entirely positive from the point of view of candidates and those who wish the party well. There is apparently compelling evidence that Republican tactics have worked just as they were intended. In the 1978 elections, the first in which the full weight of the new Republican activities was felt, the party picked up seats in both the House and the Senate, followed that up with a very strong performance in 1980, and sustained fewer losses than many anticipated in 1982. The influx of money and expertise appeared to save many marginal candidates.[23]

However, the rise of the mighty Republican apparatus has not brought unalloyed pleasure to all of its candidates, and there is even evidence that in some cases it has been counterproductive. Inexperienced first-time challengers are much more enthusiastic about the national committees and their services than are the party's incumbents. One participant in a neophyte campaign sounded the typical appreciative note: "I was really impressed. They had good polls, they did mailings, they paid for so many things and had very exact kinds of measuring tools. They were most cooperative." But more experienced campaigners often wish the party would simply give them financial help and otherwise stay away. One characterized the RNC as "arrogant. They tried to tell us how to run the campaign, and the advice was worthless." A manager for a House incumbent was more specific in his indictment:

> I think the campaign committee is a superfluous bureaucracy. It doesn't do a thing for incumbents. I think it's a great organization for the president, a great organization to sustain your fundraising mailing lists, but beyond their giving money, the most valuable thing they have is their campaign seminars for challengers.
>
> The RNC has a beautiful actuality service, a nicer office than I do, and sixteen cute little girls whose daddies are from Texas and gave to the Eagles [an organization of large contributors]. But it doesn't run on Sundays or after six in the afternoon. How the hell can you get something on drive time Monday morning? That's the living proof of bureaucracy.

Another problem some Republican candidates identify is the difficulty generated by the committees' national outlook and their lack of familiarity with local problems. For example, the 1982 national party advertising theme, of staying the course with President Reagan, struck the right note in areas where the president remained popular, but was unhelpful, or even detrimental, in the many communities in which the severe economic recession was associated with the president's economic policies.[24] As one Republican incumbent who lost in 1982 argued, "To put out one theme and expect it to play in 435 districts is like Ford making one color car." [25] By 1984, even a vice chairman of the NRCC, Representative Mickey Edwards of Oklahoma, was questioning the national theme strategy. "The Republican party has been treating congressional races as if they were miniature presidential races," Edwards observed. "If anything, they are glorified state legislative races. You win not by tying into the grand march of history, but by concentrating on the individual, unique aspects of each district." [26]

The campaign of H. L. ("Sonny") Callahan, an experienced Alabama Republican challenger (and former Democrat) who won in 1984, exemplified the problem identified by Edwards. Callahan accepted an offer of NRCC advertising production assistance but clashed repeatedly with the national party staffers about the content of the ads. As an NRCC staffer who chose to remain anonymous described it, "he would trash everything that we did. We tried to put our stuff on the air and he would take our stuff off the air." [27]

These complaints would not be of much serious interest if there were hard evidence that the party role did in fact make a substantial difference to campaigns. But the apparently stunning recent Republican successes can be looked at in a framework that makes the party's role in them more problematical. For example, formally accurate statistical models predicted that the Republicans would lose roughly twice as many House seats in 1982 as they did. However, another measure—seats lost by the president's party in his first midterm election—shows that the average since 1950 is eighteen, eight *less* than the Republicans lost in 1982. On the Senate side, the Republicans did better than average in 1982 by not losing any seats. However, in 1962 and 1970, the president's party actually *gained* Senate seats in comparable midterm elections. Nor was the party's 1984 congressional performance historically impressive. Despite the Reagan presidential landslide, the Republicans made only a minor dent in the House Democratic majority and lost two seats in the Senate. Other scattered evidence casts some doubt on the efficacy of the Republican campaign machine. A study of eight closely contested 1982 congressional races found "no differences between winners and losers in terms of RNC and NRCC fieldmen support." Further, national party support did not always translate into electoral success in the district— "winners tended to receive a relatively greater percentage of their funds from individuals." [28]

However, the important point may be that the entire political establishment—both Democrats and Republicans, political analysts from both the media and academia—*believes* that what the Republicans do makes a difference. There is also the indisputable fact that the Republican party's new efforts have coincided with their longest period of Senate control in the past half-century.

Although the parties of the 1980s no longer controlled nominations for political office and had severely attenuated grass roots, they were developing a new role in which they paid for or supplied campaign technology. The Republican national party organization was able to use its sizable financial resources to recruit a number of candidates, but these candidates ran campaigns indistinguishable from those of self-starting entrepreneurs. The party did not ask them to adhere to a party line, nor did it set the themes of their campaigns. Once in office, successful candidates enjoyed the perquisites of all incumbents and became even less reliant on the party. In many ways, the party had become a kind of super-PAC—more powerful and far-ranging than any individual PAC and better able to coordinate multiple campaigns, but not strong enough to reassume its traditional functions.[29] We discuss this further below, and, in our final chapter, we will consider its implications more fully. But first let us look at the relationships between the major actors in current campaigns—parties, PACs, and consultants.

Parties, Pacs, and Consultants in Campaigns

One reading of the developments considered in this chapter might be that in the last few years, American campaign practices have come almost full circle. As the traditional parties declined, political consultants, armed with the relevant technological skills, moved forward to take their place. Additionally, independent groups arose, like NCEC on the left and NCPAC and CSFC on the right, which were a source of low-cost or no-cost professional services to candidates. Then the Republican party, and to some extent the Democratic party, retaliated—by positioning themselves either to fund or to provide the same services, with neither ideological nor mercenary incentives. To what extent have parties reassumed the central role in campaigns? What is their relationship to the consultants and political action committees who have usurped many of their traditional functions?

Perhaps naturally, the consultants, the PACs offering campaign services, and the party professionals have somewhat critical views of each other's work, particularly in the Republican community, where the overlap has become greater and the competition more obvious. Party staff see the consultants as putting the candidates second to their own profits and the special-interest groups as an unwelcome development. As Mitch Daniels described the party's role in campaigns:

> I think it's a very healthy thing to create a source of support for candidates that is not tied to a special interest and is not purely on a mercenary basis. We care about candidates, back them to the hilt, and don't ask anything from them except their own best efforts. We're going to be there every day, not just when the bill is overdue.

The consultants and independent PACs, on the other hand, believe that the party committees are too bureaucratized, inflexible, and riddled with patronage. As a NCPAC operative observed: "The NRCC doesn't have 'campaign managers,' they have 'administrative aides.' They homogenize all campaigns. There are NRCC 'managers' that have lost two or three races. They go back to their friends at the committee and get another campaign to screw up." One consultant said of the national committee field staff deployed to campaigns: "We don't allow them to interfere. By 'them,' I mean typically a field person, a young guy, this is his first real campaign. He may desire to get involved. His activities might be counterproductive. We won't allow it." Another is more direct: "The political staffs of the committees are on salary, and if they were any good, they would be running their own firms. All the good talent is freelancing." The perspective of both sides is thoughtfully summed up by Vince Breglio, a former director of the NRSC who now heads his own independent consulting company:

> I've been on both sides, and the fact of the matter is that campaigns do get ripped off by their consultants. But my own personal view is that by the very nature of the party structure, the party will never accomplish its goal because really talented people can't survive in the pressure cooker of the committees. Whenever an incumbent senator or congressman calls up and says "Hire X," you have to hire X. You can't maintain the highest professional standards of advancement until you move away from that into the private sector, where you are controlling the dynamics that make an organization efficient. The national committees will never have the kind of efficiency or personnel that will allow them to take over some of the functions they'd like to.

In the final analysis, both the consultants and the party committees admit that the future is likely to include them both, although the admission is somewhat grudging. From a consultant's point of view, the chief advantage of working with the committees is that they are clients with a long-term existence and "repeat business," unlike some individual candidates; they can be depended upon to pay their bills; and they make the consultant's life easier. Still, most consultants think of the committees primarily as organizations that can help them with their individual candidates and not as ends in themselves. From the party's point of view, the consultants are a necessary evil in a technology-dominated campaign system. It is the role of the party to attempt to displace and replace the consultants as much as possible and, where this is not possible, to control their behavior through the party's financial resources.

However, to summarize the argument of this section, the party is not the only repository of campaign resources, technical or financial. There are an increasing number of candidates in both parties and of all ideological persuasions who are wealthy enough to use their own money to purchase the needed resources and technical help. There are also the independent political action committees—from the National Committee for an Effective Congress on the left to the Committee for the Survival of a Free Congress on the right—that are increasingly well positioned to provide these campaign needs. An adept and promising candidate can shop for money and other resources among other special-interest groups—labor, business, feminist, environmental, senior citizens, moralistic—or whatever. For better or worse, the parties' renascence has not yet returned us to a party-based campaign system, nor to a system in which most candidates who become officeholders owe much to their party organizations. In our final chapter, we analyze the broader political effects of this state of affairs and the forces that might hinder or favor its continuation.

Notes _____

1. Larry J. Sabato, *The Rise of Political Consultants: New Ways of Winning Elections* (New York: Basic Books, 1981), 336.
2. Marjorie R. Hershey has long argued that "learning theories" explain much candidate behavior. See Hershey, *Running for Office* (Chatham, N.J.: Chatham House, 1984), and her earlier *The Making of Campaign Strategy* (Lexington, Mass.: D. C. Heath, 1974).
3. *The 1981 New Jersey Legislative General Election: Contributions and Expenditures* (Trenton, N.J.: New Jersey Election Law Enforcement Commission, December 1982), vol. 1, 99; *New Jersey Campaign Financing: 1983 Legislative General Election,* (Trenton, N.J.: New Jersey Election Law Enforcement Commission, January 1985), vol. 1, sec. 4.
4. All the statistics in the discussion of state parties come from a mail survey of state party chairs conducted from October 1983 through February 1984 by the Advisory Commission on Intergovermental Relations, in cooperation with the Democratic and Republican National Committees. It is likely that the survey somewhat overstates state party activity, since 30 percent of all

state party organizations (10 Republican and 20 Democratic) did not respond; it seems reasonable to assume the nonrespondents would be concentrated among the less active and well-staffed organizations. The results are published in Timothy Conlan, Ann Martino, and Robert Dilger, "State Parties in the 1980s," *Intergovernmental Perspective* 10 (Fall 1984): 6-13.

5. See Larry J. Sabato, *PAC Power: Inside the World of the Political Action Committees* (New York: Norton, 1984), 93-99.

6. Richard P. Conlon, "Commentary," in *Parties, Interest Groups and Campaign Finance Laws,* ed. Michael J. Malbin (Washington, D.C.: American Enterprise Institute, 1980), 187.

7. Quoted in Elizabeth Drew, "A Reporter at Large: Politics and Money: I," *The New Yorker,* December 6, 1982, 54ff.

8. Nelson W. Polsby, *Consequences of Party Reform* (New York: Oxford University Press, 1983), 139.

9. A substantial portion of this money did not go directly into political ventures but was spent on overhead, such as the expenses of the direct mailings themselves.

10. Paul Weyrich, "Authors' Replies," in Malbin, *Parties, Interest Groups and Campaign Finance Laws,* 96.

11. See Richard A. Viguerie, *The New Right: We're Ready to Lead* (Falls Church, Va.: Viguerie Company, 1981), 68-69; Alan Crawford, *Thunder on the Right* (New York: Pantheon, 1980), 228.

12. Viguerie, *The New Right,* 88.

13. *Congressional Quarterly Weekly Report,* April 21, 1984, 915. New Right uncertainty about how to deal with the Republican party was again apparent when Viguerie considered running for lieutenant governor in the 1985 Virginia Republican primary.

14. Paul Weyrich, "The New Right: PACs and Coalition Politics," in Malbin, *Parties, Interest Groups and Campaign Finance Laws,* 81.

15. See James L. Gibson et al, "Assessing Party Organizational Strength," *American Journal of Political Science* 27 (May 1983): 206.

16. Sarah McCally Morehouse, "The Politics of Gubernatorial Nominations," *State Government* 53 (Summer 1980): 128. See also Malcolm E. Jewell, *Parties and Primaries: Nominating State Governors* (New York: Praeger, 1984), parts IV and V.

17. A distinction developed by Austin Ranney, *Curing the Mischief of Faction* (Berkeley and Los Angeles: University of California Press, 1975), 134ff.

18. Xandra Kayden, "The Nationalizing of the Party System," in Malbin, *Parties, Interest Groups and Campaign Finance Laws,* 269.

19. Christopher Arterton, "Political Money and Party Strength," in *The Future of American Political Parties,* ed., Joel L. Fleishman (Englewood Cliffs, N.J.: Prentice-Hall, 1982), 109.

20. Sabato, *The Rise of Political Consultants,* 271.

21. The "reforms" of the Democratic party and their effects are the subject of several studies, including Polsby, *Consequences of Party Reform;* William J. Crotty, *Political Reform and the American Experiment* (New York: Crowell, 1977); and Jeane J. Kirkpatrick, *Dismantling the Parties: Reflections on Party Reform and Party Decomposition* (Washington, D.C.: American Enterprise Institute, 1978).

22. T. B. Edsall, "The GOP Money Machine," *Washington Post National Weekly Edition,* July 2, 1984, 6.

23. See Larry Sabato, "Parties, PACs and Independent Groups," in *The American Elections of 1982,* ed. Thomas E. Mann and Norman J. Ornstein (Washington, D.C.: American Enterprise Institute, 1983): 72-110.
24. See the findings in Alan I. Abramowitz, "National Issues, Strategic Politicians, and Voting Behavior in the 1980 and 1982 Congressional Elections," *American Journal of Political Science* 28 (November 1984): 710-21.
25. *Congressional Quarterly Weekly Report,* July 2, 1983, 1351.
26. Ibid. See also *National Journal,* December 15, 1984, 2402.
27. Stuart Rothenberg, *Winners and Losers* (Washington, D.C.: Free Congress Research and Education Foundation, 1983), 100.
28. Ibid., 94.
29. A concept developed in Arterton, "Political Money and Party Strength."

Campaigns and American Politics

10

> *You can look around the floor of the House and see a handful—*
> *twenty years ago, you saw a lot of them—today you can see just a*
> *handful of hacks that were put there by the party organization, and*
> *there are very, very few of them left. It is just mostly people who*
> *went out and took the election.*
>
> —U.S. representative, 1983[1]

As we have shown in the preceding chapters, the importance of the individual candidate's campaign has risen as the role of the political parties has declined. The parties have become only one of a number of actors in candidate-centered campaigns, and often not the most significant one. We contend that the examination of campaigns is important to anyone thinking about the future course of American politics and governance. In this chapter, we explain why.

Political parties have been integral—indeed central—to the functioning of our democratic system. From James Bryce in the last century, who wrote that "parties are inevitable. . . . No one has ever shown how representative government could work without them"[2] to E. E. Schattschneider in this one, who argued that "democracy is unthinkable save in terms of the parties,"[3] serious political analysts have "shared an underlying agreement that effective parties are desirable and probably essential in American politics as in democratic politics elsewhere."[4] The vital roles that parties play in democratic systems are many, but can be broadly classified in terms of their functions for the electorate, as political organizations, and in government.[5] To the extent that the American parties fail to fulfill these functions, our understanding of the way American democracy operates must be reconsidered.

Of the three major party roles, campaigns are most directly related to the party as political organization, because the nomination and election of candidates are at the heart of the party's organizational role. Candidate-centered campaigns have at a minimum provided the parties with a major competitor, and indeed, at the present time, one that is acknowledged to be dominant. However, the effects of candidate-centered campaigns have spilled over in important ways to the parties' other major functions. In the next section we discuss the various roles of the parties more fully, by describing the long-term decline in their ability to fulfill these roles and explaining the extent to which candidate-centered campaigns have been both causes and effects of party decline.

The Decline of Parties

In the 1960s and 1970s, scholars became increasingly disturbed by the apparent decay of the American parties in all their aspects. Concern about the parties stemmed from the implications of their decline for the democratic process. Referring to their role in democratic systems, one observer warned, "When parties are absent or . . . have become Cheshire cats of which very little is left except the smile, pathologies multiply." [6] Such pathologies include a state of political affairs in which political debate is "more negative and bitter, and policy compromises are much harder to come by." [7] Scholars observed signs of party decay everywhere, pervading all its roles.

Within the electorate, parties seemed increasingly unable to perform their key function of structuring the voters' choice.[8] As we discussed in chapter 3, the electorate's psychological identification with the parties steadily weakened. Not only were fewer voters partisan identifiers at all, but those who were reported increasingly weaker attachments, as shown by their growing propensity to split their tickets. Perhaps most damning was the voters' simple lack of interest in the parties as salient political objects. From 1952 to 1980, the proportion of the electorate that could not think of anything at all to say about America's parties—either good or ill—rose from slightly under a tenth to somewhat over a third.[9] The parties were, increasingly, not supported or rejected, but regarded by voters as irrelevant. By a margin of 45 to 37 percent, the American public in 1983 believed that "organized special interest groups" spoke to their concerns better than the parties did.[10]

The decline of the parties' organizational role—as the vehicle for nomination and election—is what the body of this book bears witness to. Local party organizations and their vaunted machines almost entirely passed into history. Little more than a tenth of all Democratic and Republican county organizations now have permanent headquarters, and even fewer have paid staff.[11] As we have seen, state party organizational strength has rebounded a bit from its nadir, but, as we saw in chapter 9, "the evidence is not overwhelming."[12] At the national level, traditionally the weakest link in the party chain, growth was impressive. The fact remained, however, that the direct primary robbed the parties of their monopoly on nominations, just as the advent of television and computerized direct mail robbed them of their monopoly on campaign communication. Moreover, campaign finance laws have made the increasing amounts of money required to wage campaigns via television and the mail more difficult to obtain from the parties than from alternative sources, such as political action committees, the candidate's personal resources, and direct solicitation of the public.

The parties' role in government suffered as well. Parties were traditionally able to structure government policy because one of them usually controlled both major policymaking institutions—the presidency and the Congress. Until the turn of the century, the president's party controlled the Senate almost 90 percent of the time, and the House more than two-thirds of the time. Most of the rare out-party victories occurred in midterm elections; only twice in more than a hundred years—in the disputed Hayes-Tilden election of 1876 and the second election of Grover Cleveland, in 1892—did the president fail to carry both houses in a presidential election year. Between 1900 and 1954, despite the Populist and Progressive crusades against party control, the trend grew even stronger. The president's party controlled the Senate better than 90 percent of the time and the House more than 80 percent of the time. Not once in all the presidential elections between McKinley's second campaign and Eisenhower's first did the president fail to bring in both houses of Congress with him.

Events changed dramatically in the 1950s, however. After 1954, the president's party controlled the Senate barely half the time, and the House even less than that. Further, party control meant less and less, as both John Kennedy and Jimmy Carter found to their chagrin. Despite majorities in both houses, neither president was able to enact major components of his program. Lyndon Johnson, the only other president of the period to have party control, was more successful at first, but his success stemmed in large measure from the powerful emotions generated by Kennedy's assassination.

Officeholders who appealed to an increasingly nonpartisan electorate to gain victory, and often achieved it without any significant reliance on the party for assistance during the campaign, had no compelling reason to vote their party; for them, as for voters, the parties were simply becoming irrelevant. As a member of the Democratic party leadership in the House observed:

> Nobody in the United States Congress ever talks about the Democratic or Republican party. I have never heard a member of the Congress refer to a colleague and urge a vote for him because he was in the same party. Most Democrats and Republicans could not recall three items on the platform of their party.... We have 435 parties in the House.[13]

The result of these developments was that, as the 1980s began, the parties were weaker than they had ever been. It was on the parties' organizational role that the candidate-centered campaigns had the most negative impact, but they impinged on other party functions as well. Campaigns that presented candidates to the public as individuals rather than as partisans hastened the decline of party identification as a means of structuring voters' choice: "The voters did not decide all of a sudden that parties were bankrupt political institutions and mandate their decline. Rather, voters reacted gradually over the last quarter of a century *to the way in which politics was presented to them*." [14]

As we have seen, candidates for executive office—presidents and governors—appealed to the voters on the basis of leadership and competence, while House members—and, increasingly, senators as well—emphasized their service to their constituencies. Voters responded to these appeals as they heard them; they punished Jimmy Carter for the state of the nation and rewarded Ronald Reagan. At the same time, they reelected a large majority of legislators in both parties, in approval of the way they had fulfilled their stated roles and irrespective of whether they shared either the partisanship or the policy preferences of successful or unsuccessful presidents.

Thus officeholders who were voted in as the result of candidate-centered campaigns increasingly emphasized electoral considerations in their decisionmaking calculus. Describing the culture of the House, a top staffer for the Democratic leadership distinguished between the "street-corner guys" and the "Atari guys." The former, a dying breed epitomized in 1985 by House Speaker Tip O'Neill and his Republican counterpart, Minority Leader Bob Michel, came to Congress originally through strong local party organizations. Their major career goal was to achieve seniority, and thus important committee positions. Their orientation was hierarchical; when faced with a tough question, their response was to find out what the chairman or the leader thought about it.

In contrast, the "Atari guys" of the candidate-centered era arrived in Washington as a result of their own efforts. Many, like Democrat Tim

Wirth of suburban Denver and Republican Newt Gingrich, until 1984 the sole member of his party in the Georgia House delegation, represented areas that had been traditional strongholds of the other party. Many seemed supremely uninterested in their committee assignments; they sought instead to become national spokesmen for the "big issues" and were often notably nondeferential to the House establishment. Wirth, for example, became widely known for his views on telecommunications policy, and Gingrich openly clashed with the leadership on the question of proper behavior for junior House members and members of the minority. The same House staffer mused on the behavior of this new breed in their officeholding roles:

> They talk about issues, but little gets accomplished. They just talk. They don't care about bills or chairmen; they just care about sending messages. When they vote, they think, "What kind of ad can they run against me?" The biggest turnout at the caucus meetings is never for legislative discussions, but to see the new party TV ads—they say, "Wow! This is great—I can save myself with this ad!"
>
> The only committees they care about getting on are Budget and Ways and Means so they can talk about the big macroeconomic issues, or Defense so they can talk about the big foreign policy issues, or Energy and Commerce so they can get PAC money. The Budget Committee is great because . . . they don't have to make hard program choices, they can just debate the macroeconomic issues.
>
> What do they want? They want to be famous. For the old guys, friendships crossed party lines. For these new guys, it's message-sending that crosses party lines.

No wonder that through most of the 1970s, party cohesion in both the House and Senate, as measured by the number of votes on which a majority of legislators of one party opposed a majority in the other party, continued to decline.[15] Increasingly, executives and not parties set the legislative agenda; increasingly, legislators decided whether or not to support this agenda based almost purely on an electoral calculus. As one observer commented: "There is no venality in all this. . . . We are simply living with the consequences of the separation of powers and the single-member district electoral system when there are no parties to contain the centrifugal forces." [16]

Was party in the electorate, as organization, and in government in permanent and irreversible decline? So it seemed. In 1982 the American Political Science Association commissioned a set of papers assessing the state of the discipline. In the contribution dealing with the study of political parties, Leon Epstein, a distinguished parties scholar, asked his colleagues, "Are professional students of politics now champions of a lost cause, trying with words to roll back a tide of American anti-partyism?." [17]

The Parties Resurrected? Maybe _____

The picture may not be quite so bleak, however. In the past few years, some of the political scientists who exhibited the most pessimism about the future of the parties (and with it perhaps the broader American future as well) have seen signs of party renascence. One who had argued in the 1970s that the weakened parties "may eventually bring the nation to a free floating politics in which prediction is hazardous, continuities are absent, and governmental responsibility is impossible to fix,"[18] was more optimistic by the 1980s: "There is still hope and time available. The need for stronger parties is becoming evident."[19] Another student of party decline had second thoughts by 1984: "It is not inconceivable that the decline of political parties could begin to reverse in the near future."[20] The same year a third well-known scholar argued, "The two parties show signs of strength as great, if not greater than, they have at any time in the past fifty years. It should be clear by now that the grab bag of assumptions, inferences, and half-truths which have fed the decline of party thesis is simply wrong."[21] What occasioned this substantial shift in tone was a series of events, occurring mostly around and after the election of Ronald Reagan in 1980, and apparently signaling the reversal of the decay of the party in all its major roles.

Party in the Electorate

There was, first, the matter of party identification in the electorate. Although approximately a third of the voters stubbornly continued to call themselves independents, the proportion of Republicans crept upward, mainly at the expense of the Democrats—some indication that Ronald Reagan's admirers were extending their commitment beyond the party's titular leader to the party itself. Further, political conversion might be a lagging indicator; in September 1984, 49 percent of ABC/*Washington Post* poll respondents said that the Republican party's stands on issues were similar to their own, as opposed to 38 percent who so characterized the Democrats.

There were other signs that Reagan's strong leadership was polarizing the electorate in a partisan way. Between July and September 1984, the ABC/*Washington Post* poll also found the Republicans gradually overtaking the Democrats in the public's perception of which party could do a better job at solving the problems the nation faced. Ticket splitting for House and Senate races dropped 7 percent between 1980 and 1982, and the proportion of survey respondents who could find no way to characterize the two parties, either positively or negatively, dropped eight points in the same period. The president himself polarized partisans in a truly dramatic fashion. Harris polls charting every president since Kennedy had found that Democrats and Republicans tended to disagree fairly modestly in their assessment of presidential performance in office. Most, for example, agreed that Jimmy Carter was not doing a very good job—only ten percentage points separated the assessments of the two groups of partisans. Richard Nixon held the previous record for polarization, with a twenty-seven-point difference between Democrats and Republicans. However, in October 1983, the partisan discrepancy in views of Ronald Reagan was a full thirty-four points, and a September 1984 CBS/*New York Times* poll charted an unprecedented gulf of fifty-six points.[22] Thus, there were modest signs that the electorate might finally be engaging in a realignment toward the Republicans that had previously been "akin to waiting for the Second Coming—much discussion, not much happening."[23]

Party as Organization

The strengthening of the party organizations at the national level continued apace. Both congressional campaign committees engaged in extensive candidate recruitment and "nursing" activities. Fred Asbell of the NRCC estimated that his organization was involved in a "major way" with sixty to sixty-five House candidates, or almost half of all NRCC-targeted districts in 1984. Martin Franks, Director of the DCCC, put the figure for his committee at thirty to thirty-five—"up from zero in 1980."[24]

In addition to stepping up their traditional activities, both committees engaged in new endeavors. The opening of the Democrats' media center permitted them to produce the low-cost, high-quality boilerplate advertising that the NRCC had offered for several years; the Republicans for the first time emulated their Senate committee colleagues and did tracking polls in selected targeted House districts.

There were some signs that the efforts were bearing fruit. Analysts pointed to a sharp drop over time in the number of uncontested House seats beginning in about 1960, but escalating in 1980 and 1982. They attributed this growing competition at least in part to the strengthened parties.[25] At lower levels, there were increasing reports of state party activity in areas such as coordinated mailings for legislative candidates. In states like New Jersey, party subsidies for such endeavors extended to the level of county office. Thus at all levels of the parties there were signs of organizational activities.

Party and Governance

Finally, there were apparent dramatic shifts in the legislative behavior of officeholders, at least at the federal level. We referred earlier to
the disintegrating cohesion of party voting patterns in both the House
and Senate through much of the century. However, the Reagan administration may have polarized legislators in much the same way as it polarized voters. By 1983, the inclination of Democratic legislators to vote
with the majority of their fellow partisans had reached a level un-
matched since 1908.[26] Additionally, there was a strong ideological cast to
the partisan divisions, with the Republican members becoming more
conservative across all major issue areas (economic measures, social policy measures, and foreign policy measures) and the Democrats more liberal. The strength of these partisan divisions cut across all regions. Even
though, for example, Republican legislators from the Northeast were
more liberal than the rest of their party, and southern Democrats in both
houses were more conservative than other Democrats, there was no
Republican regional group that was more liberal than any Democratic
group—northeastern Republicans were still more conservative as a
group than southern Democrats.[27] Other studies found that the interrelated elements of party and ideology outweighed factors like PAC contributions. Although PACs responded to legislative votes when they
considered making later contributions, the recipients did not change
their positions to accommodate them on major issues like the B-1 bomber, the windfall profits tax, the Chrysler bailout, or dairy subsidies.[28]

Staffers who worked in the Senate before and after the advent of
the Reagan administration found that their day-to-day experiences
confirmed these statistical findings. As one observed:

> The Senate Democrats had less cohesion before Reagan. They were fat
> and happy. Before Reagan the caucus [Senate policy committee] was
> irrelevant. Now it's energized. It meets every week and is very well
> attended. There's an emerging consensus on the big issues like defense
> and the budget. Party unity on the [1985] budget resolution was even
> higher than the Republicans'.

Thus, if "the ultimate test of party linkage is the behavior of the
party member in government,"[29] the signs seemed to indicate that in
the 1980s, officeholders were finally passing that test. Some analysts
tied the increased party voting in the legislature directly to the party
organizational activity we discussed earlier. They hypothesized that the
stepped-up party efforts that produced similar campaigns and similar
issues across the country was at least partly responsible for the parties'
more like-minded legislators. The campaign committees were seen as
having a nationalizing and centralizing effect.[30]

With voters demonstrating an increasing ability to distinguish between the parties, and with the amount of split-ticket voting decreasing, the parties appeared to be regaining some of their lost effectiveness in all their roles. And if party meant more, then it would follow that candidate-centered campaigns would mean less.

The Parties Resurrected? Maybe Not

Although the evidence we have just presented seems impressive, the old saying "One swallow does not a summer make" applies powerfully in this case as well. As analysts, we should be extremely wary of drawing conclusions for the long term from short-term data. The cautious observer might note that the increases in Republican party identification in 1984 were also seen in 1980—only to disappear within a year or two. The ABC/*Washington Post* polls that reported only a ten-point Democratic lead among party identifiers in September 1984 had found an even smaller seven-point difference in 1980. However, midway in the period, when the Reagan administration was presiding over the deepest recession in fifty years, the Democrats had regained their accustomed eighteen-point lead over the Republicans.

The effect of party organizational activity was also difficult to quantify. Although some analysts attributed the less-than-predicted Republican House losses in 1982 to the various efforts of the party,[31] others pointed out that the Republican showing was the worst for a president in his first midterm election since 1922.[32] Moreover, the operatives at the campaign committees were at best tentative in their agreement with political scientists' observations that their endeavors might in fact influence the voting behavior of the legislators they supported. They were still sharply aware of the effects of candidate-centered campaigns. Fred Asbell of the NRCC attributed the similarity of congressional campaign themes not to any "line" laid down by the party but rather to the consultants who used the committee as a clearinghouse. The DCCC executive director agreed with the proposition that "when someone has a call on you [referring to the committee's campaign contributions and other activities], it does have an impact," but in describing how the party might try to use it, continued, "It has to be subtle.... You call a media person or pollster who's something of a guru to said member." [33]

Campaign committee staff also recognized that even grateful challengers, once elected, became incumbents able to command contributions from political action committees and other nonparty sources; they expected party resources as their due, whatever their legislative behavior. A cautious political scientist noted, "Once in office, members of Congress may be invulnerable to party pressure based on past or prospective allocations of party campaign resources." He observed that the Republican party bureaucracy "has not developed substantial influence over policy-making by Republican officeholders. Indeed, influence tends to run the other way." [34]

The party's influence on contributions from PACs was also limited. A survey of PAC directors found that political action committees were more likely to seek information and take contribution cues from their largest and most influential colleagues than from the parties. Corporate and trade associations looked for guidance more to the Business-Industry Political Action Committee (BIPAC), labor committees to the AFL-CIO's Committee on Political Education (COPE), and liberal ideological organizations to the National Committee for an Effective Congress (NCEC) than any of them did to the political parties. [35] The parties' lists of targeted races competed with the Chamber of Commerce's lists of "opportunity races," COPE's "marginal committee" lists, and the NCEC and NCPAC "ideological" lists.

Finally, the effect of party activity on competition levels was erratic. Although the number of uncontested congressional seats had, as we have noted, dropped sharply after 1960, especially in presidential years, it suddenly rose quite dramatically in 1984, to a level more than twice as high as in 1980. Of the fifty-three uncontested seats in 1984, forty-four were held by Democrats and twenty-six of those were in the South, despite the resources the Republican party could offer challengers and its much improved southern performance.

It is also necessary to maintain some perspective about the high levels of party cohesion in congressional voting. Although it is true that the Democrats were more unified in their opposition to the Republicans during the Reagan administration than at any time since 1908, it was also the first time they had found themselves on the defensive against an activist and ideological president. Their behavior was most similar to the Republicans' reaction to the Democratic activists John Kennedy and Lyndon Johnson in the 1960s. Who was to say that, given a different president with a different legislative agenda, they would not return to the pattern in which their cohesion levels were lower, and almost identical, under the Republican Richard Nixon and the Democrat Jimmy Carter, and make the Reagan years merely a blip on the chart?

Further, the proportion of "party votes," although rising, remained less than half. [36] This meant, on the majority of roll call votes, either that most legislators of both parties voted the same way, or that partisans distributed themselves more randomly. Nonparty votes were often on the classic pork barrel issues that legislators point to when they run for reelection as constituency ombudsmen. Let us consider two typical questions that senators faced in 1984 when analysts were observing the high party cohesion and ideological tone on the big issues.

The first involved amending legislation that regulated the travel of oversized tractor-trailer trucks on highways, regulations that had previously been under the purview of the states. The two Republican senators from Pennsylvania sought to amend the legislation so that it would divert the "killer trucks" from their state to roads in New York and New Jersey. In this case, Republican senator Alfonse D'Amato joined forces with his Democratic colleague, Daniel Patrick Moynihan, and the two Democratic senators from New Jersey to defeat the Pennsylvanians by a margin of two to one. There was no "party line" on this vote; the six senators merely prevailed personally on colleagues for whom they had done similar favors on parochial issues. As a staffer for one of the senators commented, "We had the issue on the merits, but nobody voted on the merits. The six senators stood in the well and lobbied. They just divided up the names they were going to lobby."

In another instance senators were drawn into a dispute over committee jurisdiction for an arcane deregulation issue involving the transportation industry. The chief antagonists on the measure were both Republicans, Oregon's Robert Packwood, chairman of the Committee on Commerce, Science, and Transportation, and North Dakota's Mark Andrews, chairman of the Department of Transportation subcommittee of the Appropriations Committee. Packwood took the "usual" Republican line favoring deregulation. Andrews opposed it in this case because of the loss his "out of the way" state would suffer when corporations were no longer required to provide service. The calculations of other senators revolved around which of their feuding colleagues could do them the most damage on future pork barrel issues in their states. A Senate staffer explained: "Nobody made it a party issue. The question was, was it worse to have Andrews cut your state out of the next transportation appropriation bill, or Packwood never let your next bill out of committee?" For the constituency-minded legislator, such issues loom larger than their votes on the defense bill or the budget. They do not forget the political wisdom embodied in Jeff Greenfield's admonition to campaigning incumbents that "one amendment to the Internal Revenue Code to protect an important industry is better than a 98 percent voting record on the scorecard of an interest group." [37]

It was also on such arcane and low-profile issues that legislators felt more able to reward political action committees. The impact of political action committees could outweigh ideology or party when powerful organized interests on only one side were arrayed against elements of the unorganized public. Purchasers of defective automobiles did not have a PAC to threaten retribution if a "lemon law" was not passed, nor were citizens who had received improper medical care or faulty legal advice organized to lobby on behalf of regulation of professionals. A legislator also pointed out what statistical analysis of voting behavior and PAC contributions could not reveal: "There are various degrees of being for a bill—co-sponsoring it, or fighting for it in committee, in debate, on the floor, or in a leadership role on the floor. PAC funds can determine a member's intensity as well as position." [38]

The overall note we sound in this section, therefore, is one of caution. Many of the trends of the last five years may be transitory; others are subject to the classic debate over whether a glass is half-empty or half-full. It appears to us that the objective environment still contains many more of those forces that impel candidates away from parties and party discipline and toward the continuation of candidate-centered campaigns and what they imply for the behavior of both voters and candidates who later become officeholders.

Candidates and Parties: A Longer View

Whatever the nature of the American political landscape, one element has always remained constant—the major force driving most candidates for political office has been the desire to win. The story of candidate and officeholder behavior in campaigns and afterward is always the story of the activities that candidates believe will optimize the chances of winning. When the political parties controlled nominations, directed campaigns, brokered policy, and cued voter decisions, candidates had no rational alternative to participation in this party system, broadly understood. They had to participate in it to achieve their goal—winning.

However, developments in recent years have given candidates new means of winning. Voters who were less firmly bound psychologically to the parties were more open to nonpartisan appeals. New technologies provided an alternative to the party symbol and organization for communicating those appeals to voters. Structural changes in government increased officeholders' ability to give voters what they wanted independent of the party. These changes included legislative reorganization that weakened the power of the party leadership and increased governmental programs—entitlement programs, special tax considerations, and so on—that individual members could claim credit for.

These interdependent developments are likely to become permanent parts of the political landscape. All of them argue for a continued diminution of the party role in setting candidates' fates, and a continued increase in the ability of politicians to affect their own destinies. There are no countervailing trends that would clearly benefit parties. Parties can thus be only as important as candidates permit them to be. In the next section, we will elaborate on the most significant of the trends benefiting candidates, and thus candidate-centered campaigning, and consider under what circumstances candidates might conceivably find it advantageous to have strengthened parties.

The Critical Role of Technology

Analyses of the factors that brought an end to party primacy (including our own in chapter 3) properly place emphasis on the role of technological advances, especially television and the computer. The parties had survived other kinds of massive social change. Although the upheavals at the end of the nineteenth century that generated the Populist and Progressive threats to their hegemony were massive indeed, parties found ways to adapt to potentially devastating reforms like the Australian ballot and, particularly, the direct primary. In many ways, as we have seen, they were certainly stronger in the first half of the twentieth century than they were in the golden age of parties, in the last half of the nineteenth.

But what made television and the computer unique was that for the first time in history, they provided candidates everywhere with a highly effective alternative means of conveying information about themselves to the mass of voters. The impact of newspapers, magazines, and radio paled in comparison with what television offered: a powerful combination of visual and aural messages. Now candidates could literally enter voters' homes and give party organizations a competitor they never had before.

If television provided the means for "wholesale" communication, the computer, with its ability to locate the precise voters that candidates needed to reach, furnished the means for "retail" communication. As Morris Fiorina has commented: "Candidates would have little incentive to operate campaigns independently of parties if there were no means to apprise the citizenry of their independence. The media provide the means." [39]

In principle, there is no reason why these media cannot also be used by the parties; indeed, the institutional advertising and direct mail efforts they increasingly engage in show that they are. But parties no longer have a *monopoly* on the major forms of political communication. Once candidates learned that they could independently compete with party organizations and had the vehicle of the direct primary to do it, why should they choose to give up their independence and control of their message to the parties?

The Matter of Money

One possible development could force candidates to become more reliant on their parties, and that is a campaign finance system that forced them to go to their parties for sustenance. If money has always been the mother's milk of politics, the enormous costs of the new campaign technology has made raising money, and lots of it, more imperative than ever. Giving parties a greater role in the financing of elections is always the first suggestion of reformers intent on strengthening the parties and ending candidate-centered politics. As the chairman of the American Political Science Association's Committee on Party Renewal argued, "First, we need to revise the election finance laws so that . . . campaign funds are channeled through the parties rather than independently to candidates." [40] Another leading student of the parties' main competitors, PACs and consultants, suggests that national and state party committees "should be permitted to give any party candidate at least several times the amount of money a single PAC can contribute, and tax credits for gifts to the party should be expanded." [41] Not unnaturally, party staff share these views. As a former director of the NRCC says, "If Congress and the [Federal Election Commission] are serious about wanting to help rebuild the parties, then they will have to look at us as something more than just super-PACs, and grant us major new authority and maneuvering room." [42]

This observation brings us to the crux of the matter. It is the officeholders in Congress who pass the legislation regarding campaign financing for candidates—in other words, themselves. No proposal being seriously advanced even entertains the notion that parties should play the major role in the process. Republicans generally support taking the lid off the parties and permitting them to contribute greater amounts but, at the same time, leaving political action committees free to operate as well. They favor having more money available to candidates, but not merely party money. This view is consistent with the Republicans' greater access to the business money that comprises an increasing proportion of the PAC fund pool, and their long-time position as a minority party wishing to aid challengers who have difficulty raising money from nonparty sources. The relatively impoverished Democrats, on the other hand, show little enthusiasm in the current environment for an increased party role. To further unleash the Republican money machine would mean, as Representative Al Swift comments, that the Democrats "would start every game on the goal line and [the Republicans would] start every game on the 40-yard line." [43]

Instead, many Democrats support public funding for congressional races and limits on both contributions and expenditures by individuals,

PACs, and parties. Representative David Obey, who has led the fight for public financing for several years, states its proponents' basic argument: "It's time Congress was taken off the auction block.... I detest what money and the candidates' need for money is doing to the House."[44] Not surprisingly, Republicans, who regard finance limits as an incumbents' protection act for the majority Democrats in the House and who philosophically reject the additional bureaucracy and expenditure that public financing would bring, are generally unenthusiastic about Obey's proposal.

Therefore, so long as the major players have diametrically opposed views about the direction of revision in the campaign finance laws—and disagreement is certain to continue—if change comes at all, it will be only incremental at best and is extremely unlikely to give the parties a dominant role.[45]

Ideology as a Vehicle for Party Coherence

In the discussion so far, we have argued that candidates no longer need parties to get their messages across and that parties no longer monopolize the resources (workers in the old system, money in the new one) for the delivery of messages. Is there some other resource of importance to candidates that parties could provide?

One strong possibility is that the party symbol could once again serve, as it historically did, as a kind of shorthand cue to voters of what the candidate's message is, in a way that would be to the advantage of the candidates. To be sure, it would be a different and more powerful message than it was in the past, because, thanks to technology, it would have to be a national message rather than a parochial one. If most candidates accepted the notion that the party symbol was of use to them personally and acted on that assumption by running as partisans, it would give more policy content to campaign debate and produce more coherence in government action on major issues, *because candidates would see such a state of affairs as beneficial to their own electoral interests.*

There are two circumstances under which we might expect candidates to see the party symbol as a useful vehicle for their own campaigns and officeholding behavior. The first is when the national debate over policy is phrased in terms of such sharply different alternatives that all politicians are virtually forced to choose. The second is when one party is such a clear favorite among voters that identification with it becomes a likely ticket to reelection. Let us consider the conditions that permit either of these circumstances to emerge and examine how likely either one of them is to produce a long-term tendency that favors stronger parties.

Structured Policy Debate. Sea changes of one sort or another have occurred in American politics approximately every forty years and have brought with them major realignments of party strength.[46] The era of Jacksonian democracy, the Civil War and the rise of the Republicans to power, the industrial revolution and McKinley's crushing of Bryan and the Democrats, and the Great Depression and the Roosevelt New Deal are the major landmarks. In each era, the parties defined the terms of the national policy debate, and the party that won the debate emerged as the major party.

Two conditions were necessary for each of these realignments to occur. First, there had to be a set of major issues on which there were two clear sides so that a meaningful debate could take place. Second, there had to be a presidential candidate who either in his campaign or once in office would take a clear stand on one side of the debate and had the vision and leadership qualities which would make him its symbol. Jackson, Lincoln, and Franklin Roosevelt played major roles in winning the debate for their side; Bryan played a major role in losing it for his.

Beginning in the 1960s, the kinds of issues arose that could potentially produce a debate leading to another historical realignment. But the leaders were not there. Kennedy was assassinated. Johnson, with his call "Come, let us reason together," preferred a consensus politics. Nixon gave up on converting Democrats, called for an "ideological majority" rather than leading his party, and was swept away by Watergate. Carter never decided between his instincts as both a fiscal conservative and a working class populist. But then Ronald Reagan came to the presidency. Like Roosevelt, he was elected primarily as a rejection of his predecessor and turned his negative mandate into a positive one.[47] His dominance of the political landscape produced the ideological and policy coherence that observers have noted, as officeholders and their opponents measured whether it was to their electoral advantage or disadvantage to stand with him or against him.

The Emergence of a New Republican Majority? But how likely is the "Reagan effect" to endure beyond his last term of office? We have already seen the public, which greeted his first election by shifting in a notable way to self-professed Republican identification, swing back at least once (in 1982) when disenchanted with his economic policies. If the economy remains sound, then the debate will shift to other concerns—foreign policy, social issues, the environment, and entitlement programs—where public opinion is not always supportive of the positions of President Reagan and his party. If the Reagan economic program should not be successful in the long term, then 1986 is likely to repeat 1982, when many Republican candidates did not see running with the president as an advantage. The party unity of 1981 collapsed in

1982, and "there is no evidence that the strong GOP party organization was able to influence defecting Republicans to support the party leadership."[48] When party definition depends overmuch on presidential leadership, "either his party becomes a flock of sheep or the party falls apart."[49]

But, the reader might ask at this point, if in fact Reagan is successful, why couldn't he accomplish what Roosevelt did, and make the Republican party a majority for a generation? If the Republican gains of 1984 should be more enduring than those of 1980 and the public more solidly Republican in identification, then the majority of strong office hopefuls would stream to the Republican party, as they did in the past to the Democrats. It would be to candidates' personal advantage to be identified with the party that the majority of the public supported. Strong presidential leadership would be necessary only in the short run, and the loss of Reagan's inspiration would not be fatal. Future presidents, at least until the next set of realigning issues arose, could preside over the consolidation of the new agenda, as they did after past realignments.

The answer is that after the last two major realignments, in 1896 and 1932, candidates were essentially stuck with the party. Lacking any other means of communication, they had to rely on the persuasiveness of the party's message—and hope it would carry them to victory. The majority party became a vast umbrella, a coat of many colors; the minority party became either a collection of "me toos," advocating little more than a tinkering with the majority party agenda, or a reactionary remnant doomed to lose. Most legislators were either insulated from presidential failures by the strongly partisan nature of their constituencies or, if in the relatively few marginal constituencies, at the mercy of the "surge and decline" of the president's fortunes.[50]

Unlike those of 1896 or 1932, however, the politicians of today are not tied to their party or its presidents in sending their messages. What President Reagan might accomplish is the elimination of the long-time Democratic advantage in partisan identifiers and numbers of incumbent officeholders, and a change in the issue agenda. When Democrats calculate how to fit in to this new state of affairs, though, they need not worry too much about constraints placed upon them by the symbolic baggage of their nominal party affiliation. If Utah could award its Democratic governor 55 percent of the vote at the same time it was giving the Democratic presidential candidate 21 percent (as happened in 1980), or Nebraska could reelect a Democratic senator with 53 percent while giving his party's presidential candidate 29 percent (as happened in 1984), then Democrats can win anywhere with attractive appeals, divorced from a party hypothetically buried in a Republican realignment. Unlike earlier realigning periods, *it is now the candidate's choice whether he or she wishes to identify strongly with the party.* Strong candidates, not strong parties, produce the competitive political environment we now observe.

The opportunities for candidates to shape their own appeals are breathtakingly evident in a dialogue that took place between New York Republican representative Jack Kemp and New Jersey Democratic senator Bill Bradley in September 1984. Both men were to win decisive victories in November, both were regarded as national and party spokesmen on the issues of taxation and tax reform, and both were widely perceived as leading candidates for their parties' future presidential nominations. Legislative proposals each offered—"Bradley-Gephardt" and "Kemp-Kasten"—were to figure heavily in the major economic debates of 1985, and the superficially remarkable part was that the ideas they put forth were amazingly similar—both calling for a vastly simplified flat tax system that eliminated all but the most politically popular deductions in the current system.[51] Part of that dialogue follows:

> MR. KEMP: Bill. . . . People have a choice. Mondale wants to raise tax rates and you and I and Reagan want to lower them. . . .
> Q [from interviewer]: Senator, do you oppose Mr. Mondale's tax increase proposals?
> MR. BRADLEY: Yes.
> Q: Representative Kemp, if the alternative before the House was Bradley-Gephardt, would you vote for it?
> MR. KEMP: Oh sure, I've said that publicly.
> Q: If Kemp-Kasten were before the Senate?
> MR. BRADLEY: We ought to head in the same direction. I'm going to look at getting one bill.[52]

Kemp rode the crest of his party's popularity on the economy to national fame and was, indeed, through his early advocacy of supply-side economics and the Kemp-Roth proposal—the centerpiece of Reaganomics—an architect of that Republican package. He made his reputation by championing supply-side economics when the Republican mainstream economic message still centered on austerity and monetarism. Bradley is no Johnny-come-lately either. His support of the flat tax goes back to his entry into the Senate in 1978. Like his fellow Democrat and 1984 presidential aspirant Gary Hart, he used the current political environment to shape a persona divorced from the party. Like Hart in 1980, he withstood the Reagan landslide in 1984 and indeed gained his own landslide reelection with a margin greater than the president's. Bradley and Kemp epitomize why a partisan realignment in the classic sense of 1896 and 1932 is not likely to come again. Skillful politicians who want to win will not permit it, and they have the independent resources to carry out their determination.

Candidates, Campaigns, and Parties:
A Conclusion_____

In this final chapter, we have argued that the current candidate-centered campaigns are a major decentralizing force in American politics and work to make candidates—who become our political officeholders—independent actors. The American political parties have been the institutions most threatened by the new self-sufficiency of candidates. Voters, responding to candidates' messages, have exhibited increasing psychological independence from the parties and a willingness to split their tickets, thereby diminishing the traditional role of the party in the electorate. Candidates, by creating personal campaign organizations, have subverted another traditional party role.

As our survey of their recent organizational activities indicates, the political parties have not ignored the assaults on their role. The rapid emergence of institutionalized national party organizations and, to a lesser extent, of state party organizations, is in some ways as dramatic a departure from traditional American politics as the appearance of candidate-centered campaigns. Bankrupt in the early 1970s and offering virtually no services to candidates, the national party organizations between them raised approximately $300 million for the 1984 elections and offered candidates not only money but the wide range of campaign technologies we have described. Republican organizations, in particular, "have attained a degree of institutional permanence that they have never known before, and have carved out a secure niche for themselves by virtue of their fund-raising and campaign-services capabilities." [53] Centralization rather than their traditional decentralization is the parties' appropriate response to the imperatives of technology-centered politics. Robert Huckshorn and John Bibby are among those who see these developments as "counter trends which may reflect continuing strength, viability, and durability of the parties." [54] However, it still seems unlikely that the parties can reverse the events that have made them the servants rather than the masters of successful independent politicians. These office-seekers are unlikely to cede their newfound independence and flexibility, and the parties are likely to prosper only to the extent that strong candidates see it in their interest to have strong parties. Those who are both most optimistic about the prospects for party revival and most desirous of it acknowledge this truth. Huckshorn and Bibby see the most favorable outcome for the parties as one in which "skilled incumbents may well be able to develop leadership and governing resources which permit parties to play a significant role in this new and changing environment." [55] David Price, both a political scientist and a recent state party chair, writes:

The point is not that candidates and officeholders should sacrifice their political interests and values for the sake of the party but rather that a *range* of viable strategies of campaigning and governance are available, some of which tend to reinforce and others to undermine party strength. It is important to bring to light the implications of these strategies and practices for the welfare of the parties, and for politicians to give these implications greater weight in the choices that they make.[56]

To date, politicians pondering the implications have seemed most inclined to encourage the parties to perform those functions that are helpful to candidates' reelections, but most distant from their "presentation of self"[57] and the messages they communicate to voters. These include voter identification programs, get-out-the-vote activities, maintenance of contributor lists, and acceptance of useful strategic information.[58] They have resisted changes that would seriously impede their ability to run their own races and make their own cases—most notably, limits on sources of nonparty campaign money or handing over control of their messages to the parties. So long as they continue to do so—and from their perspective, it is most difficult to see why should not— candidate-centered campaigns will also continue, and the role of the parties will be limited.

Candidates and their campaigns will therefore remain important to those who wish to understand American voting behavior, political mobilization, electoral outcomes, and policymaking. We hope that the description and analysis in this book is a step in shaping and deepening that understanding.

Notes _____

1. As quoted in *Congress Off the Record: The Candid Analyses of Seven Members*, ed. John F. Bibby (Washington, D.C.: American Enterprise Institute, 1983), 43.
2. James Bryce, *The American Commonwealth* ed. Louis Hacker (1888; reprint, New York: Putnam, 1959), vol. 1, 119.
3. E. E. Schattschneider, *Party Government* (New York: Holt, Rinehart and Winston, 1942), 1.
4. Leon Epstein, "The Scholarly Commitment to Parties," paper presented at the Annual Meeting of the American Political Science Association, Denver, Colorado, September 2-5, 1982, 1-2.
5. For representative discussions, see Samuel J. Eldersveld, *Political Parties in American Society* (New York: Basic Books, 1982), chapter 1; Martin P. Wattenberg, *The Decline of American Political Parties* (Cambridge, Mass.: Harvard University Press, 1984), 1-6.

6. Walter Dean Burnham, "Foreword," in Wattenberg, *The Decline of American Political Parties*, xii.
7. Wattenberg, *The Decline of American Political Parties*, 128.
8. See Norman H. Nie, Sidney Verba, and John R. Petrocik, *The Changing American Voter* (Cambridge, Mass.: Harvard University Press, 1976).
9. Wattenberg, *The Decline of American Political Parties*, 63. See also Richard J. Trilling, *Party Image and Electoral Behavior* (New York: Wiley, 1976).
10. Larry J. Sabato, *PAC Power: Inside the World of the Political Action Committees* (New York: Norton, 1984), 163.
11. David E. Price, *Bringing Back the Parties* (Washington, D.C.: CQ Press, 1984), 25.
12. Epstein, "The Scholarly Commitment to Parties," 16.
13. Democratic representative Thomas Foley, as quoted in Austin Ranney, *The Referendum Device* (Washington, D.C.: American Enterprise Institute, 1981), 70.
14. Wattenberg, *The Decline of American Political Parties*, 125. Emphasis added.
15. See the data on party cohesion in David W. Brady, Joseph Cooper, and Patricia A. Hurley, "The Decline of Party in the U.S. House of Representatives, 1887-1968," *Legislative Studies Quarterly* 4 (August 1979): 381-408; *Congressional Quarterly Weekly Report*, January 9, 1982, 61-64.
16. Morris P. Fiorina, *Retrospective Voting in American National Elections* (New Haven: Yale University Press, 1981), 210.
17. Epstein, "The Scholarly Commitment to Parties," 20.
18. Gerald Pomper, "Impacts on the Political System," in *American Electoral Behavior*, ed. Samuel Kirkpatrick (Beverly Hills, Calif.: Sage, 1976), 137.
19. Gerald Pomper, *Party Renewal in America* (New York: Praeger, 1980), 15.
20. Wattenberg, *The Decline of American Political Parties*, xvi.
21. Joseph Schlesinger, "The New American Political Party," paper presented at the Annual Meeting of the American Political Science Association, Washington, D.C., August 30-September 2, 1984, 1.
22. These data appear in Wattenberg, *The Decline of American Political Parties*, xvii; John Kenneth White and Dwight L. Morris, "Shifting Coalitions in American Politics: The Changing Partisans," paper presented at the Annual Meeting of the American Political Science Association, Washington, D.C., August 30- September 2, 1984; the CBS/*New York Times* polls of September 12-16 and November 8-14, 1984; and the ABC/*Washington Post* poll of September 7-11, 1984.
23. White and Morris, "Shifting Coalitions," 5.
24. Transcribed remarks at the Roundtable on National Recruitment of Congressional Candidates: Trends and Consequences, Annual Meeting of the American Political Science Association, Washington, D.C., August 31, 1984.
25. Schlesinger, "The New American Political Party," 17.
26. See note 15 and *Congressional Quarterly Weekly Report*, December 31, 1983.
27. As calculated by *National Journal*, May 12, 1984, 904-20.
28. See Henry W. Chappell, "Campaign Contributions and Congressional Voting," *Review of Economics and Statistics* 61 (1982): 77-83; Henry W. Chappell, "Campaign Contributions and Voting on the Cargo Preference Bill: A Comparison of Simultaneous Models," *Public Choice* 36 (1981): 301-12; William P. Welch, "Campaign Contributions and Legislative Voting: Milk Money and Dairy Price Supports," *Western Political Quarterly* 35 (December 1982): 478-95; Diana Evans Yiannakis, "Contributions and House Voting on

Conflictful and Consensual Issues: The Windfall Profits Tax and the Chrysler Loan Guarantee," paper presented at the Annual Meeting of the American Political Science Association, Chicago, September 1-4, 1983.

29. Schlesinger, "The New American Political Party," 31.
30. Transcribed remarks by Gary C. Jacobson at the Roundtable on National Recruitment of Congressional Candidates.
31. Gary C. Jacobson and Samuel Kernell, "Strategy and Choice in the 1982 Congressional Elections," *P.S.* 15 (Summer 1982): 423-30.
32. Alan I. Abramowitz, "National Issues, Strategic Politicians, and Voting Behavior in the 1980 and 1982 Congressional Elections," *American Journal of Political Science* 28 (November 1984): 710-21.
33. Transcribed remarks by Fred Asbell and Martin Franks at the Roundtable on National Recruitment of Congressional Candidates.
34. David Adamany, "Political Parties in the 1980s," in *Money and Politics in the United States,* ed. Michael J. Malbin (Chatham, N.J.: Chatham House, 1984), 111, 114.
35. Sabato, *PAC Power,* 46.
36. See note 26.
37. Jeff Greenfield, Running to Win (New York: Simon and Schuster, 1980), 241.
38. Sabato, *PAC Power,* 133, 135.
39. Morris P. Fiorina, "The Decline of Collective Responsibility in American Politics," *Daedelus* 109 (1980), 33.
40. Pomper, *Party Renewal in America,* 15-16.
41. Larry J. Sabato, *The Rise of Political Consultants: New Ways of Winning Elections* (New York: Basic Books, 1981), 331.
42. Steven F. Stockmeyer, "Commentary," in *Parties, Interest Groups and Campaign Finance Laws,* ed. Michael J. Malbin (Washington, D.C.: American Enterprise Institute, 1980).
43. *Congressional Quarterly Weekly Report,* July 16, 1983, 1453. The Republican position is spelled out in a series of articles in the Republican party's "journal of thought and opinion," *Commonsense* 6 (December 1983).
44. *Congressional Quarterly Weekly Report,* July 16, 1983, 1451.
45. For an extended discussion of this point and of the further complications introduced by independent expenditures, unlimited personal spending by candidates, and constitutional issues, see Sabato, *PAC Power,* chapter 6.
46. Among the notable studies of realignment and realigning elections are James Sundquist, *Dynamics of the Party System,* rev. ed. (Washington, D.C.: Brookings Institution, 1983); V. O. Key, "A Theory of Critical Elections," *Journal of Politics* 17 (1955): 3-18; Walter Dean Burnham, *Critical Elections and the Mainsprings of American Politics* (New York: Norton, 1970); and Paul A. Beck, "A Socialization Theory of Partisan Realignment," in *The Politics of Future Citizens* (San Francisco: Jossey-Bass, 1974).
47. See the analysis in Gerald Pomper et al, *The Election of 1980* (Chatham, N.J.: Chatham House, 1981); Paul R. Abramson, John H. Aldrich, and David W. Rohde, *Change and Continuity in the 1980 Elections* (Washington, D.C.: CQ Press, 1982).
48. Adamany, "Political Parties in the 1980s," 110.
49. *American Political Science Association,* "Toward a More Responsible Two-Party System: A Report of the Committee on Political Parties," *American Political Science Review* 44 (1950): Supplement, 94.

50. Angus Campbell, "Surge and Decline: A Study of Electoral Change," *Public Opinion Quarterly* 24 (1960): 397-418.
51. Bradley's and Kemp's respective cosponsors were Representative Richard Gephardt of Missouri and Senator Robert Kasten of Wisconsin.
52. *New York Times*, September 30, 1984, section 4.
53. Price, *Bringing Back the Parties*, 297.
54. Robert J. Huckshorn and John F. Bibby, "State Parties in an Era of Political Change," in *The Future of American Political Parties*, ed. Joel L. Fleishman (Englewood Cliffs, N.J.: Prentice-Hall, 1982), 99.
55. Ibid.
56. Price, *Bringing Back the Parties*, 301.
57. Erving Goffman, *The Presentation of Self in Everyday Life* (New York: Doubleday, 1959). Richard Fenno applies Goffman's analysis to representative's behaviors toward their constituents. See Fenno, *Home Style: House Members in their Districts* (Boston: Little, Brown, 1978), chapters 3 and 4.
58. Xandra Kayden makes some of these points in *Campaign Organization* (Lexington, Mass.: D. C. Heath, 1978), 172-73.

Methodological
Appendix

The data used in this book come from three sources: the academic and "popular" literature on the subject, our own experiences as strategic participants or observers in a number of campaigns in several states and for a variety of offices, and forty-two structured personal interviews conducted by one or both of us between late 1982 and late 1984. The subjects of the interviews were candidates, officeholders and members of their staffs, campaign managers and other campaign workers, party personnel at the state and national level, personnel at political action committees, pollsters, media consultants, and political reporters. Several were interviewed more than once.

These interviews ranged in length from one to four hours, and most have been preserved on tape. We requested that they be "on the record" and for attribution. In most, but not all cases, our subjects agreed. Our promise of confidentiality to some individuals, or on some subjects, has been preserved. Many respondents who are named have moved on to other positions; the job titles we attribute to them are those they held in the campaigns in question or at the time we interviewed them. All quotations in the text that are not footnoted come from our formal taped interviews. Aside from occasional minor editing to convert conversational English into intelligible written prose, they come directly and without modification from transcriptions of the tapes.

We cannot count or formally list the many informal conversations with these interviewees and other participants or observers in campaigns with which we were centrally or peripherally involved, but these numerous encounters were also very significant in shaping our view of campaigns and in giving us the "verstehen" to write this book. In most of the campaigns we observed, including both Democratic and Republican ones, we were not neutral observers. Rather, in many cases, we were committed, paid participants. Because of our participant status, we had access to many aspects of a campaign that simply would not have been available to someone not completely trusted by the campaign.

We do not claim that our formal interviews constitute any sort of "scientific" sample of the campaigners' universe. Such a sample is probably impossible to construct in any case. However, as the text makes clear, the data are gathered from a broad spectrum. The positions our informants held varied enormously. The campaigns we describe and analyze include races for the state legislature, the House of Representatives, the Senate, and governorships. They include winners and losers, Democrats and Republicans, incumbents and challengers, and they span the country.

Generally, we saw our interviews as an opportunity to fill in gaps in our knowledge and sought out those who could do this. There seemed little point in asking busy people about things we already knew from the literature or from our own experience. The people we interviewed and the timing of the interviews were, of course, somewhat affected by events and "targets of opportunity." However, for the most part, they were connected to the stages of campaigns we describe in the book and the corresponding stages of our research. Generally, campaign and party personnel were interviewed first, then polling and media consultants and reporters, and finally organizational personnel. As indicated, we went back a second time, and sometimes even more than that, to some very patient respondents who could advise us on multiple topics.

With this kind of research plan, there could not be a single formal questionnaire we could administer to everyone. We approached each interview with a list of questions, sometimes the same ones, and intensively instructed ourselves beforehand about the campaigns in which our respondents had participated. No one we approached declined to speak with us, although some were, at least in our judgment, more forthcoming than others. The interviews are almost exactly evenly divided between people we knew personally when we began and people we approached "cold," or with a recommendation from someone else we had interviewed. Whether we knew someone personally had almost no bearing on how "good" the interview turned out to be.

Our data also include confidential candidate polls, strategic memos, and similar materials that their authors or their clients supplied to us, generally with an assurance of confidentiality. Any scholar who has tried to obtain such material, even about a campaign long over, knows that there are few "state secrets" guarded so closely! We especially appreciate the trust respondents displayed in us by giving us access to these materials and permission to use them in some form. We are strongly convinced that our ability to obtain such material, and the almost uniformly high level of cooperation and friendly reception we received, stemmed from the respondents' knowledge that we had participated in campaigns—had "been there"—and were not merely students of them. The fact of that participation was much more important than which side we had supported in any given contest.

All of the political advertising material we quote was in fact broadcast. Some of it was supplied to us in the form of scripts or the original tape cassettes prepared for broadcast, and some of it was taped during actual air play. All of it is preserved in the original form in which we acquired it.

Suggested Readings

General

Agranoff, Robert. *The New Style in Election Campaigns.* rev. ed. Boston: Holbrook, 1976.

Greenfield, Jeff. *Running to Win.* New York: Simon and Schuster, 1980.

Hershey, Marjorie R. *The Making of Campaign Strategy.* Lexington, Mass.: D. C. Heath, 1974.

——. *Running for Office.* Chatham, N.J.: Chatham House, 1984.

Kayden, Xandra. *Campaign Organization.* Lexington, Mass.: D. C. Heath, 1978.

Kelley, Stanley, Jr. *Political Campaigning: Problems in Creating an Informed Electorate.* Washington, D.C.: Brookings Institution, 1960.

——. *Professional Public Relations and Political Power.* Baltimore: Johns Hopkins University Press, 1956.

Kingdon, John W. *Candidates for Office: Beliefs and Strategies.* New York: Random House, 1968.

Leuthold, David A. *Electioneering in a Democracy.* New York: Wiley, 1968.

Mandel, Ruth B. *In the Running: The New Woman Candidate.* New York: Ticknor and Fields, 1981.

Nimmo, Dan, and Robert L. Savage. *Candidates and their Images.* Santa Monica, Calif.: Goodyear, 1976.

Voting Behavior

Campbell, Angus, Gerald Gurin, and Warren E. Miller. *The Voter Decides.* Evanston, Ill.: Row, Peterson, 1954.

Campbell, Angus, Philip E. Converse, Warren E. Miller, and Donald E. Stokes. *The American Voter.* New York: Wiley, 1960.

Fiorina, Morris P. *Retrospective Voting in American National Elections.* New Haven: Yale University Press, 1981.

Hadley, Arthur T. *The Empty Polling Booth.* Englewood Cliffs, N.J.: Prentice-Hall, 1978.

Lazarsfeld, Paul, Bernard Berelson, and Hazel Gaudet. *The People's Choice.* New York: Columbia University Press, 1944.

Wolfinger, Raymond E., and Steven J. Rosenstone. *Who Votes?* New Haven: Yale University Press, 1980.

Political Parties

Cotter, Cornelius P., James L. Gibson, John F. Bibby, and Robert Huckshorn. *Party Organizations in American Politics.* New York: Praeger, 1984.

Eldersveld, Samuel P. *Political Parties in American Society.* New York: Basic Books, 1982.

Fleishman, Joel L. *The Future of American Political Parties.* Englewood Cliffs, N.J.: Prentice-Hall, 1982.

Ladd, Everett C., and Charles D. Hadley. *Transformations of the American Party System.* New York: Norton, 1975.

Polsby, Nelson W. *Consequences of Party Reform.* New York: Oxford University Press, 1983.

Pomper, Gerald M., ed. *Party Renewal in America.* New York: Praeger, 1980.

Price, David E. *Bringing Back the Parties.* Washington, D.C.: CQ Press, 1984.

Ranney, Austin. *Curing the Mischiefs of Faction.* Berkeley and Los Angeles: University of California Press, 1975.

Sundquist, James L. *Dynamics of the Party System: Alignment and Realignment of Political Parties in the United States,* rev. ed. Washington, D.C.: Brookings Institution, 1983.

Wattenberg, Martin P. *The Decline of American Political Parties 1952-1980.* Cambridge, Mass.: Harvard University Press, 1984.

Presidential Campaigns

Asher, Herbert. *Presidential Elections and American Politics: Voters, Candidates, and Campaigns Since 1952.* Homewood, Ill.: Dorsey Press, 1984.

Barber, James David, ed. *Race for the Presidency: The Media and the Nominating Process.* Englewood Cliffs, N.J.: Prentice-Hall, 1978.

Hess, Stephen. *The Presidential Campaign.* Washington, D.C.: Brookings Institution, 1978.

Kessel, John H. *Presidential Campaign Politics.* Homewood, Ill., Dorsey Press, 1984.

Lamb, Karl A., and Paul A. Smith. *Campaign Decision-Making: The Presidential Election of 1964.* Belmont, Calif.: Wadsworth, 1968.

Wayne, Stephen J. *The Road to the White House,* 2d ed. New York: St. Martin's Press, 1984.

White, Theodore H. *America In Search of Itself: The Making of the President: 1956-1980.* New York: Harper and Row, 1982.

Congressional Campaigns

Clem, Alan L. *The Making of Congressmen: Seven Campaigns of 1974.* North Scituate, Mass.: Duxbury, 1976.

Fenno, Richard F., Jr. *Home Style: House Members in Their Districts.* Boston: Little, Brown, 1978.

——. *The United States Senate: A Bicameral Perspective.* Washington, D.C.: American Enterprise Institute, 1982.

Fiorina, Morris P. *Congress: Keystone of the Washington Establishment.* New Haven: Yale University Press, 1977.

Fishel, Jeff. *Parties and Opposition: Congressional Challengers in American Politics.* New York: David McKay, 1973.

Froman, Lewis A., Jr. *Congressmen and Their Constituencies.* Chicago: Rand McNally, 1963.

Goldenberg, Edie N., and Michael W. Traugott. *Campaigning for Congress.* Washington, D.C.: CQ Press, 1984.

Hinckley, Barbara. *Congressional Elections.* Washington, D.C.: CQ Press, 1981.

Huckshorn, Robert J., and Robert C. Spencer. *The Politics of Defeat: Campaigning for Congress.* Amherst: University of Massachusetts Press, 1971.

Jacobson, Gary C., and Samuel Kernell. *Strategy and Choice in Congressional Elections.* New Haven: Yale University Press, 1981.

Maisel, Louis Sandy. *From Obscurity to Oblivion: Running in the Congressional Primary.* Knoxville: University of Tennessee Press, 1982.

Mann. Thomas E. *Unsafe at any Margin: Interpreting Congressional Elections.* Washington, D.C.: American Enterprise Institute, 1982.

Mayhew, David R. *Congress: The Electoral Connection.* New Haven: Yale University Press, 1974.

Rothenberg, Stuart. *Winners and Losers: Campaigns, Candidates and Congressional Elections.* Washington, D.C.: Free Congress Research and Education Foundation, 1983.

State and Local Campaigns

Banfield, Edward C. *Big City Politics.* New York: Random House, 1966.

Coffman, Tim. *Catch a Wave: A Case Study of Hawaii's New Politics.* Honolulu: The University Press of Hawaii, 1973.

Gosnell, Harold F. *Machine Politics: Chicago Model,* 2d ed. Chicago: University of Chicago Press, 1968.

Jewell, Malcolm E. *Parties and Primaries: Nominating State Governors.* New York: Praeger, 1984.

———. *Representation in State Legislatures.* Lexington: University Press of Kentucky, 1982.

———, and David M. Olson. *American State Political Parties and Elections.* Homewood, Ill.: Dorsey Press, 1982.

Mileur, Jerome M., and George T. Sulzner. *Campaigning for the Massachusetts Senate.* Amherst: University of Massachusetts Press, 1974.

Miller, Warren, and Teresa E. Levitan. *Leadership and Change: The New Politics and the American Electorate.* Cambridge, Mass.: Winthrop, 1976.

Nie, Norman H., Sidney Verba, and John R. Petrocik. *The Changing American Voter.* Cambridge, Mass.: Harvard University Press, 1976.

Rosenthal, Alan, and Maureen Moakley. *The Political Life of the American States.* New York: Praeger, 1984.

Smith, Thomas F. X. *The Poweriticians.* Secaucus, N.J.: Lyle Stuart, 1982.

Wilson, James Q. *The Amateur Democrat: Club Politics in Three Cities.* Chicago: University of Chicago Press, 1962.

Campaign Management and Techniques

Blumenthal, Sidney. *The Permanent Campaign: Inside the World of Elite Political Operatives.* Boston: Beacon Press, 1980.

Bruno, Jerry, and Jeff Greenfield. *The Advance Man.* New York: William Morrow, 1971.

Hiebert, Ray, et al. *The Political Image Merchants: Strategies in the New Politics.* Washington, D.C.: Acropolis Books, 1971.

Mauser, Gary A. *Political Marketing: An Approach to Campaign Strategy.* New York: Praeger, 1983.

Nimmo, Dan. *The Political Persuaders.* Englewood Cliffs, N.J.: Prentice-Hall, 1970.

Roll, Charles W., and Albert H. Cantril. *Polls: Their Use and Misuse in Politics.* Cabin John, Md.: Seven Locks Press, 1980.

Rosenbloom, David. *The Election Men.* New York: Quadrangle, 1973.

Sabato, Larry J. *The Rise of Political Consultants: New Ways of Winning Elections.* New York: Basic Books, 1981.

Steinberg, Arnold. *The Political Campaign Handbook: Media, Scheduling, and Advance.* Lexington, Mass.: D. C. Heath, 1976.

Media

Clarke, Peter, and Susan H. Evans. *Covering Campaigns: Journalism in Congressional Elections.* Stanford, Calif.: Stanford University Press, 1983.

Diamond, Edwin, and Stephen Bates. *The Spot: The Rise of Political Advertising on Television.* Cambridge, Mass.: MIT Press, 1984.

Hess, Stephen. *The Washington Reporters.* Washington, D.C.: Brookings Institution, 1981.

Patterson, Thomas E. *The Mass Media Election: How Americans Choose Their President.* New York: Praeger, 1980.

___, and Robert D. McClure. *The Unseeing Eye: The Myth of Television Power in National Elections.* New York: G.P. Putnam's Sons, 1976.

Ranney, Austin. *Channels of Power: The Impact of Television on American Politics.* New York: Basic Books, 1983.

Sigal, Leon. *Reporters and Officials.* Lexington, Mass.: D. C. Heath, 1973.

Trent, Judith S., and Robert V. Friedenberg. *Political Campaign Communication.* New York: Praeger, 1983.

Wyckoff, Gene. *The Image Candidates: American Politics in the Age of Television.* New York: Macmillan, 1968.

Campaign Finance

Adamany, David W., and George E. Agree. *Political Money: A Strategy for Campaign Financing in America.* Baltimore: Johns Hopkins, 1979.

Alexander, Herbert E. *Financing Politics: Money, Elections, and Political Reform*, 3d ed. Washington, D.C.: CQ Press, 1984.

___, ed. *Campaign Money: Reform and Reality in the States.* New York: The Free Press, 1976.

Heard, Alexander. *The Costs of Democracy.* Chapel Hill: University of North Carolina Press, 1960.

Jacobson, Gary C. *Money in Congressional Elections.* New Haven: Yale University Press, 1980.

Malbin, Michael J. *Money and Politics in the United States.* Chatham, N.J.: Chatham House, 1984.

___. *Parties, Interest Groups and Campaign Finance Laws.* Washington, D.C.: American Enterprise Institute, 1980.

Overacker, Louise. *Money In Elections.* New York: Macmillan, 1932.

Sabato, Larry J. *PAC Power: Inside the World of the Political Action Committee.* New York: Norton, 1984.

Index

Defensive, need for candidates to stay off - 177-178, 179
Democratic Congressional Campaign Committee (DCCC) - 55, 95, 210, 231
Democratic National Committee - 214
Democratic party
campaign funding and - 54-55, 202
changing role of - 210-213
getting-out-the-vote by - 190-191
in 19th century America - 21
and Populist movement - 26-27
procedural reforms of - 213-215
recent presidential election results and - 7
Democratic Senatorial Campaign Committee (DSCC) - 55
Democratic Study Group (DSG) - 214
Democrats, challengers among - 93-94
Democrats for the Eighties - 214
Designated marketing areas - 146
Deviating election - 7
Dewey, Thomas E. - 40
Diamond, Edwin - 57
Dilger, Robert - 222
Direct mail advertising - 145-146
last minute - 175
used in congressional campaigns - 148-150
Direct mail solicitations - 50, 68, 91-92
for Democratic party contributions - 55
for Republican party contributions - 52-53
Direct primary - 30, 227
DMAs. *See* Designated market areas
Doak, David - 111, 115, 178, 201
Doggett, Lloyd - 124
Dolan, John T. ("Terry") - 206
Door-to-door campaigning - 91
Douglas, Stephen - 21, 23
Drew, Elizabeth - 58, 69, 82, 222
Dukakis, Michael - 123
Duquin, Lorene Hanley - 112
Durenberger, Dave - 87, 100, 179

Economic conditions, voting choices and - 8
Edgar, Bob - 63-64

Edsall, T. B. - 193, 222
Edwards, Mickey - 218
Ehrenhalt, Alan - 113, 143
Eisenhower, Dwight D. - 39, 41
Eldersveld, Samuel J. - 244
Election day, getting-out-the-vote on - 188-191
Electronic journalism - 156-157
End Poverty in California. *See* EPIC movement
Energy and Commerce Committee (House) - 69
EPIC movement - 32
Epstein, Leon - 229, 244, 245
Ertel, Alan - 139
Eubank, Robert B. - 58
Evaluation phase, as part of voter attitude formation - 13
Evans, Susan H. - 15, 81, 112, 166, 192
Exon, J. J. - 142
External campaign - 59, 60

Farley, James A. - 2
Farmers' Alliances - 26
Federal Election Commission - 169
Fenno, Richard, Jr. - 83, 112, 113, 247
Fenwick, Millicent - 121, 125-126, 127, 130, 134, 140, 161, 162, 171-172, 173, 175
Field organizations
during campaigns - 10
Fiorina, Morris P. - 245, 246
Fishel, Jeff - 15
Fisher, Harry N. D. - 57
Flanigan William H. - 14, 82
Fleishman, Joel L. - 58, 222, 247
Florio, Jim - 91
Flushing crews - 189
Flynn, Edward J. - 2
Foley, Tom - 78
Ford, Gerald - 210
Fossel, Jon - 140
Frank, Barney - 203
Franks, Martin - 231, 246
Free media - 115, 145-165. *See also* News coverage; News interview programs; Newspaper coverage; Radio coverage; Television coverage
paid media used to gain - 177
as part of final phase of campaigns - 175-177

DATE DUE

MAR 2 6 1994			

DEMCO 38-297

WHITMAN COLLEGE LIBRARY